Blacks in American Films:
Today and Yesterday

by

EDWARD MAPP

The Scarecrow Press, Inc.
Metuchen, N. J.   1972

Copyright 1971 by Edward Mapp

"The Library of Congress Cataloged the Original Printing of
This Title as:".

PN
1995
.9
.N4
M3
1972

Mapp, Edward.
  Blacks in American films: today and yesterday. Metuchen, N. J., Scarecrow Press, 1972 ₍c1971₎

  278 p. illus. 22 cm.

  Bibliography: p. 255–267.

  1. Negroes in moving-pictures. 2. Moving-pictures—U. S.—History.   I. Title.

PN1995.9.N4M3   1972   791.43′0909352   72–172946
ISBN 0–8108–0458–1   MARC

Library of Congress   71 ₍60–2₎

CONTENTS

DEDICATION

Generations of moviegoers remember Prissy,
the simple-minded black servant girl who evoked the
wrath of Scarlett O'Hara in the baby delivery sequence
of Gone with the Wind. The author recollects a chance
meeting in 1952 with the actress who portrayed Prissy.
He recalls as well his subsequent involvement in her
project at that time, a new concept of William Shakespeare's A Midsummer Night's Dream. Unfortunately
this production was never realized. Reading the part
of Demetrius under her direction, one soon discovered
the full range of her acting ability. It became clear
at once that this gifted black actress possessed a mas-
tery of the English speaking language remote from the
"who dat say dat?" kind of dialogue assigned her in
American motion pictures. The story unfolded in the
following pages is part hers and she is in part it.
Therefore this book is dedicated to Butterfly McQueen.

Butterfly McQueen, to whom this work is dedicated, won film
fame for her portrayal of Prissy in Gone With the Wind.   (Photo
by permission of Metro-Goldwyn-Mayer Inc.)

Chapter 1

INTRODUCTION

During the last decade, the American motion picture
industry produced a progressively increasing number of films
in which a Negro was a major character. The objective of
this book is to ascertain, by the use of informal qualitative
content analysis, the portrayal of the Negro as a major
character in these recent American films. Of necessity,
the terms "Negro," "black," "Afro-American" will be used
interchangeably hereinafter.

Only movies made by American companies anywhere in
the world for commercial distribution are included. Although the
African is portrayed frequently in American motion pictures by
some of America's leading black actors (Jim Brown in Dark of
the Sun, Sidney Poitier in Something of Value, Raymond St. Jacques in Mr. Moses), these characterizations are excluded, because these are of a different genre appropriate to other works.

Black films made by black producers such as George
P. Johnson and Noble Johnson (Lincoln Motion Picture Co.),
Ebony Pictures, The Birth of a Race Co., Oscar Micheaux,
Bert Williams, and others will not be considered in this
book. These were aimed at black audiences, denied wide
distribution and are therefore atypical.

Since this work is concerned solely with the portrayal
of the Negro, any characterizations of other ethnic groups by
Negro actors and actresses will be excluded.

The book emphasizes an objective assessment of the

7

content of the Negro portrayal.   No effort is made to determine the effects of the portrayals on the motion picture
audiences.

More than thirty-five years ago, Edgar Dale alluded
to the enormous power available to the motion picture industry in its characterization of ethnic groups:

> One way in which prejudice may be shown is
> through using the characters as clowns or buffoons.
> While some might object to classifying this as a
> form of race prejudice, nevertheless none of us
> would like to have our own race constantly pre-
> sented in this light. [1]

As recently as July 2, 1968, a Columbia Broadcasting
System television program, sponsored by the Xerox Corporation, called attention to the misrepresentation of Negroes by
the motion picture medium.   The show, entitled Black History: Lost, Stolen or Strayed, used clips from films to make
its point.

> It also presented a chillingly revealing visual his-
> tory of the Negro in American films from Uncle
> Tom's Cabin through The Birth of a Nation and a
> host of happy darkies, smilin' Aunt Jemimas and
> shufflin' Stepin Fetchits--all of them either lazy,
> ignorant, whisky-drinking, craps-playing, easily
> scared or stupid, with a loyal 'good nigger' oc-
> casionally thrown in for dramatic relief. [2]

Clifford Mason believes that motion pictures have substituted new subtle stereotypes for the old blatant ones.   Referring to several of Sidney Poitier's recent film portrayals,
Mason states:

> ... [Poitier] thinks these films have been helping
> to change the stereotypes that black actors are
> subjected to.   In essence, they are merely con-
> trivances, completely lacking in any real artistic
> merit.

...he remains unreal, as he has for nearly two decades, playing essentially the same role, the antiseptic, one-dimensional hero. [3]

In the light of his changing role in American society, an attempt to ascertain the evolution of the portrayal of the Negro in American motion pictures appears appropriate. This work is an effort to systematically examine the major characterizations of Negroes in American motion pictures during a time when Negroes were engaged actively in the struggle for an improved status in the United States.

Previous Research

Peter Noble's The Negro in Films, published in 1948 and reprinted in 1969, still is the major work on the subject. Noble, a British film critic, traced the experience of the Negro from the earliest silent films up to the motion pictures of the post-World War II period. Noble's inclusion of references to the Negro in documentaries, British and European films may be considered an asset or liability depending on one's interests in these categories. [4]

In 1950, V. J. Jerome, then Chairman of the Communist Party's National Cultural Commission, authored The Negro in Hollywood Films, a Marxist indictment of American films of the forties dealing with racial themes. Jerome believed that newly emerging film stereotypes would perpetuate the oppression of black people. Almost two decades later, this concept was to become part of a broader controversy. [5]

Royal Colle attempted an investigation of the image of the Negro in newspapers, magazines, radio, television as well as motion pictures. The broad scope of Colle's research curtailed intensive attention to any one medium. [6]

Samuel Bloom[7] did a case study of the movie Lost

Boundaries, and Daniel Wilner[8] did one for Home of the
Brave. Each study tried to determine audience reaction to
the particular film in question.

In her descriptive study of occupational roles represented by Negroes in selected mass media, Daisy Balsley
analyzed forty films produced from 1956 to 1958.[9]

The comments and attitudes of the Negro press concerning the portrayal of the Negro in films were researched
by Singer Buchanan in 1968. Buchanan used the files of the
Chicago Defender and the Pittsburgh Courier as his primary
research tools.[10]

William Burke examined the presentation of the Negro
in American films between 1946 and 1961 in a selective
analysis of twenty-nine films.[11]

Reference should be made to three masters' theses
completed in the University of Southern California's Cinema
Department. Terry Theodore made an analysis of eight
selected films released between 1949 and 1961 which depicted
social relations between Negroes and whites. Theodore, as
part of his research, created a radio program symposium of
authoritative views on the Negro in the American motion picture.[12] Donald Fernow included the Negro problem as a
section of his thesis on the treatment of social problems by
the motion picture medium.[13] Arun Chaudhuri duplicated in
his thesis much of the material in Noble's work.[14]

To date, no previous books on this subject reflect
changes which have occurred in the medium since 1961 with
regard to the Negro.

There are two fundamental categories of studies which
are tangentially related to this work. The first includes
studies of the portrayal of the Negro in other media. Seymour Gross and John Hardy made a survey of the charac-

terization of the Negro in American literature.[15] Beulah
Johnson investigated the treatment of the Negro woman in
the American novel for a doctoral dissertation at New York
University in 1955.[16] There are a number of works on the
Negro in the American theatre. Among the most notable are
those written by Edith Isaacs[17] and Loften Mitchell.[18] Although the Isaacs' work, recently reprinted, is dated by more
than two decades, it is still definitive for the period covered.

The second category of study related to this one is
that which investigates the motion picture depiction of other
special groups. Studies by Nasir,[19] Schwartz,[20] and Worden[21] reported on the portrayal of the Arab, the educator,
and the Protestant minister, respectively.

In conducting research for this book, standard procedures of historical criticism were applied to a wide variety
of primary and secondary sources dealing with the Negro in
American motion pictures. Histories, biographies, unpublished theses, pamphlets, articles, correspondence, press
clippings and other materials were examined, questioned and
evaluated. The aim was to establish the history of the Negro in motion pictures from the earliest occurrence up to
1962.

The next step was a systematic identification of all
post-1962 films with major Negro characterizations as defined
and delimited above. Personal knowledge, motion picture
directories, and film reviews in newspapers and periodicals
were used for this purpose. Once these identifications were
made, the procedures of content analysis were instituted.
Bernard Berelson suggests that content analysis offers a
highly objective and scientific method for the description of
communication content.

> The requirement of objectivity stipulates that the
> categories of analysis should be defined so pre-
> cisely that different analysts can apply them to
> the same body of content and secure the same re-
> sults. [22]

The establishment of categories of analysis and the
construction of a content schedule was the first step. Categories were derived from existing content schedules with
appropriate modifications to the needs of this work.

> A character, or person, or a class of persons
> is sometimes used as a coding unit in content
> analysis. All relevant information about the
> character is sifted out of the article or story
> [or movie] and classified. [23]

> It is certainly desirable that the student be fa-
> miliar with the definitions, units, codes, and
> categories other researchers have used before
> them. He can save valuable time by following
> the disciplined measures others have devised. [24]

The content schedule was tested for reliability with
the assistance of volunteers, who viewed several films and
applied the schedule to each Negro characterization. Modifications were made, as indicated, with some categories
added, others deleted, and still others sharpened to eliminate certain ambiguities.

> ...the general categories of a content analysis
> must be stated in analyzable forms appropriate
> to the particular content under investigation. [25]

Once more, the schedule was tested and the raters
were in agreement on better than 80 per cent of the items.

The films comprising the sample were viewed by the
author, some of them twice. Most films were seen in local
motion picture theatres and on home television. Notes were
taken on all aspects of the characterizations. Audio tapings

(recorded by the author) and production scripts (whenever obtainable) were consulted for data essential to the completion of the schedule and as an accuracy check. A content schedule was completed for each characterization in the sample.

Notes

1. Edgar Dale, The Content of Motion Pictures (New York: The Macmillan Co., 1935), p. 55.

2. George Gent, "Television: Exit Darkies, Enter Blacks," The New York Times, July 3, 1968, p. 71.

3. Clifford Mason, "Why Does White America Love Sidney Poitier So?," The New York Times, September 10, 1967, pp. 1, 21.

4. Peter Noble, The Negro in Films (London: Skelton Robinson, 1948).

5. V. J. Jerome, The Negro in Hollywood Films (New York: Masses & Mainstream, 1950).

6. Royal D. Colle, "The Negro Image and the Mass Media," (Unpublished Ph.D. dissertation, Cornell University, 1967).

7. Samuel W. Bloom, "A Social Psychological Study of Motion Picture Audience Behavior; A Case Study of the Negro Image in Mass Communication," (Unpublished Ph.D. dissertation, University of Wisconsin, 1956).

8. Daniel M. Wilner, "Attitude as a Determinant of Perception in the Mass Media of Communication: Reactions to the Motion Picture, 'Home of the Brave'," (Unpublished Ph.D. dissertation, University of California, Los Angeles, 1951).

9. Daisy F. Balsley, "A Descriptive Study of References Made to Negroes and Occupational Roles Represented by Negroes in Selected Mass Media,"

(Unpublished Ph. D. dissertation, University of
Denver, 1959).

10.   Singer A. Buchanan, "A Study of the Attitudes of
      the Writers of the Negro Press Toward the De-
      piction of the Negro in Plays and Films: 1930-
      1965," (Unpublished Ph. D. dissertation, The
      University of Michigan, 1968).

11.   William L. Burke, "The Presentation of the Ameri-
      can Negro in Hollywood Films, 1946-1961:
      Analysis of a Selected Sample of Feature Films."
      (Unpublished Ph. D. dissertation, Northwestern
      University, 1965).

12.   Terry Theodore, "The Negro in Hollywood: A
      Critical Study of Entertainment Films Con-
      taining Negro Themes," (Unpublished M. A.
      thesis, University of Southern California, 1962).

13.   Donald L. Fernow, "The Treatment of Social Prob-
      lems in the Entertainment Film," (Unpublished
      M. A. thesis, University of Southern California,
      1952).

14.   Arun Chaudhuri, "A Study of the Negro Problem in
      Motion Pictures," (Unpublished M. A. thesis,
      University of Southern California, 1951).

15.   Seymour L. Gross and John Hardy, eds., Images of
      the Negro in American Literature.   (Chicago:
      University of Chicago Press, 1967).

16.   Beulah V. Johnson, "The Treatment of the Negro
      Woman as a Major Character in American
      Novels, 1900-1950," (Unpublished Ph. D. dis-
      sertation, New York University, 1955).

17.   Edith J. Isaacs, The Negro in the American Thea-
      tre, (New York: Theatre Arts, 1947).

18.   Loften Mitchell, Black Drama: The Story of the
      American Negro in the Theatre, (New York:
      Hawthorn Books, 1967).

19.   Sari Nasir, "The Image of the Arab in American
      Popular Culture," (Unpublished Ph. D. disserta-

tion, University of Illinois, 1962).

20. Jack Schwartz, "The Portrayal of Education in American Motion Pictures, 1931-1961," (Unpublished Ph. D. dissertation, University of Illinois, 1963).

21. James Worden, "The Portrayal of the Protestant Minister in American Motion Pictures 1951-1960," (Unpublished Ph. D. dissertation, Boston University, 1962).

22. Bernard Berelson, Content Analysis in Communication Research (Glencoe, Illinois: The Free Press, 1952), p. 16.

23. Ralph O. Nafziger & David M. White, Introduction to Mass Communications Research, (Baton Rouge: Louisiana State University Press, 1963).

24. Ibid., p. 189.

25. Berelson, op. cit., p. 164.

Chapter 2

SILENT FILMS

One of the earliest American films to portray the Negro was The Wooing and Wedding of a Coon in 1905, described by the producers as a genuine Ethiopian comedy, whatever that connoted. According to Peter Noble, the film "unashamedly poked fun and derision at a coloured couple."[1]

A similar film during this period was The Masher in 1907. The production is illustrative of the slapstick and derogatory manner in which Negroes were depicted in American and European films during the pre-World War I era.

> The film shows a lady-killer who is unsuccessful in his wooing with everyone with whom he tries to flirt. Finally he becomes successful with a lady wearing a veil, who quickly responds to his flirtation. However, when he makes further advances and lifts her veil, he discovers to his consternation that the lady of his choice is coloured.[2]

In most of these early films, Negroes were played by white actors.

Also appearing at this time were two widely distributed series of short comedies known as the "Rastus" films and the "Sambo" films. The central character of each series was a black buffoon who appeared to have not the slightest intelligence.[3]

When the Negro was not made an object of ridicule, he was portrayed as the devoted slave who knew his place. Between 1910 and 1915 a number of such films were made,

16

including Dion Boucicault's The Octoroon and Edward Sheldon's
The Nigger, stories involving miscegenation and passing.

> In all the films made during this period dealing
> with octoroons and mulattos the apparent shame
> and degradation of being even the smallest degree
> non-white was exploited to the full, with the ob-
> vious implication that there was something prac-
> tically sub-human in being black. [4]

There were virtually no favorable portrayals of Negroes in this period. Noble cites, as a single exception, an
early Charles Ray film, The Coward, in which a colored
minister was given a sympathetic characterization.

Motion pictures of Harriet Beecher Stowe's famous
novel Uncle Tom's Cabin were made in 1909, 1914, 1918 and
1927. The first, in 1903, directed by Edwin S. Porter, of
The Great Train Robbery fame, cast a white actor in the role
of Uncle Tom. Negro actor, Sam Lucas, played Tom in
the 1914 version.

> Thus for the first time, a film about Negroes ac-
> tually used coloured actors and thenceforth with
> notable exceptions...the practice of using burnt-
> corked whites to play Negro roles gradually fell
> into disuse. [5]

The 1927 production for Universal, perhaps the best remembered version, was to have employed the noted stage actor,
Charles Gilpin, as Tom. After discussions with Harry Pol-
lard, the film's director, concerning the manner in which
the novel would be filmed, and in particular the characterization of Tom, Gilpin relinquished the role in favor of James
B. Lowe.

> It is said he went back to his old job as lift-man
> [elevator-operator] rather than play a well-paid
> screen role, the treatment of which, in his opin-
> ion, helped to malign his people. [6]

This gesture established a precedent which was emu-
lated by all too few Negro actors in the future. It must be
noted that Uncle Tom's Cabin, an anti-slavery novel and the
first of the important abolitionist works, has not been re-
garded with esteem by Negroes and their sympathizers for
many years. The book, like many individuals, organizations
and movements, has outlived its function in the black American's struggle for equal treatment. More than twenty years
ago, Noble observed:

> The Uncle Tom who possessed the qualities of
> brotherly love and humility was, in his time, an
> argument against slavery, but Negroes have in
> recent years discovered militancy, and the meek
> Beecher Stowe character now offends the sensi-
> bilities of most coloured thinkers, writers and
> workers. In the eyes of most Negroes, Uncle
> Tom has long been a figure of contempt, and his
> name associated with a kind of submissive, ser-
> vile, passive Negro, the 'good nigger' who would
> not fight against oppression. [7]

If Uncle Tom's Cabin was one milestone in the evolution of the motion picture portrayal of the Negro, The Birth
of a Nation certainly was another. Based upon Thomas
Dixon's novel, The Clansman, the film became D. W. Griffith's
monumental achievement. Film historian Lewis Jacobs says,

> The film was a passionate and persuasive avowal
> of the inferiority of the Negro. In viewpoint it
> was, surely, narrow and prejudiced. Griffith's
> Southern upbringing made him completely sympa-
> thetic towards author Thomas Dixon's exaggerated
> ideas and the fire of his convictions gave the film
> a rude strength. At one point in the picture a title
> bluntly editorialized that the South must be made
> 'safe' for the whites. The entire portrayal of the
> reconstruction days showed the Negro, when freed
> from his white domination, as an ignorant, lustful
> villain. Negro Congressmen were pictured drink-
> ing heavily, coarsely reclining in Congress with

bare feet upon their desks, lustfully ogling the white women in the balcony. [8]

If the Negro press can be considered the voice of Negro opinion, especially in matters pertaining to racial injustice, that voice was explicit on The Birth of a Nation. The Chicago Defender commented:

> The film viciously plays our race up to the public as being one of rapists and murderers. [9]
>
> No more vicious and harmful bit of propaganda has ever been put on the screen. [10]

Thomas R. Cripps reports on an early effort of the National Association for the Advancement of Colored People to marshall public opinion against the showing of the film that defamed the Negro race:

> For Negroes, their failure in the fight against 'Birth of a Nation' was another reminder that... the Wilson era was a time of troubles characterized by a Jim Crow federal government, lynching, and the seedtime of a new Ku Klux Klan. The controversy also demonstrated the seriousness with which films had come to be regarded both as creators and reflectors of opinions and attitudes after only two decades of existence. [11]

On the lighter side, Hal Roach's widely known series of Our Gang comedies first appeared in the silent film era. A colored child, "Farina," often became the brunt of the gang's jokes. Those who opposed the series saw "Farina" as a Negro object of derision emanating from racial prejudice. Those who accepted the series claimed that "Farina" had achieved true racial integration as a black member of an otherwise white social group. Noble refers to the positive effects of the series:

> ... for a large number of popular Hollywood films

with a very wide appeal to indicate dozens of times,
in a series lasting over a number of years, that
there is no objection to white and coloured children
playing together, seems to be a significant point.
...12

The situation of the Negro in American silent films
was indeed bleak. With few exceptions, Negroes were portrayed by white actors. The films poked fun at the black
man, portrayed him as a devoted slave, or depicted him in
a heinous manner. The major production of the era was the
vicious, anti-Negro film, The Birth of a Nation. It remained
to be seen whether the advent of talking pictures offered the
hope of progress for the Negro on the screen.

Notes

1. Peter Noble, The Negro in Films (London: Skelton
   Robinson, 1948), p. 28.

2. Ibid.

3. Ibid.

4. Ibid., p. 29.

5. Ibid., p. 31.

6. Ibid., p. 32.

7. Ibid.

8. Lewis Jacobs, The Rise of the American Film, A
   Critical History With An Essay, "Experimental
   Cinema in America, 1921-1947." (New York:
   Teachers College Press, 1968), p. 177.

9. Chicago Defender, July 7, 1930, p. 10.

10. Chicago Defender, July 26, 1930, p. 10.

11. Thomas R. Cripps, "The Reaction of the Negro to

the Motion Picture Birth of a Nation," The
Historian, **XXV** (May, 1963), p. 362.

12.   Noble, op. cit., p. 45.

Paul Robeson's film re-creation of his stage success in Eugene
O'Neill's Emperor Jones in 1933 was a landmark for the Negro
in films. (Photo courtesy of Film Images/Radim Films, Inc.,
New York, N.Y.)

Chapter 3

TALKIES BETWEEN THE WARS

Motion pictures made history in 1927 when Al Jolson's
songs, although not the dialogue, were recorded in The Jazz
Singer. Ironically, for the Negro, who made no direct gain
from his debut, Jolson appeared in black face.

Now that music and sound could be heard on the screen,
Hollywood imported Negro dancers, singers and musicians
from the New York theatre and night-clubs for "all colored, all
singing, all dancing" film epics of the thirties. The pioneer all-
Negro movie made in Hollywood was Hearts in Dixie in 1929.
About the film, Noble says:

> ... we were given no new slant on Negro life and
> thought, just the same old hackneyed routine. The
> story was so slight as to be almost nonexistent, but
> apparently we were to be compensated for this by a
> succession of endless musical numbers, spirituals,
> prayer meetings, cotton-picking and the like. [1]

Films such as the Twentieth Century Fox production
Hearts in Dixie (1929) and Metro-Goldwyn-Mayer's Hallelujah
(1929) directed by King Vidor, were significant for bringing talented Negro performers such as Stepin Fetchit, Clarence Muse,
Daniel Haynes and Nina Mae McKinney to the screen. Hearts in
Dixie was the story of the sacrifice of an aging black man for
his young son, interspersed with the doltish antics of the not yet
familiar Fetchit. Hallelujah's plot, about a country fellow who
momentarily falls for the charms of a bad woman, was trite
even in 1929. Reacting critically to both films in the September
1st issue of Film Weekly, black singer Paul Robeson said:

> The box office insistence that the Negro shall fig-
> ure always as a clown has spoiled the two Negro
> films which have been made in Hollywood, 'Halle-
> lujah' and 'Hearts in Dixie.' In 'Hallelujah' they
> took the Negro and his church services and made
> them funny. [2]

> Hollywood can only visualise the plantation type of
> Negro--the Negro of 'Poor Old Joe' and 'Swanee
> Ribber.' It is [sic] absurd to use that type to ex-
> press the modern Negro as it would be to express
> modern England in the terms of an Elizabethan
> ballad. [3]

Robeson's 1936 appearance as Jim in Universal's Show
Boat confirms his comments. That small singing role, with
its sentimental "Old Man River," was clearly incommensurate
with Robeson's earlier achievement as star of Emperor Jones.
Robeson's film re-creation of his stage success in Eugene
O'Neill's Emperor Jones in 1933 had been a landmark for the
Negro in films. The part of Brutus Jones was most de-
manding, requiring rotating histrionic demonstrations of hu-
mility, strength, suspicion and fear. He sang (Water Boy,
John Henry, Jacob's Ladder) in the film as well.

> To have a black man playing the star part in a
> film in which the white actors were of lesser im-
> portance was indeed something of a filmic revolu-
> tion. Indeed it was enough of a social revolution
> to make the film a financial failure. [4]

Negro cinematic progress in the thirties is actually a
tale of exceptions. The dignified portrayal of a Negro physician by Clarence Brooks in the 1932 Arrowsmith was another
singular instance of fair treatment of the Negro by sound
films of the period.

The first film production of Fannie Hurst's novel,
Imitation of Life, released in 1934, featured two important
Negro characterizations. Louise Beavers portrayed Delilah,

an aunt Jemima type, who reveals her secret recipe for pan-
cakes to her white employer, enacted by Claudette Colbert.
When Colbert promotes this into an enormously profitable enterprise, Beavers elects only to continue on as servant and
eventually have a big funeral with white horses leading the
cortege. Ned Sparks, playing another role in the film, explains Delilah thus: "Once a pancake--always a pancake."
Interpreted as a racial slur, this line evoked resentment
among Negro audiences. Another Negro actress, Fredi
Washington, played Delilah's discontented mulatto daughter,
Peola. Her role was concerned with a sub-plot on the issue
of "passing." Noble considers this role "the most interesting...in the cast."

> She is...sensitive, tempestuous and grows bitterly
> indignant when she sees that the white girl with
> whom she has been reared is getting all the fine
> things of life while she is subjected to humiliation
> and unhappiness. [5]

While this author finds Peola's militancy admirable
and certainly uncommon for the thirties, it must be noted
that she bases her claim for social justice on her whiteness
rather than on her blackness.

In the middle thirties, two black performers, Stepin
Fetchit and Bill Robinson, became popular with mass movie
audiences. Fetchit developed the lethargic, shuffling, stupid,
colored servant in numerous films including Stand Up and
Cheer and David Harum. Robinson portrayed the grinning,
dancing, fawning servant in the Shirley Temple movies The
Littlest Rebel, The Little Colonel and Rebecca of Sunnybrook
Farm, as well as other films. The plots may have been
varied but the Fetchit/Robinson characterizations were always
essentially the same, the happy Negro.

On rare occasions, films gave their audiences brief glimpses of possible Negro discontent, even if only in pseudo-historical context. The 1935, So Red the Rose, starring Margaret Sullavan and directed by King Vidor, was such a film. Clarence Muse appeared as Cato, leader of a slave uprising. Noble's telling description of one sequence explains, to a degree, why some critics attacked the film:

> But in the old Southern homestead sits the mistress of the house, a proud daughter of the Confederacy (Margaret Sullavan). She is worried in case the sound of rebellion should reach to the manor house, where her father, the traditional Southern colonel, is dying. The girl knows that his heart will break if he realises that his devoted servants and slaves have turned upon him; so with a heart-warming simplicity she strides fearlessly into the slave quarters, and breaks up the rebellion by slapping one of the ring-leaders in the face, and shaming the rest of the rioters with a reminder that they are all her dear, dear friends and they must continue to be 'good' for the sake of her dying father. Confronted by the brave little woman whom they have loved since she was a child, the slaves break down and cry, chanting hymns and following her to the manor. [6]

Warner Brothers brought The Green Pastures, Marc Connelly's award-winning play, to the screen in 1936. Despite fine performances by Rex Ingram as De Lawd and Eddie "Rochester" Anderson as Noah, the film did much to perpetuate a popular mythology of the Negro.

> Well-intentioned, it merely gave filmgoers once more the happy, religious, hymn-singing black man, whose idea of Heaven seems to consist mainly of long white night-gowns, hymn-shouting and fish-fries. [7]

Between 1932 and 1937, Mervyn Le Roy made two socially conscious dramas at Warner Brothers which included

Negro parts. I Am a Fugitive from a Chain Gang (1932)
dealt with the injustices of the labor camp system in the
South.   Everett Brown appeared as a Negro prisoner who assists the star, Paul Muni, to escape.   Noble says, "The
feeling which remained...was that the Negro is an ordinary
human being, capable of great friendship, loyalty and courage."[8] They Won't Forget was a film indictment of the pe-
culiarly Southern custom, lynching.   Clinton Rosemond played
a Negro janitor, who is persecuted by Southern police officers for a crime of which he is innocent.   The controversial
nature of these two film themes suggests rare courage on the
part of the studio and Mr. LeRoy.

- Margaret Mitchell's Gone with the Wind, produced by
David O. Selznick in 1939, occupies an historic place in the
Negro's struggle for advancement in American motion pictures.   Negro actress, Hattie McDaniel, received an Academy
of Motion Picture Arts and Sciences award for the best performance of the year in a supporting role in this film.   She
was the first and only member of her race to be so honored,
even if the "Oscar" statuette was bestowed upon her for portraying "Mammy," house-slave and nursemaid to Scarlett O'-
Hara.   Also appearing in Gone with the Wind was Butterfly
McQueen, who acted the role of Prissy, an addlebrained Negro girl.   Miss McQueen repeated this stereotypical characterization with minor comic variations in numerous subsequent films.   In his autobiography, Malcolm X recalls his
ethnic embarrassment upon viewing this role as a youth.[9]
The National Association for the Advancement of Colored
People and other concerned pressure groups waged a campaign to have the film's more offensive aspects softened or
eliminated.   For example, Scarlett's reference to "free niggers" was changed to "freedmen."[10]   On the basis of its

lengthy footage, tremendous financial returns, artistic and technical merit, subject matter and point of view, Gone With the Wind resembled The Birth of a Nation.

During the early days of sound films, then, Negro film stereotypes were implemented by a sound track. Although serious portrayals of the Negro were exceptional, sound films did provide a broader showcase for Negro musical talent.

Notes

1. Peter Noble, The Negro in Films (London: Skelton Robinson, 1948), p. 50.

2. Quoted in Noble, op. cit., p. 54.

3. Quoted in Noble, op. cit., p. 48.

4. Noble, op. cit., p. 57.

5. Noble, op. cit., p. 62.

6. Noble, op. cit., p. 67.

7. Noble, op. cit., pp. 68, 69.

8. Noble, op. cit., p. 71.

9. Malcolm Little, The Autobiography of Malcolm X, (New York: Grove Press, 1964), p. 32.

10. Murray Schumach, The Face on the Cutting Room Floor: The Story of Movie and Television Censorship, (New York: Morrow, 1964), p. 102.

Chapter 4

DURING WORLD WAR II

As one might expect in time of war, the communications media, including motion pictures, concentrated on the war effort. War dramas, morale-building musicals and escapist light comedies were the film fare of the day. During this period, as in times past, there were a few motion pictures which attempted sympathetic presentations of Negroes in minor roles.

At a time when Dorie Miller was being honored as one of the first heroes of World War II, stories about our fighting services were filmed without Negroes in the cast.

> ... Admiral Chester W. Nimitz, commander in chief of the Pacific Fleet, pinned the Navy Cross on the twenty-two-year old black's chest, and the sailor returned to America to tour the nation in a War Bond drive. Then he went back to sea in the Pacific and served until Thanksgiving Day of 1943, when he went down with most of his ship's seven-hundred-man crew in the torpedoing of the aircraft carrier 'Liscome Bay.'
>
> Miller was only one of many noncombatant blacks who deserted the galleys and wardrooms to engage the enemy during World War II. [1]

When total exclusion was not practiced, a policy of adding one Negro to a war film was substituted. As a result, movie-goers saw Ben Carter in Crash Drive, Rex Ingram as Tambul in Sahara, and Kenneth Spencer as Wesley Epps in Bataan. About the latter role, Burke comments,

29

> In a film in which the Negro character is supposed-
> ly treated 'fairly,' Epps is too busy working to par-
> ticipate in most group scenes. When he does ap-
> pear among a sizeable number of his comrades, he
> is distinctly relegated to the background in discus-
> sion. [2]

Peter Noble, [3] and other researchers on the Negro in
motion pictures, tended to attribute an inordinate significance
to the mere inclusion of Negroes in these films. A research-
er, consciously or not, brings an interpretation to even the
simplest film sequence. As an example, Noble describes in
positive terms one of Ingram's scenes in <u>Sahara</u>:

> ...he uses his hands as a cup for the dripping
> water which quenches the thirst of the other men.
> Each of the whites drinks out of the water in the
> hands of the Negro, and none of them appears to
> find this extraordinary... [4]

Noble, who is white, implies that even in a situation
of extreme thirst, a white man might view drinking from a
black man's hands as an "extraordinary" act. On the other
hand, a black man might well see this entire episode as another version of "the devoted servant" stereotype foisted upon blacks by whites. As outlined by Lawrence Reddick in
1944, the list of stereotypes is fairly comprehensive: [5]

1.   The savage African
2.   The happy slave
3.   The devoted servant
4.   The corrupt politician
5.   The irresponsible citizen
6.   The petty thief
7.   The social delinquent
8.   The vicious criminal
9.   The sexual superman
10. The superior athlete

11. The unhappy non-white
12. The natural-born cook
13. The natural-born musician
14. The perfect entertainer
15. The superstitious churchgoer
16. The chicken and watermelon eater
17. The razor and knife "toter"
18. The uninhibited expressionist
19. The mental inferior.

Categories number 13 and 14 above figured prominent-
ly in the all-Negro musicals and the "Jim Crow" sequences
of other musicals produced during the war years. An abundance of talent was available for these musical presentations.
Among the "forced to grin" musical artists appearing were
Ethel Waters, Lena Horne, Bill Robinson, Fats Waller,
Count Basie, Duke Ellington, Cab Calloway, Hazel Scott,
Louis "Satchmo" Armstrong and Katherine Dunham. The vehicles were Stormy Weather, Cabin in the Sky, Thank Your
Lucky Stars, and Thousands Cheer, among others. [6] The
costumes were usually garish exaggerations of the fashions
of the time. The main tragedy was that gifted individuals
were required to demean themselves, as exemplified in the
lyrics sung by Miss Dunham in the 1942 Star Spangled
Rhythm, "You ain't only classy, you are Haile Selassie."

Beyond the musical and war film categories, there
were several other motion pictures which in some measure
defined the status of the Negro in films between 1940 and
1945.

Canada Lee, a Negro actor of some reknown, made
Lifeboat for Twentieth Century Fox in 1944. He appeared as
Joe, the only Negro, in a group of survivors set adrift in a

lifeboat after a ship-sinking. The scarcity of serious film
parts for Negro actors attached to this role a respectability
it might not have warranted otherwise. For most of the film,
the character remained in the background, following orders,
answering when addressed. Burke observes:

> While the personal stories of all the other passen-
> gers are developed to a greater or lesser extent,
> Joe's remains untold. Indeed, including even the
> German [Nazi], Joe is the only human on board who
> has no one of significance with whom to share
> something of himself. [7]

Leigh Whipper, another well-known Negro actor, gave
outstanding performances in two important films made in
Hollywood during the war. As an outspoken preacher in The
Ox-Bow Incident he tries to dissuade a posse from a lynching.

> As he declares, he comes from a race which has
> had to bear the brunt of lynch law, and lynching
> is no way to settle things for either black or white
> people. [8]

As a western ranch hand in Of Mice and Men, Whipper befriends Lenny and George, the two main characters of the
story.

A comparatively unknown actor, Ernest Anderson, had
the good fortune to be cast in a Bette Davis film entitled In
This Our Life. The role is an integral part of the film and
essential to its denouement. Refreshingly, the characterization of Parry Clay does not fit the too familiar stereotypes:

> The Negro boy, ... is portrayed as a hard-working,
> ambitious youngster who works as a clerk during
> the day and studies to be a law student in his spare
> time. [9]

Even judged by the standards of today, the portrayal

would be deemed realistic.

Fighting a war against totalitarianism may have fostered a democratic spirit which manifested itself in films of the period. Black houseboys and maids become the sidekicks and confidants of their white employers, as in the relationship of Sam (Dooley Wilson) to Rick (Humphrey Bogart) in Casablanca and Angelique (Flora Robson) to Clio (Ingrid Bergman) in Saratoga Trunk. Curiously, the latter film represented another type of retrogression in that once again a white actress, Miss Robson, donned black make-up to portray a non-white.

There were two major film productions during the war years which belied the notion of an improved treatment of the Negro by American films. Tennessee Johnson, a complimentary film biography of the 17th president of the United States, purportedly depicted the events which led to his impeachment. The focus of the film is Johnson's conflict with Thaddeus Stevens, who favored equal rights for the former slaves.

> In the U.S.A. most liberal film critics were indignant that in the middle of a war such a film could still be made by a Hollywood studio, and several reviewers of the daily newspapers deplored the fact that whenever the Civil War was featured in a motion picture the North was shown as the villain, principally because of its advocation of the abolition of slavery. [10]

Tales of Manhattan was another motion picture that marked a backward step for the Negro in American films. All-black production numbers in movie musicals were scarcely new, but a segregated sequence in a dramatic production was unprecedented. As though the "Jim Crow" treatment was not sufficiently insulting, the script required Paul Robe-

son and Ethel Waters to expend their professional talents on
an incredible episode.   A coat containing considerable money
is dumped from an airplane flying over some shacks inhabited
by Southern Negroes.

> A tasteless and naive sequence saw such eminent
> artists as Paul Robeson, Ethel Waters... demeaning
> themselves by impersonating supersitious 'niggers,'
> thanking the Lord for his goodness in sending them
> the money from the skies, praying, kneeling, sob-
> bing, and behaving generally in the same old credu-
> lous, sub-human manner. [11]

An analysis made in 1945, of 100 motion pictures involving Negro characters, revealed that in 75 instances the
portrayal was disparaging and stereotyped.   In only 12 cases
were Negroes presented in a favorable light as individual human beings. [12]

During the war years, it would appear that efforts to
bring realism to the film image of the Negro succeeded only
in isolated offerings.   Although more Negro performers acted
in films, the specter of the old stereotypes prevailed.

Notes

1.   Phillip T. Drotning, Black Heroes in Our Nation's
     History: A Tribute to Those Who Helped Shape
     America, (New York: Cowles, 1969), p. 179.

2.   William L. Burke, "The Presentation of the Ameri-
     can Negro in Hollywood Films, 1946-1961:   An
     Analysis of a Selected Sample of Feature Films,"
     (Unpublished Ph.D. dissertation, Northwestern
     University, 1965), p. 129.

3.   Peter Noble, The Negro in Films (London: Skelton
     Robinson, 1948).

4.   Noble, op. cit., p. 198.

5.   Lawrence D. Reddick, "Educational Programs for

the Improvement of Race Relations: Motion Pictures, Radio, the Press and Libraries," Journal
of Negro Education, 13 (Summer 1944), p. 369.

6. Lena Horne and Richard Schickel, Lena (New York:
    Doubleday, 1965), p. 172.

7. Burke, op. cit., p. 137.

8. Noble, op. cit., p. 195.

9. Noble, op. cit., p. 197.

10. Noble, op. cit., p. 209.

11. Noble, op. cit., p. 210.

12. The Writers' War Board, How Writers Perpetuate
     Stereotypes, 1945, p. 5.

Among the "forced to grin" musical artists was Bill Robinson in <u>Stormy Weather.</u>   (Photo from author's collection)

Chapter 5

1946 - 1961

After World War II, the American motion picture industry turned its attention, at least temporarily, to making films about the problems confronting racial and religious minorities. The post-war period brought forth a questioning of values. William Katz notes that:

> One of the biggest problems faced by Americans of the postwar years was that of making America a land of liberty and justice for all. Many whites had returned from Europe and Asia believing that if the idea of a 'master race' was wrong for our enemies, it was wrong for America too. [1]

Home of the Brave, a stage play about anti-semitism, underwent a change of theme in its transition to the screen. The first Hollywood film to give full-length coverage to the Negro problem introduced James Edwards as Moss. As a black soldier fighting for his country in the Pacific, Moss becomes a victim of white G.I. bigotry. His consequent paralysis and eventual recovery is linked to a psychological exploration of reaction to race. The film reaches its climax when a psychiatrist deliberately provokes Moss with the line, "You dirty nigger get up and walk!"[2] This was strong language for 1949 audiences. Secrecy surrounded the production of the film.

Another Negro interest film, Pinky, was produced by Twentieth Century Fox in the same year. Jeanne Crain, a white actress, appeared in the title role, as a nurse who returns to the South after passing for white in Boston. Her washerwoman grandmother (Ethel Waters) expects Pinky to accept the substandard status accorded to blacks. After much conflict within the plot, Pinky rejects her white suitor, decides against more "passing" up North, wins justice from a white Southern court of law, and opens a nursing school for blacks on the property she has inherited from grandmother's white aristocratic employer. V. J. Jerome, then editor of Political Affairs, attacks the resolution of the problem and the characterizations:

> Yes, Pinky offers a solution. A reformist, segregationist, paternalistic solution. It is a 'solution' which, as in all past Hollywood films, builds on acceptance of the 'superiority' of the whites and ends in endorsement of Jim Crow--in this case, 'liberal,' 'benevolent,' Social-Democratic Jim Crow.
>
> Pinky, perhaps for fear that the New Stereotype is as yet imperfect for the function of Pinky's role, abounds in hideous stereotypes of the past. Pinky's grandmother, Aunt Dicey, who has accepted her oppressed status and moves about with an Uncle Tom loyalty to the 'good' white folk, fulfills the old-style 'Mammy' cliché, notwithstanding Ethel Waters' brave attempt to invest the part with some dignity. Another stock-character Negro, Jake, is the 'bad' shiftless type, the loose loafer and money-loving schemer, with 'comic relief.' Then there is Jake's 'woman,' who 'totes a razor.'[3]

The concept of "new stereotypes" which Jerome introduces became a theme of other writers in connection with subsequent film characterizations of the Negro. The issue will be treated later in this work.

A semi-documentary film released about the same time was Lost Boundaries. It told of a Negro physician and his family, and of the consequences of their "passing" for

white in a New England community.   As was the case with
Pinky, any of a number of qualified light-complexioned Negro
actors such as Ellen Holly, Fredi Washington, Jane White,
Hilda Simms, Harold Scott or Frank Silvera were not engaged for the film.   Instead, white actors were cast as the
four Negro leads.   The motion picture, largely white in its
orientation, seemed to be unconcerned with true black attitudes and opinion.   As Bloom observes in his case study of
the film:

> ...the film, looks at passing somewhat differently
> than Dr. Albert Johnston, the original creator
> of this autobiographical story.   Dr. Johnston and
> more particularly his son Albert, speak vividly of
> the gamut of opposition from his own race which
> the permanent passer must run.   The film side-
> steps this side of the issue.   In fact, when the
> movie's hero makes the decision to pass, it ap-
> pears that the decision is forced upon him more by
> fellow Negroes than by whites.   Whereas Dr. John-
> ston actually encountered all his early career diffi-
> culties from white people and the discriminatory
> practices of white society, the film inverts this
> theme, making his ordeal an intra-Negro affair... [4]

Atlanta's ban on the film, on the ground that it was
"likely to have an adverse effect on the peace, morals, and
good order of the city," was upheld by the Fifth Circuit
Court of Appeals in RD-DR Corp. v. Smith. [5]

It should be apparent that the worst element of these
1949-vintage films was a lack of honesty.   They raised phony
issues, played with them in unrealistic fashion, and finally
threw in happy endings.   Millions of black Americans, who
had no intention of "passing," were deeply concerned with
ghetto-living, unfair employment practices, housing discrimination and similar problems, ignored by these movies.

Nineteen hundred and fifty was a proud year for the

Negro in American films. Metro Goldwyn Mayer brought
William Faulkner's Intruder in the Dust to the screen with
Juano Hernandez in the role of Lucas Beauchamp. Despite
possible attempts to stereotype this character with an out-
landish costume, Hernandez gives an imposing performance
from start to finish. Burke says:

> Lucas's portrayal becomes a statement about a
> Southern black who will not be a 'nigger.' While
> the tale focusses upon a Southern community as it
> reacts to this fact--its meanings for the bulk of
> white population, a liberal minority, white trash
> and the Negro population too--both the internal and
> external conflicts in this film arise for all from
> the fact that Lucas is what he is, and stands ac-
> cused of murdering a white man. [6]

In the same year, a promising young actor named
Sidney Poitier was introduced to motion picture audiences in
the film, No Way Out. Poitier takes the role of Luther
Brooks, a medical intern, who is accused by Ray Biddle
(Richard Widmark) of professional malpractice. Biddle, a
psychopathic criminal, insists that his brother's death was
caused by Brooks. Needless to say, after a near race riot
and an attempt on his life, Dr. Brooks is vindicated. Praising the film, Poitier biographer Carolyn Ewers writes:

> To begin with, the Negroes in the film were played
> by Negroes, and their problem isn't trying to be
> white but simply trying to live decently under diffi-
> cult, trying conditions. [7]

The strong dialogue of the film, including several racial
slurs, presaged some of the films of the next decade.

In 1947 Jackie Robinson broke the color barrier in
big league baseball and became the National League's "Rookie
of the Year." In 1950, Hollywood filmed The Jackie Robinson Story with Robinson in the lead and Ruby Dee as Mrs.

Robinson. The script did not avoid revealing the racial obstacles which Robinson had to overcome in his bid for success. Mr. Robinson's direct involvement with the film gave
it a fidelity which was missing from a subsequent film biography, The Joe Louis Story (1953), starring Coley Wallace.
The presentation of the Negro in American films between the years 1946 and 1961 should be evaluated in terms
of lapses as well as advances.

At least three important motion pictures followed the
tired tradition of casting white performers in non-white roles
which might more practically have been portrayed by Negroes.
A succession of tragic mulattos was presented including Ava
Gardner in a new version of Showboat (1951), Natalie Wood
in Kings Go Forth (1958), Julie London in Night of the Quarter
Moon (1959), and Susan Kohner in a remake of Imitation of
Life (1959). Ellen Holly, a light-complexioned Negro actress,
was considered for the latter role but was passed over in
favor of the white actress. [8]

Butterfly McQueen revived her "stupid maid" characterization in such films as Mildred Pierce (1946) and Duel in
the Sun (1946).

The all-Negro musical still served up a one-dimensional view of Negro life. The craps-shooting, the garish costumes, the razor blade as weapon, the orgiastic gyration,
the over-display of dentures were present in varying degrees
in The St. Louis Blues (1958), purportedly the biography of
W. C. Handy, "father of the blues"; Porgy and Bess (1959),
the Gershwin folk opera; and Carmen Jones (1954). In his
study Burke comments:

> It is not necessary to elaborate further upon the
> 'pagan' treatment of the American Negro in this
> film adaptation of the classic 'temptress' plot.

In company with dozens of similar films, it returns
to the unmasked treatment of the black as Savage
and Ecstatic. [9]

Once again, as in the case of Hattie McDaniel, a performer gained recognition for an unfavorable Negro characterization. For Carmen Jones, Dorothy Dandridge received
the Academy of Motion Picture Arts and Sciences nomination
for the best performance by an actress in a leading role.
Although Dandridge did not win an "Oscar," it was the first
time a Negro actress had achieved a nomination in the "lead"
category.

Much discord surrounded the production of Porgy and
Bess which co-starred Dandridge with Sidney Poitier. The
controversy loomed large with the "on," "off," "on" again
commitment of Poitier to the film. In her biography, Ewers
quotes Poitier as saying,

> I hated doing Porgy and Bess, but pressure was
> brought to bear from a number of quarters and
> there was a threat of my career stopping dead still.
> I toyed with the idea of being steadfast, but I
> weakened ultimately and I did it. I didn't enjoy do-
> ing it and I have not yet completely forgiven my-
> self. [10]

Poitier and the other Negro players in the cast won
their dispute on the style of speech to be used in the film.
Standard English speech was spoken rather than the "yassuh"
Negro dialect of the original script. It is interesting to note
Harry Belafonte's reaction to this musical and another, almost identical in its presentation of the Negro. He rejected
the lead in Porgy and Bess, while accepting the lead in Carmen Jones. [11]

As in other eras, famous works of literature provided
the substance of Negro characterizations on film. In seven

motion pictures, produced between 1946 and 1961, two recur-
rent themes emerge relative to the Negro. Either he is sac-
rificed on behalf of the redemption of a white heroic figure
or he is seen as a happy subservient inhabitant of the glori-
ous old South.

Dorothy Baker's Young Man with a Horn came to the
screen in 1950 with Kirk Douglas as Rick Martin and Juano
Hernandez as Art Hazard. As an older Negro jazz musician,
Hazard teaches the young Martin all he knows about playing
trumpet. They become fast friends. After gaining success,
Martin insults Hazard, thoughtlessly. Deeply hurt, Hazard
crosses against oncoming traffic and is killed. The incident
brings first guilt, then catharsis to Martin.

In the Warner Brothers film The Breaking Point
(1950), Hernandez appears as Wesley Park, side-kick of
Harry Morgan (John Garfield). The script, based upon an
Ernest Hemingway story, requires Wesley, who is black, to
tell Harry, who is white, "I'm all set. All I worry about is
you." This canine loyalty to Harry gets Wesley shot in the
next scene.

In the 1961 film adaptation of William Faulkner's Sanc-
tuary, famed folk singer Odetta portrays Nancy. Confessing
to a crime she did not commit, Nancy goes to the gallows so
that the white heroine (Lee Remick) will be free for a second chance at happiness.

The Southern Negro folk tales of Joel Chandler Harris
came to the screen in 1947 as Walt Disney's Song of the
South. Negro actor James Baskett, as Uncle Remus, sang
"Zippity Doo Dah" and told stories which were visualized by
Disney animation. Lawrence Lemarr summarized the argu-
ment for and against the picture as follows:

> ...one opposing school of thought maintained that
> the story material was a reflection on the Negro
> and that it was antebellum and Uncle Tomish, while
> the other asserted that it was a mere whimsical
> fairy tale and that no harm would be suffered
> through its filming. [12]

Baskett was given a special award by the Academy of Motion
Picture Arts and Sciences for his role in the picture.   A
performance in a stereotyped characterization was rewarded
once more.

Eleven years later, in the Stanley Kramer production
of The Defiant Ones (1958), which was not based upon a literary work, Sidney Poitier is seen joined to actor Tony Curtis, as they portray two fugitives from a chain gang, one
black, one white.   Once their chains are disconnected, the
two men race for a freight train.   Poitier leaps aboard but
Curtis has fallen behind and will not make the train.   Poitier
leaves the train in an impulsive decision to share the fate of
his white companion, who has previously scorned him.

Although Poitier appeared in the Warner Brothers production of Robert Penn Warren's Band of Angels in 1959, the
film did little to enhance his career.   It is not even mentioned in his biography by Carolyn Ewers but the distinguished
Negro novelist, John O. Killens, had a distinct impression of
the movie:

> In one particular scene, Clark Gable, who was Sid-
> ney Poitier's good massa, was coming from New
> Orleans via the Mississippi River back to his plan-
> tation.   When the boat neared the shore, all of his
> happy faithful slaves were gathered there singing a
> song of welcome to old massa.   White people in the
> theatre were weeping, some slyly, some unasham-
> edly, at the touching scene, when suddenly my
> friend and I erupted with laughter, because we
> thought that surely, in the time of Montgomery and
> Little Rock, this must have been put into the film

for comic relief. [13]

Perhaps Killens would have found even more anachronistic the 1960 motion picture debut of Archie Moore, light heavyweight boxing champion of the world. The heroic figure to countless Negro youths portrayed "nigger" Jim in Metro Goldwyn Mayer's film, The Adventures of Huckleberry Finn. This was the third production of the Mark Twain classic in three decades, substantiating Hollywood's preference for Southern-oriented material.

Progress can be evaluated in terms of where one has yet to go as well as in terms of from where one has come. Temporarily disregarding the former and concentrating on the latter, there were several American motion pictures with a more positive image of the Negro between 1946 and 1961.

Edge of the City (1957) presented one of the more human portrayals of the Negro ever encountered in films. The character of Tommy Tyler (T. T.) played by Sidney Poitier is endowed with such qualities as courage, loyalty, compassion, humor, tenderness, generosity and understanding. He is pictured as a loving husband and father who earns his living as foreman of a gang of longshoremen. T. T.'s tastefully decorated brownstone apartment includes a large record collection and a television set. Middle class in his orientation, this character appreciates life's basic satisfactions. The film depicts several scenes of social integration between black and white characters. Praising the movie, Albert Johnson states:

> The most constructive contribution of Edge of the
> City to film history is one sequence in which Poi-
> tier talks philosophically to his white friend, using
> language that rings so truthfully and refreshingly
> in the ears that one suddenly realizes the tremen-
> dous damage that has been nurtured through the
> years because of Hollywood's perpetration of the

dialect-myth. [14]

Johnson recognizes that the film, as satisfactory as it was, had its limitations. He comments:

> ...any hint of successful integration must be con-
> cluded by death, usually in some particularly gory
> fashion, and so, Poitier gets it in the back with a
> docker's bale-hook.
>
> ...its conclusion was disturbing; audiences wanted
> to know why the Negro had to be killed in order for
> the hero to achieve self-respect. [15]

Darryl F. Zanuck released an opulent technicolor movie rendition of Alec Waugh's Island in the Sun in 1957. The story centers on the romances of two interracial couples on the fictitious isle of Santa Marta. The script permits the attraction between Margot (Dorothy Dandridge) and a white British civil servant to progress naturally, culminating in their departure together for England at the film's end. Concomitantly, the affection between David Boyeur (Harry Belafonte) and Mavis (Joan Fontaine) is denied fruition, by even so much as a caress or kiss. The evasive Hollywood treatment appeared even more conspicuous in a film such as this one, which claimed a mature theme. Failing to recognize that whites are also cast in films that have little to do with reality, Johnson contends:

> The entire film is certainly important as a study
> of the tropical myth in racial terms, and even
> Dandridge's character, though she comes out of the
> whole business fairly happily, is not entirely free
> from the stereotype of the Negro as sensualistic,
> for at one point, she performs a rather unusual
> Los Angeles-primitive dance among the Santa Marta
> natives, an act that is quite out of character, if
> one knows anything at all about the problems of
> class consciousness among the Negroes themselves
> in the West Indies. [16]

Any lack of authenticity in the character of Ralph Burton in The World, the Flesh, and the Devil (1959) may have been overlooked amid the bizarre theme of the film.   The plot deals with the relationships among three survivors of an atomic holocaust.   Sarah, an attractive young white woman, is faced with making a choice between a handsome middle aged white man and an equally handsome black man, portrayed by Harry Belafonte, who also co-produced the movie. The film establishes the fact that Ralph, a miner, is industrious, versatile, cultured, mechanically talented and extremely racially sensitive.   Challenged by the white man into a rifle duel for the affections of Sarah, Ralph appears unarmed in his personal stand against shooting as an answer. Burke considers Ralph too good to ring true, saying:

> Here again is the Negro as 'a fine, decent man' of cheerful stripe whose beaverish activity following the most calamitous of catastrophes would warm the heart of any Puritan; whose moral and ethical conduct in a distinctly amoral situation lies beyond reproach, and whose final decision it is to die, if he must, for the hopeful improvement of others. [17]

Although the script does not demand Ralph's sacrifice, neither does it resolve the racially complicated "eternal triangle."

In 1960, the cinematic portrait of the Negro in the military was more finely etched than it was in either Bataan or Home of the Brave.   Columbia's All the Young Men gave us Sidney Poitier as Sgt. Towler, on active duty in the Korean war.   Towler gives orders to his Caucasian subordinates, rebuffs derogatory epithets such as "nightfighter," donates his blood to a wounded white marine, and prevents the molestation of a Korean woman by a white southerner.   Poitier is supposed to have remarked:

> Why spend a million dollars producing a picture

about war, that makes no salient point about war, pro or con, and is hardly a work of art?[18]

Sgt. Towler, however, did represent a Negro character not witnessed before on the American motion picture screen.

Three dramatic plays, critically acclaimed on Broadway, were transferred to the motion picture medium, unsuccessfully.

Philip Yordan's Anna Lucasta, the tale of a reformed prostitute, was filmed for the second time in ten years. Unlike the first version, which had a white cast, the 1959 film co-starred Eartha Kitt and Sammy Davis Jr.[19]

The 1953 film of Carson McCullers' Member of the Wedding enabled Ethel Waters to recreate her stage portrayal of Berenice, cook and domestic, for a family with a strange adolescent daughter.

Richard Wright's Native Son (1951) was filmed in Argentina with the author taking the lead role of Bigger Thomas, enacted on stage earlier by Canada Lee. The story highlighted the social pressures in the North which frustrated and antagonized a young Negro man of limited intelligence, driving him to murder a young white woman.[20]

The "behind the scenes" activities, real or imagined, of jazz musicians, especially Negro jazz musicians, seems to hold a strange fascination for the mass communicators.

All the Fine Young Cannibals (1960) is a movie primarily about four young white persons driven by various neuroticisms. However, the film does contain a major Negro character who figures in the story line. Ruby Jones, portrayed by Pearl Bailey, is a once famous blues and jazz singer, now on the decline. Her scenes are either played in night clubs or in her bedroom. Depending upon alcohol to extinguish the torch of a broken love affair, Ruby accepts, even welcomes, the imminence of death. Chad, the white protagonist, admires and befriends Ruby. She in return provides Chad with important musical contacts in New York. When Ruby dies, a rather unusual funeral sequence reinforces the Negro as "the uninhibited expressionist" from Reddick's list of Negro stereotypes. Burke comments:

> ...this film tries to be set in the decade of the 1920's. As such, perhaps it is histrionically appropriate to find a Harlem funeral at which massed Ecstatics rock to the rhythm of a jazz band, in the style of the great jazz funeral parades of the New Orleans of that time. [21]

Paris Blues (1961) cast Sidney Poitier and Paul Newman as expatriate jazz musicians in a Paris night club. As the plot unfolds, we learn that Poitier is a refugee from American racial prejudice and injustice. Contributing a look of authenticity, Louis Armstrong appears briefly in a jam session scene. Romantic interest for Poitier in the film is provided by songstress-actress Diahann Carroll, who plays a teacher on holiday in Paris.

Two years earlier, Harry Belafonte made Odds Against Tomorrow (1959), in which he too portrayed a night club musician, a familiar occupation for Negroes in films. Although Ingram (Belafonte) is a man ensnared by unmet gambling debts and a marriage that has failed, there is still insufficient motivation for his sudden, and fatal, turn to crime. Because Ingram is the brunt of another character's overt racial prejudice, we tend to romanticize him and see him as more hero than criminal. The melodrama was filmed by Harbel Productions, Belafonte's own company, with a script by John O. Killens. Killens is among those who believe that the plight of Negroes in American motion pictures cannot be

improved significantly without the involvement of black
writers:

> ...there's never been a crop of black writers for
> film or television. If you don't work in these two
> media, you do not reach the multitudes. Holly-
> wood makes great pretensions of doing controversi-
> al movies. But the great debate in America today
> is Negro freedom. This is the fundamental contro-
> versy. How does the Negro artist break through
> this wall of censorship?[22]

Although the film industry has yet to employ the "crop"
to which Killens refers, Lorraine Hansberry and Louis Peterson, two black playwrights, did bring their major dramatic
efforts to motion pictures in 1961. Coincidentally, both plays
dealt with attempts of Negro families to live in racially integrated neighborhoods.

Peterson's drama, Take a Giant Step, introduced
Johnny Nash as Spencer Scott, young Negro adolescent. Spence
is misunderstood by Lem and Mary, his parents, by his
white school teacher and by his white friends. His aged
grandmother is his sole companion and confidante. As Abramson notes:

> Lem and Mary speak in behalf of the cultural de-
> mands made of Negroes by society and by them-
> selves when they accept their role as prescribed
> by society. They uphold the status quo, Spence,
> still in process of defining his personality, must,
> of necessity, counter their arguments in terms of
> his own emerging identity image.[23]

> It is significant that he does not take a step back-
> ward into the servitude originally prescribed by
> his parents.[24]

> The giant step that is taken is from irresponsible
> childhood through frustrated adolescence into ma-
> turity still undefined.[25]

Hansberry's Pulitzer Prize winning play, A Raisin in
the Sun, also involved the intra-relationships of its family,
the Youngers.   Walter Lee, portrayed by Sidney Poitier, is
a 35-year old Negro chauffeur who cannot provide adequately
for his wife, Ruth, his mother, Lena, his little son, Walter
Jr., and his sister Beneatha.   Poitier, himself, states:

> There is that about Walter Lee,...that is hard to
> find in terms of character structure.   There is a
> central kernel from which all of Walter Lee blos-
> soms.   He has an obsession--he wants to and has
> not been able to carve for himself a badge of dis-
> tinction.   The only acceptable one, the only one he
> recognizes, would be some material symbol of his
> life's worth.
>
> This is a guy who has no sense of direction; his
> wherewithal is that failure rather than success
> would be his lot.   Nevertheless, he has gigantic
> needs--kookie though they may be--and the conse-
> quences of not filling them would be gigantic. [26]

Appreciation of Hansberry's Negro characters was not
unanimous.   Some critics considered the story nothing more
than a soap opera made successful by America's collective
guilt over the Negro question.   It is true that we have seen
these types before--Lena, "a tyrannical but good-natured
matriarch"; Walter, "a frustrated young man surrounded by
too many women"; Beneatha, "a free-thinking college student,"
but it is equally true that we have never seen them before as
Negroes. [27]

Perhaps more to the point, this film represents a
milestone in that motion picture audiences were given a
glimpse of real life black people, motivated by fundamental
and universal issues.   Burke explains:

> ...this story is unique in the degree to which it
> directs sensitive attention to honest forms and ex-

pressions of Negro reality, as opposed to low-level
melodramatic treatment of mere themes. A care-
ful tracing of the dramatic terms of development
reveals the considerable richness of character where
all the Negroes are concerned. The foremost fact
of this film is the essential humanity of its characters. They are not mere stereotypes. [28]

Notes

1. William Loren Katz, Eyewitness: The Negro in
   American History, (New York: Pitman, 1967),
   p. 457.

2. Home of the Brave (United Artists, 1949).

3. V. J. Jerome, The Negro in Hollywood Films (New
   York: Masses & Mainstream, 1950), p. 28.

4. Samuel W. Bloom, "A Social Psychological Study of
   Motion Picture Audience Behavior: A Case Study
   of the Negro Image in Mass Communication,"
   (Unpublished Ph. D. dissertation, University of
   Wisconsin, 1956), p. 128.

5. Richard S. Randall, Censorship of the Movies, The
   Social and Political Control of the Mass Medium,
   (Madison: The University of Wisconsin Press,
   1968), p. 24.

6. William L. Burke, "The Presentation of the Ameri-
   can Negro in Hollywood Films, 1946-1961: An
   Analysis of a Selected Sample of Feature Films,"
   (Unpublished Ph. D. dissertation, Northwestern
   University, 1965), p. 197.

7. Carolyn H. Ewers, Sidney Poitier: The Long Journey, (New York: The New American Library,
   1969), p. 61.

8. Ellen Holly, "Living a White Life-for a While,"
   The New York Times, August 10, 1969, p. D13.

9. Burke, op. cit., p. 248.

10. Ewers, op. cit., p. 89.

11. Bob Thomas, "Power is Difference to Richer Bela-
    fonte," The Plain Dealer, August 11, 1957, p.
    10 quoted in George E. Simpson and J. Milton
    Yinger, Racial and Cultural Minorities, 3rd ed.,
    (New York: Harper, 1965), p. 480-481.

12. Pittsburgh Courier, July 26, 1947, p. 10.

13. John O. Killens, "Hollywood in Black and White,"
    in Boroff, David, The State of the Union,
    (Englewood Cliffs, New Jersey: Prentice-Hall,
    1966), pp. 102-103.

14. Albert Johnson, "Beige, Brown or Black," Film
    Quarterly, 13:1 (Fall 1959), p. 39.

15. Ibid.

16. Johnson, op. cit., pp. 40-41.

17. Burke, op. cit., pp. 277-278.

18. Ewers, op. cit., p. 94.

19. Sammy Davis, Jr., Jane Boyar and Burt Boyar,
    Yes I Can: The Story of Sammy Davis, Jr.,
    (N.Y.: Farrar, Straus & Giroux, 1965), p. 425.

20. Doris E. Abramson, Negro Playwrights in the
    American Theatre, 1925-1959, (New York:
    Columbia University Press, 1969), p. 136.

21. Burke, op. cit., p. 280-281.

22. Killens, op. cit., p. 106.

23. Abramson, op. cit., pp. 231-232.

24. Ibid., p. 238.

25. Ibid.

26. Ewers, op. cit., pp. 92-93.

27. Abramson, op. cit., p. 254.

28. Burke, op. cit., p. 287.

Chapter 6

1962

The eyes and ears of the world were upon the United
States in 1962, with special focus on the South. This was
the year in which no less than eight Negro churches were
burned in the state of Georgia. This was also the year in
which President John F. Kennedy issued an executive order
barring racial and religious discrimination in federally-fi-
nanced housing. Finally, it was in 1962 that Mississippi
Governor Ross Barnett defied a federal government court order for the admission of James Meredith, Negro graduate
student, to the University of Mississippi. Despite Barnett's
attempt at "interposition," Meredith, accompanied by federal
marshals, was enrolled at the University. The ensuing riots
on and near the campus resulted in two deaths and other cas-
ualties. Edward W. Brooke became the first Negro elected
to the office of state attorney general (Massachusetts) in the
United States.[1]

With the exception of Sidney Poitier's performance in
Pressure Point, the appearances of Negroes in American motion pictures during 1962 were limited to supporting roles in
several productions which even film critics did not consider
as serious film fare. This paucity of movies with Negro
portrayals was underscored even further by the recent re-
membrance of A Raisin in the Sun (1961).

It appears that all the portrayals observed during
1962 included one or more of Reddick's familiar Negro

stereotypes. [2]

Beah Richards acts the part of Viney, servant in the Keller household, for the motion picture, The Miracle Worker. Based upon the successful Broadway play, the film provided little more than stage entrances and exits for this version of "the devoted servant."

Woody Strode appears as Pompey in Man Who Shot Liberty Valance. Pompey is employee and side-kick to Tom Doniphon (John Wayne), one of the film's heroes. The other characters, who are white, address him merely to give orders. On the few occasions in which he emerges from the background, he is being sent on an errand. Pompey is one of two people to share a secret pertinent to the plot. This is a phenomenon common to Negro portrayals as will be noted in subsequent characterizations. Pompey's unexplained and unquestionable loyalty to Doniphon makes him "the devoted servant." Ransom Stoddard (James Stewart) conducts school classes which Pompey attends. While reciting lines from the Declaration of Independence, Pompey falters over, "We hold these truths to be self-evident, that all men are created equal." Stoddard reassures him with a double entendre, "That's all right, Pompey, a lot of people forget that part." Pompey's "You know I don't drink," said to Doniphon, establishes his moral character. Pompey is heroic too, carrying Doniphon out of a house aflame. When Doniphon dies, Pompey sits by the coffin in obvious grief. [3]

James Edwards performs the role of Corporal Melvin, a soldier who has experienced communist brainwashing, in the motion picture, Manchurian Candidate. Joe Adams plays a psychiatrist in the same motion picture. The film-makers obviously wanted to integrate their production and both performers make token appearances that are more visual than substantive.

The Twentieth Century Fox film, Hemingway's Adventures of a Young Man, presents Juano Hernandez in a characterization that is brief but worthy of mention because of
his performance. The entire movie consists of a series of
unrelated episodes in the life of Nick Adams, supposedly the
young Hemingway. After leaving home, as a young man,
Adams encounters an assortment of picturesque characters.
Among these is Ad Francis (Paul Newman in a cameo role).
Francis, a former boxing champion, now down on his luck,
is accompanied by an older man, a Negro called Bugs.
Both men make Adams welcome. In the few scenes of this
sequence, Bugs is seen catering to every need of Ad Francis.
He is solicitous, protective and totally immersed in his care
of the "punchy" pugilist. When Francis experiences an apparent mental decline, arguing with the well-meaning Adams,
Bugs has no choice but to send the latter on his way. The
Negro, Bugs, is solely occupied with the well-being of another person. This is a familiar part for Juano Hernandez,
who portrayed almost identical characters in Young Man with
a Horn and The Breaking Point, both mentioned in the last
chapter. Hernandez lends stature to almost any role he undertakes and Hemingway's Adventures of a Young Man was
no exception, for the Times critic said he "is dignified and
doleful."[4] None the less, the character of Bugs comes within the province of Reddick's "a devoted servant" stereotype.
That Bugs serves Ad Francis out of loyalty rather than for
monetary gain is of little consequence. He is "a devoted
servant."

Falling in the same category is the film portrayal of
Elvira Stitt done by Maidie Norman in Warner Brothers'
What Ever Happened to Baby Jane? Elvira is a sleep-out

maid-housekeeper for two retired actresses, Blanche and
Jane Hudson. Elvira's loyalty is to the nicer sister, Blanche
(Joan Crawford), who is confined to a wheel chair. Elvira
dislikes Jane (Bette Davis), who is obsessed by a jealousy
and hatred of Blanche. When Jane stealthily opens Blanche's
personal mail, it is Elvira who informs Blanche. Elvira also reluctantly accepts extra time-off from work, granted by
Jane, fearing Blanche might need her. Following her sudden dismissal, part of Jane's insane plot against Blanche,
Elvira returns unsummoned to the Hudson household. Anx-
iety over the welfare of her employer is written on her face
as she approaches Blanche's room. Sneaking up behind Elvira, the demented Jane bludgeons her to death. Even Elvira's demise is told in terms of her mistress. We hear
the fatal blow as the camera pans to the look of horror in
Blanche's eyes, which confirm Elvira's murder. Like Bugs,
in his relationship to Ad Francis, Elvira is solicitous, protective and totally immersed in her care of the invalid rec-
luse, Blanche. Elvira Stitt is still another example of Reddick's "devoted servant."

    The motion picture version of The Connection brought
Carl Lee, son of the late black actor, Canada Lee, to the
screen in the role he created in Jack Gelber's Off-Broadway
play. Lee portrays Cowboy, "the connection" referred to by
the title. Several narcotics addicts reveal themselves to
each other as they await Cowboy and their "fix." The camera emphasizes the story's dismal setting in a loft apartment, even focusing upon cockroaches on the wall. There is
no plot, as such, merely characterizations. Arriving in the
middle of the film, Cowboy performs an integrative function;
he is the link between the other characters. Time observed
another image for Cowboy.

> Cowboy appears as a Negro dressed entirely in
> white--that is to say, as a union of opposites, as
> a completeness possible perhaps only in God. He
> comes moreover as a redeemer. One by one, and
> through the veil of a sanctuary, he leads the junk-
> ies through a door marked TOILET. One by one
> he injects them with an elixir that washes away
> their wretchedness...[5]

The notion of a "redeemer" was an ironical choice of

words to associate with the film, which indeed required a

sort of redemption. The Connection played for two perform-

ances on opening day, then was withdrawn on order of the

court. The censorship involved the repeated use in the film

of a four-letter word which has been employed by some to

describe human excrement. In the context of narcotics, the

word is slang for heroin. One month later, the courts ruled

that the film was not obscene and it was cleared for showing

in New York State.

In this film, Cowboy is a character portrayed by a

Negro as distinguishable from a Negro character per se.

Kenneth Tynan notes:

> Some of the characters are Negro, others Cau-
> casian. The colour of their skin is of negligible
> importance. 'The Connection' is probably the first
> American play of which this could be said. In a
> preliminary note, the author stresses that, although
> he envisaged some of the characters as white and
> others as coloured, 'there need not be any rigidity,
> in casting.' This constitutes a minor, but vital,
> revolution. [6]

Although Cowboy traffics in drugs, he does so without

shame. He accepts his role of drug pusher as a natural

consequence of our society. While Cowboy may evade the

police, he does not run from himself. In his own words:

> COWBOY: Everything that's illegal is illegal be-
>   cause it makes more money for more

people that way.

SOLLY: That may be right. But, junk does take
            its effect.

COWBOY: We all pay our dues whatever we do. [7]

Cowboy will not accept blame for his actions. He as-
signs responsibility to the addicts for their predicament.
From Reddick's roster, he qualifies as "the irresponsible
citizen," but he is not evil enough to be labeled "the vicious
criminal."

Sammy Davis Jr. was responsible for two Negro characterizations on screen in 1962. Davis, because of his eminence as a performer, received stellar billing in the two
films but actually both assignments were in supporting roles.

Sergeants 3 was a loose remake of the movie Gunga
Din, based upon the Rudyard Kipling tale. Just two years
earlier, in 1960, Davis appeared with his friends Frank Sinatra, Dean Martin, Peter Lawford and Joey Bishop in
Oceans 11, an escapist entertainment film of no particular
significance. For Sergeants 3, the famous quintet did an en-
core of their antics. The Kipling plot and characterizations,
adapted for this film by W. R. Burnett, were subordinated to
the special talents of the five stars.

Briefly, the film was set in the wild west of the
1870's--Medicine Bend, specifically. Jonah Williams (Davis),
a former slave, is bullied by some white buffalo hunters.
Sgts. Mike Merry (Sinatra), Chip Deal (Martin) and Larry
Barrett (Lawford) rescue Jonah in the traditional western film
brawl. Grateful Jonah, "the devoted servant," attaches himself to the three soldiers, tending horses. In the course of
the plot, Chip finds himself imprisoned. He persuades Jonah
to execute his escape, promising that a feat of daring will

earn Jonah a place in the army. Gullible Jonah, "the mental
inferior," employs his mule to kick down the jail, thereby
freeing Chip.   Later, when the sergeants are captured by
war-crazed Indians (another ethnic stereotype), it is the
wounded Jonah who manages to blow the regiment's favorite
tune on his bugle ("the natural born musician"), thus saving
the day. The three sergeants are decorated for heroism and
Jonah is made a trooper. Although it is Jonah who is responsible for the military triumph, he receives no decorations.
Instead, he is admitted to the lowest military rank available,
with the implicit assumption that this represents the level of
his aspirations. [8]

    Several years prior to Sergeants 3, Davis indicated a
desire to make a western film.   His biography quotes him as
follows:

> ...I'll play anything except an Uncle Tom, but
> don't brush off the Western thing so fast. Aside
> from the fact that I happen to be better with the
> guns than most of the Schwab's Drugstore cowboys
> they're using, it also happens there were a lot of
> colored cowboys.
>
> The guys who wrote the history books happened to
> be white, and by a strange coincidence they manage
> to overlook just about everything any Negro did in
> and for America except pull barges up the...Mis-
> sissippi.   But I've got books on the early West, I
> can sit here and do an hour on authentic stories
> about Negro cowboys, an entire Negro regiment in
> the Civil War, dozens of things that have never
> been used--a wealth of fresh stuff... [9]

These remarks have special interest when reviewed in the
light of the characterization of Jonah Williams. It is true
that Sergeants 3 was an attempt at parody, which neither audiences nor critics were expected to take seriously. Nevertheless, the author has identified above three Negro stereo-

types from Reddick's list which were present in the portrayal
of Jonah.

In a completely different vein was Sammy Davis Jr.'s
portrayal of a Negro in a motion picture based upon John
Resko's autobiography, Reprieve. The film's release title,
Convicts 4, was a rather obvious attempt to capitalize on the
publicity attached to the Oceans 11 and Sergeants 3 titles.

Sentenced to prison, Johnny Resko (Ben Gazzara) is
assigned to a cell already occupied by Wino (Davis). Wino's
racial attitude is established immediately by the opening dialogue between Johnny and him.

> WINO: ...Don't call me Shine, don't amuse me.
> My name is Wino. And don't rub my head
> for luck cause I ain't your Uncle Tom...
> Don't expect me to warble 'Swing Low,
> Sweet Chariot'...[10]

In an unsuccessful attempt at intra-prison extortion,
Wino threatens Johnny:

> WINO: Hey, don't be misled by my youth. I'm a
> walking razor blade, man.[11]

Here is an unequivocal statement of Reddick's "the
razor and knife toter," but this is not the only stereotype attributed to Wino. He is also "the unhappy non-white" as illustrated by the following conversation:

> WINO: ...it's a lily-white world, man, and I
> was always a stranger.

> JOHNNY: Maybe you made yourself a stranger.

> WINO: The jobs I had, the places I lived, they
> made me a stranger. Look! for openers,
> the first job, right? Grand Central Sta-
> tion washroom attendant. I gave that up
> for something real fancy--real fancy ad-
> dress--400 Central Park South--my

name, first of the push buttons...

JOHNNY: How did you get in there? I mean,
          er...

WINO: I know what you mean. It was easy.
          My pad was second floor, beneath the
          street level, residence of the janitor.
          Yes ma'am, no sir, I'll get that fixed,
          right away ma'am. I hated every ma'am
          and every sir in New York City, man,
          every palefaced peckerwood with a de-
          cent job and a good pad. I couldn't
          lick em and I couldn't join em, Johnny.
          Left me doubled with envy. [12]

Wino is also depicted as an illiterate. He is grateful
to Johnny for teaching him to read. Since Wino is imprisoned for robbery, his release from prison, rather early in
the film, comes not unexpectedly. The final scenes of Wino's
role intimate his probable rehabilitation.

Stanley Kramer's release of Pressure Point brought
the only Negro characterization in a leading role to American
motion pictures in 1962. Kramer was no stranger to racial
theme films, having produced Home of the Brave and The Defiant Ones, cited in Chapter 5. Pressure Point stars Sidney
Poitier as a prison psychiatrist and Bobby Darin as his patient. As in The Defiant Ones, the counterpoint relationship
between the black man and the white man is the focus of the
film. All other roles are subsidiary. The character Poitier
plays was originally written as a white man. Kramer justifies the change with this comment:

> In changing the character of the prison psychiatrist
> to a Negro, we had both sound dramatic value and
> realism in mind. Obviously the psychiatrist-pa-
> tient relationship would have greater explosive
> qualities through such a switch. Realistically, we
> felt there was a chance to broaden the opportuni-
> ties available, a move that was more justified

by the fact that there are an increasing number
of qualified Negro psychiatrists in the country. [13]

Pressure Point begins with a young white psychiatrist
(Peter Falk) failing to make progress with a black patient.
He reports his professional frustration to his middle aged
black supervisor (Poitier), who recalls a similarly difficult,
but racially reversed, case at the beginning of his career.
Using the flashback technique, these recollections unfold as
the main plot of the film. During World War II, the then
young psychiatrist (Poitier) is assigned a hostile patient
(Darin) who has been imprisoned for subversive activities
with the German American Bund. In addition to his fascist,
anti-semitic, anti-Negro proclivities, the patient is dangerously psychotic.

All the characters in this film are nameless. About
the psychiatrist, our main concern, we are given little personal information. In keeping with the tradition of his profession, this psychiatrist speaks little and listens a great
deal. What we do learn about him is revealed mostly through
the lines uttered by other characters. He exercises extreme
patience when racially baited by his patient:

> PATIENT: Who ever heard of a Negro psychiatrist
> anyway? Don't you people have enough
> troubles? Boy, you must be a real
> masochist.

> DOCTOR: Why can't a Negro be a psychiatrist?

> PATIENT: Oh he can...he can but where is he go-
> ing to get his patients outside of a fed-
> eral penitentiary? Psychiatry is an ex-
> pensive thing. Your people can't af-
> ford it, you know. So the best you can
> be is a prison psychiatrist in the worst
> office they've got. You want to help
> me? Why don't you just help yourself?

DOCTOR: What do you mean?

PATIENT: This isn't the place for you. ...you
people are trying to be white, respectable, want to be doctors, psychiatrists.
Why don't you wise up?

DOCTOR: How would I do that?

PATIENT: Go back to Africa. [14]

There is no doubt about the professional worth of the
young black psychiatrist, nor any question about the quality
of his achievement in a demanding position.   In the words of
his superior:

CHIEF MEDICAL OFFICER: ...I insisted on hiring
you. You're a good man.   You had a
good record.   I liked the way you spoke
but underneath I wasn't so sure.   Apart
from taking the responsibility of giving
the job to a Negro, I couldn't dismiss
the possibility that I could have been
wrong, that you might not live up to my
expectations, which could have been unpleasant for both of us but you did.   Not
only did you justify my expectations but
you surpassed them.   Yes you did.   The
staff feels the same way. [15]

The Chief Medical Officer's praise is marred by the
thinly-veiled threat that the black psychiatrist is subject to
probation.   Yet, it takes the harsh taunting of his hostile patient to bring his insecurity to the surface.

PATIENT: All men are created equal, everything
this country is supposed to live by, right?
You personally, as far as you're concerned, Joe Miller could have written
the 'Bill of Rights.'   It's even funnier.
What have you got?   What can you do?
Can you walk on a bus or a streetcar or
a train and sit down with a little dignity
like a free human being, like a free man?

You want to see a movie, can you walk
in just any theatre? Some flapjacks
cooking in the window, can you say,
'Hey, I'll have some of those flapjacks.
You're a Negro with some brains; you
can use a little education. Can you go
to the school where you can get it best?
Maybe you see a house you like and
you've even got the money to buy it.
Can you live there?...You live in the
ghetto, north, east, south, or west, you
live where they let you live, in Harlem,
U. S. A. Now, maybe you're good at
some job. Can you go to work where
you can make something out of it? Can
you do any of those things, doctor?
And, how about your kids? Are your
kids going to do any of those things?

DOCTOR: Maybe...

PATIENT: Maybe, hah? Sure they will. Oh yeh!
In about fifty-five hundred years. Have
they got you so beat doctor that you
don't know when somebody's making
sense. Now, you hypnotize me. hah?
Well they got you hypnotized, they've
got you so mixed up that you're singing
'My Country Tis of Thee' while they
walk all over you.

DOCTOR: Right then and there, I knew what I was
frightened of. [16]

The psychiatrist was indeed frightened by his vulner-
ability in the face of such a graphic indictment of American
racial injustice. One can only conjecture as to the reasons
for having so strong a statement come, not from the victim,
the black man, but from a white fascist paranoiac. This
could only tend to vitiate the validity of the accusation.

Finally we are given the image of Reddick's "the unhappy non-white." The psychiatrist objects to the parole of
the patient, who is still dangerously ill. He is overruled,

just because he is black, we are led to believe. Although his judgment is subsequently vindicated, when the patient is hanged for the brutal murder of an elderly man, this provides no solution for "the unhappy non-white."

In a leading role for the first time, a black actor appeared as a psychiatrist. However, there was no real abandonment of traditional Negro stereotypes in the American motion pictures released during the year.

No appraisal of the status of blacks in motion pictures during 1962 could be complete without mention of the Twentieth Century Fox production, The Longest Day. Anyone viewing this "blockbuster" based upon the book by Cornelius Ryan would assume erroneously that no black Americans contributed to the European victory in World War II. "There were at least 1,700 Afro-Americans in the first wave establishing the Omaha and Utah beachheads in France on 'D Day.'"[17]

Notes

1.   Ebony, The Negro Handbook (Chicago: Johnson Publishing Co., 1966), pp. 50-51, 320.

2.   Lawrence D. Reddick, "Educational Programs for the Improvement of Race Relations: Motion Pictures, Radio, the Press and Libraries," Journal of Negro Education, Summer 1944, p. 369.

3.   Man Who Shot Liberty Valance (Paramount Pictures, 1962).

4.   The New York Times, July 26, 1962, p. 17.

5.   Time, October 5, 1962, p. M18.

6.   Jack Gelber, The Connection (New York: Grove Press, 1960), p. 10.

7. The Connection (Allen Hogdon Films, 1962).

8. Sergeants 3 (United Artists, 1962).

9. Sammy Davis, Jr., Jane Boyar and Burt Boyar, Yes I Can: The Story of Sammy Davis, Jr., (N.Y.: Farrar, Straus & Giroux, 1965), p. 421.

10. Convicts 4 (Allied Artists, 1962).

11. Ibid.

12. Ibid.

13. Stanley Kramer quoted in Royal D. Colle, "The Negro Image and the Mass Media," (Unpublished Ph.D. dissertation, Cornell University, 1967), p. 67.

14. Pressure Point (United Artists, 1962).

15. Ibid.

16. Ibid.

17. Jesse H. Walker, "Theatricals," New York Amsterdam News, June 7, 1969, p. 43.

Chapter 7

1963

The Emancipation Proclamation centennial was marked
by a gigantic march on Washington, D.C. of thousands of civil rights demonstrators, black and white. The mass media
carried the story around the world. In Mississippi, three
months after a Negro voter registration campaign got under-
way, Medgar W. Evers, a field secretary for the National
Association for the Advancement of Colored People, was slain
by a racially motivated assassin. Four black girls were
killed in the bombing of a Baptist church in Birmingham,
Alabama. James Baldwin, Negro author, wrote The Fire
Next Time, an emotionally charged book that predicted doom
for all Americans if the racial crisis should remain insolv-
able. Carl T. Rowan, a Negro, was named U.S. ambassador
to Finland.[1] Birmingham became the scene of non-violent
civil rights demonstrations under the leadership of Dr. Martin Luther King. Local police used dogs, clubs, fire hoses
and other violent tactics to dissuade the Negroes. More than
2000 demonstrators, including Dr. King, were arrested before the campaign ended.[2] President John F. Kennedy, who
was soon to be assassinated, told the nation in an historic
address that segregation was morally wrong. Before outlin-
ing his program of correction, the President noted recent
achievements:

In the last two years, more progress has been

68

made in securing the civil rights of all Americans than
in any comparable period in our history. Progress
has been made--through executive action, litigation,
persuasion, and private initiative--in achieving and
protecting equality of opportunity in education, voting, transportation, employment, housing, government, and the enjoyment of public accommodations. [3]

Of the ten American motion pictures in 1963 with Negro characterizations, four were original screen plays, three
were based on novels, three were derived from stage plays.
Two of the films, Gone Are the Days and Lilies of the Field,
included Negroes as the stars of the productions. As in preceding chapters, supporting role characterizations will be
discussed first.

Diana Sands was cast as Janice, a free-lance photog-
rapher, in An Affair of the Skin. The script was written by
Ben Maddow, director of the film, who also wrote the script
of The Balcony, the next film to be discussed. Miss Sands,
a stage actress, made her film debut in A Raisin in the Sun
(1961). As Janice, she is friend and confidante to the white
principals in the story. Although the plot attempts to involve
her in an interracial affair with a married man, Janice rejects the idea. It is her work, not romance, that concerns
her. She is temperamental, articulate, intelligent and chic.
Although she appears to have no problem as a Negro, she
does have a "mother problem." Thus, we have scenes in
which Janice purposefully makes noises simulating sexual rap-
ture in order to taunt her mother. In an emotional outburst,
Janice tells her mother to take her piano and go home. The
entire portrayal is one of a human being first, a Negro second.

The Walter Reade Sterling production of Jean Genet's
The Balcony featured Ruby Dee as "Thief," a role not racial-

ly described.   The action of the film takes place in a brothel,
where the prostitutes enact, with the aid of props, fantasy
mise en scène requested by their clients.   An accountant
(Peter Brocco), masquerading as a "Judge," badgers one
prostitute (Dee) who is pretending to be a witness, into confessing imaginary thefts.   Stretching her limbs, "Thief"
moves sensuously about the room, clad in tights.   She is
every inch "the uninhibited expressionist."   The sexual conflict between "Judge" and "Thief" is heightened by the bi-
racial casting of the two roles, carrying in each line a hint
of racial antagonism:

> THIEF: (To Judge, indicating the shoe on her
> foot which is extended) Lick it, lick it,
> lick it, lick it.   I won't do a thing until
> you lick it.   Do what I tell you.

> THIEF: I want you to crawl, I want you to crawl.

> (Judge bends over and kisses the top of
> Thief's shoe.)

> THIEF: Lick it again, again.   (Tears appear in
> her eyes.)[4]

As illustrated by the above lines, Genet's dialogue is highly
symbolic, with more than a suggestion of perversion.   Ben
Maddow's script sought to bring Bernard Frechtman's trans-
lation of the original French more in line with the American
idiom.   For example, the words "service entrance" are substituted for "tradesmen's entrance" in one of Thief's speeches.
On the basis of her occupation as a prostitute, "Thief" is the
female version of Reddick's "the sexual superman," and in
her customer's fanciful tableau she is "the petty thief."

United Artists released the motion picture version of
Lillian Hellman's stage drama, Toys in the Attic, in 1963.

Appearing in the small but noticeable role of Henry Simpson
is Negro actor Frank Silvera.

> Silvera is very light-skinned and has no conspicu-
> ous Negro features. It probably would have been
> possible for him to pass had he elected to do so.
> He played small bits first as a Negro, then as
> Latins, South Americans and other darker skinned
> races, and then roles unidentified by race.[5]

As chauffeur and mulatto lover of Albertine Prine (Gene Tier-
ney), Henry is peripherally involved in the film's sub-plot
concerning miscegenation. Contributing to the climax of the
drama, Henry reveals the hidden Negro background of Mrs.
Cyrus Walkins, wife of a white southern potentate:

HENRY:	She was in love with Julian once. She hates Walkins, wanted to leave him for years, maybe this is the money to leave with.
ALBERTINE:	How do you know about Mrs. Walkins?
HENRY:	I don't anymore. I used to. She's cousin to me.
ALBERTINE:	Did Walkins know that when he mar-ried her?
HENRY:	He doesn't know it now.[6]

The portrayal of Henry Simpson is in positive terms. He is
not "the devoted servant," in the Reddick sense. Devoted he
is, to be sure, but as Albertine's confidant rather than as
her chauffeur. Nor is Henry "the unhappy non-white." Accepted as a light-complexioned Negro by the other characters
in the film, Henry has no thought of "passing." The main
characters, who happen to be white, include the childlike
Lily, the latently incestuous Carrie and the greedy immature
Julian. As one of the film's few dignified characters, Henry

Simpson is apparently free from stereotype.

Not so flawless was the characterization of "Educated" in the motion picture, Johnny Cool. Sammy Davis, Jr., apparently not content with performing the Negro stereotype "Wino" in Convicts 4 (1962), appears as a "craps-shooter" in one dice game sequence. Since "Educated" is the only black seen in the film, the negative ethnic portrayal cannot be balanced.

In still another cameo performance during the year, Eddie "Rochester" Anderson joins an all-star cast in the Stanley Kramer production of It's A Mad Mad Mad Mad World. The film is little more than one gigantic chase for a hidden "pot of gold." Among the assorted characters in pursuit of the loot is a black taxi-cab driver portrayed by Anderson. The rather heavily etched racial joke becomes too obvious when Anderson is hurled from a falling fireman's ladder into the lap of a statue of Abraham Lincoln which just happens to be in a nearby park.

As if these last two mentioned portrayals weren't enough to justify black protest, the distinguished Negro actor Frederick O'Neal is cast in a film with the racially-taunting title, Free, White and 21. Fortunately, the low-budget movie had a limited local neighborhood release. Ernie Jones (O'Neal) is accused of the rape of a blonde Swedish "freedom rider." Trite dialogue, uneasy situations and a glaring absence of cinematic expertise destroy any latent merit to which the film might pretend. In a final bid for cheap exploitation, the audience is asked to determine the guilt or innocence of Ernie Jones.

Rape by Negroes seemed to be something of a motion picture fixation in 1963, recurring in To Kill a Mockingbird. Once again the story transpires in a small southern town.

Attorney Atticus Finch (Gregory Peck) is defending a Negro,
Tom Robinson (Brock Peters), who has been indicted for the
alleged rape-assault of a white girl.   The script tries hard
to elicit sympathy for Tom.   The tragic consequences of his
socio-economic status in southern society are revealed:

> TOM: I can't use my left hand at all.   I got it
>   caught in a cotton gin when I was twelve
>   years old.   All my muscles were tore
>   loose. [7]

We soon infer that Tom has been falsely accused, but the
legal ability and integrity of Atticus is all that stands between
Tom and his conviction by a racially biased court.   In this
milieu, we might expect Tom to be docile, cautious and even
frightened, but surely not as helpless and witless as depicted
in the following dialogue:

> TOM: ...and the next thing I know she grabbed
>   me round the legs.   She scared me so bad
>   I hopped down and turned the chair over.
>   That was the only thing, the only furniture
>   disturbed in the room, Mr. Finch, I
>   swear, when I left it.
>
> FINCH: And what happened after you turned the
>   chair over?   Tom?   You've sworn to tell
>   the whole truth.   Will you do it?   What
>   happened after that?
>
> TOM: Mr. Finch, I got down off the chair and I
>   turned around and she sorta jumped on me.
>   She hugged me around the waist.   She
>   reached up and kissed me on the face and
>   she said she'd never kissed a grown man
>   before and she might as well kiss me.   She
>   says for me to kiss her back and I said
>   Miss Mayella let me out of here.   I tried
>   to run.   Mr. Ewell cussed at her from the
>   window.   He said he's gonna kill her.
>
> FINCH: And what happened after that?

TOM: I was running so fast I don't know what
        happened. [8]

Surprising even the prosecuting attorney, Tom displays the
symptoms of "the devoted servant" in the ensuing testimony:

PROSECUTOR: How come you so all-fired anxious
             to do that woman's chores?

TOM: Looks like she...she didn't have nobody
        to help her. Like I said she...

PROSECUTOR: With Mr. Ewell and seven children
             on the place? You did all this chopping
             and work out of sheer goodness boy? You
             mighty good fellow it seems. Did all that
             for not one penny?

TOM: Yes sir, I felt right sorry for her. She
        seems...

PROSECUTOR: A white woman? You felt sorry,
             for her? [9]

As Pinky did fourteen years earlier, Tom Robinson wins justice from a bigoted southern court. The parallel ends there.
The white community accepted the judicial verdict relative to
Pinky; it did not in Tom Robinson's case. Following his
acquittal, he is murdered by local whites, who could not
abide fair play for the Negro farm worker.

        The plight of the southern black received additional
attention in Otto Preminger's The Cardinal. The role of the
black Catholic priest in this film was undertaken by Ossie
Davis. Father Gillis (Davis) visits Rome, entreating the aid
of the Pope in desegregating a Catholic school in Georgia.
Father Fermoyle (Tom Tryon), eventually the Cardinal of the
title, is the only sympathetic member of the Vatican staff.
Discouraged, Father Gillis returns to the United States.
Some time after, when Fermoyle makes an unofficial visit to
Georgia, Gillis says, "I can't believe you're here. I didn't

think anybody cared." Father Gillis is portrayed as an activist:

> GILLIS: Quite a few of the folks in my parish, they feel it's time to make some changes. So a bunch of them went and threw a picket line around that white school. Then I got a lot of phone calls and letters with no names signed. And then one night these men with white hoods, they burned my church. [10]

Heartened by the support of Fermoyle, Gillis plans to testify concerning the crime of arson. Both men are beaten by local Klan members. Now Gillis has one more reason to give testimony. Although it is not filmed, we learn in a subsequent scene that justice has been doled out. The perpetrators of the aforementioned crimes of arson and assault are found guilty of disorderly conduct, for the first time on the testimony of a black man.

In the novel, as Father Fermoyle travels through the South, he receives a vicious beating, prompted by anti-Catholic rather than anti-Negro sentiment. Otto Preminger added the Father Gillis characterization and the school desegregation issue to his film, possibly challenged by news of parochial school integration incidents in New Orleans and other places. Perhaps Father Gillis is liberated from the usual Negro stereotypes because he is a character unburdened by a prior existence in the novel. [11]

His role in The Cardinal was not the only motion picture contribution of Ossie Davis in 1963. Davis co-starred with his wife, Ruby Dee in Gone Are the Days, a film based upon his own play, Purlie Victorious. The movie is an hilarious satire on the racial mores of the old South. "What Martin Luther King is doing with love," said its author, "I am trying to do with laughter."[2]

The four major black characterizations of the story
are intentionally Negro stereotypes. Reverend Purlie Victorious Judson is "the petty thief." He has devised a scheme
which will relieve white old Captain Cotchapee (Sorrel Booke)
of a sum of money. Lutie Belle Jenkins (Ruby Dee) is "the
mental inferior." When Purlie tries to invoke a spirit of
racial pride within Lutie, she remarks, "I'm a great one for
race pride except I don't need it much in my line of work,"
which happens to be a domestic. Gitloe Judson (Godfrey
Cambridge) is "the natural-born musician." As "deputy for
the colored," a euphemism for Uncle Tom, Gitloe soothes
a cantankerous Captain Cotchapee by singing a refrain of
"Old Black Joe." Idella Landrie (Beah Richards) is "the devoted servant." When Idella is disappointed with an action
taken by Charlie Cotchapee (Alan Alda), the Captain's adult
son, she reflects, "Twenty years of being more than a mother to you!" The satirical nature of these characterizations,
even in the hands of skilled performers, is difficult to sus-
tain. Film critic Stanley Kauffmann comments, "Sometimes[13]
it gets tedious, particularly when it loses its parody vein...."

When Captain Cotchapee learns that his son has con-
spired against him in the interests of the blacks, he is enraged. Still standing, he succumbs to apoplexy, but not without hearing Purlie declare:

> PURLIE: I am released of you. The entire Negro
> people is released of you. Now, no more
> shouting hallelujah every time you sneeze
> and no more jumping jack-assed because
> you happen to be whistling 'Dixie.' We
> goin' a love you if you let us and laugh as
> we leave if you don't. Now we want our
> cut of the Constitution and we want it now.
> And not as a taste, spoon by spoon.

Throw it at us with a shovel.[14]

With the death of the Captain, a church for the blacks becomes a reality. Using Purlie's pulpit, Ossie Davis, author,
delivers a final message to his audiences:

> PURLIE: ... Today, my friends, I find, in
> being black a thing of beauty, a joy, a
> strength, a secret cup of gladness, a na-
> tive land and neither time nor place, a na-
> tive land in every Negro face. Be loyal
> to yourselves, your skin, your lips, your
> hair, your southern speech, your laugh
> and kindness. A Negro kingdom, vast, as
> any others. Accept therefore the sweet-
> ness of your blackness, not wishing to be
> red or white or yellow or any other race
> or thing but this. Farewell my deep and
> Africanic brothers. Be brave, keep free-
> dom in the family. Do what you can for
> the white folks as they in turn must do in-
> deed for you. And now may the Constitu-
> tion of the United States go with you, the
> Declaration of Independence stand by you,
> the Bill of Rights protect you, the State
> Commission Against Discrimination keep
> their eyes and ears upon you, now and
> forever, Amen. [15]

For the first time in American motion picture history, we
have an explicit statement of the "black is beautiful" credo.
The sermon is spoken to Reverend Purlie's congregation, but
it is intended for the film's audience. Kauffmann says, "...
the idea of making stereotyped conceptions ridiculous by
over-stereotyping them takes imagination... and daring."[16]
To the extent that Davis fails, the Reddick stereotypes in-
herent in the portrayals of Purlie, Lutie Belle, Gitloe and
Idella endure. The film was re-released eight years later
under the commercial title, The Man from C.O.T.T.O.N.

At some point in time, Negroes may oppose the motion picture portrayal of a black man in the occupation of

handy man but this was not the scene in 1963. As Homer
Smith, itinerant handy man in <u>Lilies of the Field</u>, Sidney
Poitier earned international acclaim as a motion picture actor. The role of Homer Smith represented a complete change
of pace for Poitier. Homer becomes involved with several
non-English speaking nuns after repairing the roof of their
farm house. The nuns, particularly Mother Maria (Lilia
Skala), are convinced that God has sent Homer to help them
build a chapel in the Arizona desert. After initial resistance,
Homer accepts the challenge. The William E. Barrett story
provided a film vehicle in which Poitier could demonstrate
his flair for comedy as well as portray a character that was
not especially written for a Negro. Unlike previous Poitier
characterizations, Homer Smith is virtually unconcerned with
race. He uses the blackness of his skin as a visual aid in
teaching English to the nuns. When Homer contacts Mr.
Ashton, a construction engineer, concerning the building of
the chapel, there is an implication of racial prejudice in the
dialogue between the two men:

> ASHTON: How did they get mixed up with you?
> How did they ever talk you into a thing
> like this?
>
> HOMER: Nobody talked me into anything.
>
> ASHTON: Well they conned me out of some adobe
> brick and some lumber. I figure I can
> write that off. But listen, if you're their
> contractor like you say, tell her to take
> her business someplace else. My terms
> are strictly cash. You understand, boy?
>
> HOMER: I understand. Hey! Boy! You need a
> good man?[17]

The deft manner in which Homer parries Ashton's affront
gives the scene its strength. A later scene between Homer

and Ashton is reconciliatory. It should be noted that the
part of Ashton was played by Ralph Nelson, director-pro-
ducer of the film. Homer is haunted by vague longings and
ambitions, which he admits:

> HOMER: I was going to build it myself. That
> way it will be built slowly and carefully.
> I wanted to really build something. You
> know? Well, well, maybe if I had had an
> education, I would have been an architect
> or even an engineer, see? You know, and
> throw the Golden Gate Bridge across San
> Francisco Bay and even maybe build a
> rocket ship to Venus or something... I'm
> not getting through to you.

> MOTHER MARIA: Now the "shapel" is being built
> and that's all that matters.

> HOMER: I wanted to build it myself.

> MOTHER MARIA: God is building out there the
> "shapel" and you sit here feeling sorry for
> yourself because you are not He. [18]

Even when the chapel is completed, largely due to his efforts,
Homer is not content. The wanderlust abides. The only
Reddick stereotype apparent in Homer is "the natural-born
musician." Quite early in the film, with an ecumenical
gusto, Homer entertains the nuns by singing a spiritual. The
catchy song is repeated throughout the film and became known
simply as "Amen."

Homer Smith is very definitely not "the sexual superman" for there is a complete absence of adult sexual behavior in the characterization. Terming this "the new unreality,"
Thomas R. Cripps states:

> ...A normal sexual role, for example, continues
> to be denied to Negroes. Sidney Poitier, in the
> widely acclaimed Lilies of the Field, is as effec-
> tively denied a full characterization by the pres-

ence of the nuns as co-stars as, say, Lena Horne was in the musicals in which she was consigned to a vaudeville act that bore no relation to the plot line. [19]

...In most middle-brow films of the 1960's, Negro characters had changed into perfectly abstinent, courageous paragons of virtue as stifling and destructive of mature characterization as the old Rastus stereotype. [20]

The portrayal of Homer Smith won for Sidney Poitier the Academy of Motion Picture Arts and Sciences award for the best performance by an actor in a leading role. He was the first and to date only black actor to be so honored.

'It has been a long journey to this moment,' said Sidney Poitier in Hollywood as he was presented with an Oscar....The long journey for Negro actors of which Poitier spoke began in silent films when the stereotypes were firmly set from which Negro actors have not yet been completely freed. [21]

Substantiation of this statement is evident in the films examined in this chapter. All but two portrayals included one or more stereotypes from Reddick's list.

Notes

1. Ebony, The Negro Handbook (Chicago: Johnson Publishing Co., 1966), pp. 51, 363, 396.

2. Time-Life Books, ed., I Have a Dream: the Story of Martin Luther King in Text and Pictures (New York: 1968), pp. 37-42.

3. Leslie H. Fishel and Benjamin Quarles, The Negro American: A Documentary (New York: Morrow, 1967), p. 514.

4. The Balcony (Walter Reade Sterling, 1963).

5. Singer A. Buchanan, "A Study of the Attitudes of the Writers of the Negro Press Toward Depiction

of the Negro in Plays and Films 1930-1965,"
(Unpublished Ph. D. dissertation, University of
Michigan, 1968), p. 114.

6. Toys in the Attic (United Artists, 1963).

7. To Kill a Mockingbird (Universal International,
    1963).

8. Ibid.

9. Ibid.

10. The Cardinal (Columbia, 1963).

11. Henry Morton Robinson, The Cardinal (New York:
    Simon & Schuster, 1950).

12. Langston Hughes and Milton Meltzer, Black Magic:
    A Pictorial History of the Negro in American
    Entertainment (Englewood Cliffs, New Jersey:
    Prentice-Hall, 1968), p. 233.

13. Stanley Kauffmann, A World on Film, Criticism
    and Comment (New York: Harper & Row, 1966),
    p. 62.

14. Gone are the Days (Hammer Brothers, 1963).

15. Ibid.

16. Kauffmann, op. cit., p. 62.

17. Lilies of the Field (United Artists, 1963).

18. Ibid.

19. Thomas R. Cripps, "The Death of Rastus: Negroes
    in American Films Since 1945," Phylon, Fall,
    1967, p. 269.

20. Ibid., p. 275.

21. Langston Hughes and Milton Meltzer, op. cit., p.
    298.

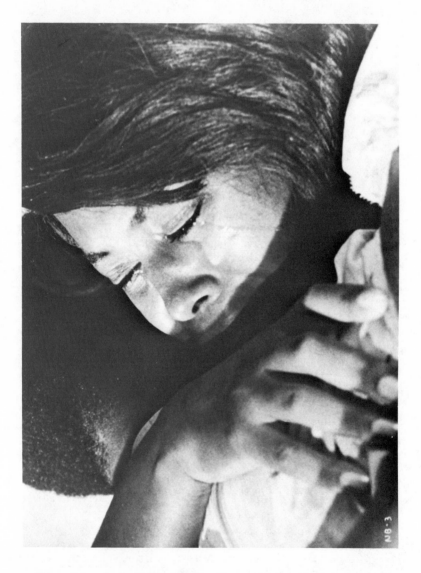

Abbey Lincoln in <u>Nothing But a Man,</u> which included some of the most vital portrayals of the Negro seen on the motion picture screen.   (Photo by permission of Donald Rugoff)

Chapter 8

1964

Racially motivated riots occurred in Negro areas of
several American cities including New York, Chicago, Philadelphia, Rochester and Jersey City. Roving gangs of unemployed black youths were involved in most of the disorders.
In what became known as "Freedom Summer," many young
volunteers went South to organize "Freedom Schools" and to
engage in voter registration programs. Three such workers,
James Chaney, Andrew Goodman and Michael Schwerner, were
murdered as a result of their civil rights activities.[1] The
Hollywood "Oscar" awarded to Sidney Poitier in April was
not the only example of distinguished achievement by a Negro
in 1964. During the year, Dr. Martin Luther King won the
Nobel Peace Prize, Cassius Clay (Muhammad Ali) became
the 24th world heavyweight champion, and Frederick O'Neal,
actor, became the first Negro to be elected president of Actors Equity Association. Passage by the 88th Congress of
the Civil Rights Act of 1964 brought new hope to black Americans in the areas of voting, education, and the use of public facilities and accommodations.[2]

The portrayal of the Negro in American motion pictures during 1964 was distinguished by a singular misuse of
Thespian talent. Of the fourteen films to include Negro characterizations, four dealt with black themes and ten did not.
The two films to receive the most critical attention were
specifically created for the motion picture medium.

As an African characterization, the part of Aly Mansuh, Moorish chief, in Columbia Pictures' film The Long
Ships, would not be mentioned in this work if it had not been
enacted by Sidney Poitier and thus become relevant to the
problem. Coming so soon after Poitier's portrayals in the
distinguished motion pictures, A Raisin in the Sun (1961) and
Lilies of the Field (1963), the retrogression represented by
this role becomes even more conspicuous. According to
Poitier, "To say it was disastrous is a compliment."[3]

In the movie, Aly Mansuh (Poitier) has one goal, the
rediscovery and restoration to Islam of a gigantic golden bell.
Poitier becomes one of the few black villains in motion pictures. When he captures Rolfe (Richard Widmark), a Viking,
he is not above inflicting torture:

> ALY: You shall die on "the mare of steel,"
>   Aminah!
>
> AMINAH: Yes?
>
> ALY: Select me a man, one of my guards. He
>   must ride "the mare of steel," before
>   the Viking.[4]

Another novel transposition between the black man and the
white man concerns the matter of enslavement:

> ROLFE: First I'd like to know what you are going
>   do with my people.
>
> ALY: Well Viking, since you are the only one
>   of importance to me, they are of course
>   to be sold as slaves, which is what we
>   customarily do.[5]

Completely absorbed in his quest, Aly defers response to
his lovely white wife's affectionate overtures until the bell is
found:

ALY: And when this time is behind us, you
        shall have everything you want. You
        shall be the most envied woman in all
        Islam. I promise.

AMINAH: I only want to share my life with you.[6]

Perhaps these episodes explain in part why black film
critic Clifford Mason prefers the role of Aly to the role of
Homer Smith or other Poitier portrayals to be discussed in
subsequent chapters. Mason submits:

At least the villain he played in 'The Long Ships'
was a fighter--on his own mission, in his own
world. And even though there was the nonsense
about a vow that kept him from making love to
Rossana Schiaffino, her attempt to warn him of
danger and his death at Richard Widmark's hands
were handled with great care for the importance
of his role. He was not killed as a mean, despicable villain, but rather as a noble enemy. Even
more important, he was nobody's eunuch or black
mammy busting his gut for white folks as if their
problems were all that's important in the world.
And so the stern 'I hated it' that he uttered in a
recent interview to tell how he felt about doing
'The Long Ships' shows the confusion in his mind
as to what constitutes dignity for Negroes in films.[7]

Though there is some substance to this argument, Mason suf-
fers from selective vision. He minimizes the incredibility of
Aly's self-imposed celibacy amid a harem setting and he does
not question the necessity for Aly's accidental death. More
importantly, Mason does not challenge the propriety of as-
signing such a secondary role to so recent an Academy
Award winner.

Rio Conchos, an otherwise ordinary "western type"
movie, can be credited with the introduction to American motion pictures of Jim Brown, former football star. Brown
portrayed Ben Franklyn, a sergeant in the Union army. The

narrow plot of the film had to do with the recovery of a
shipment of army rifles before their misappropriation by
Apaches.   Although Brown did make an auspicious debut, the
extent of his future influence upon the screen image of the
Negro could scarcely have been predicted in 1964.   In Rio
Conchos one observed a taciturn Brown participating in
scenes of physical action and heroics, as might have been
expected.

> Straining to push a wagon loaded with gun powder
> down a hill in a movie scene, this 6 foot-2, 228
> pound giant is really doing a job of acting.   If he
> wanted to, actor Jim Brown, whose physical
> strength is awesome even in the heavily muscled
> National Football League, could probably pick up
> the wagon and carry it as easily as he stiff-arms
> a hapless safety man. [8]

This description supports the notion that Franklyn (Brown) is
very much "the superior athlete," set down by Reddick.   The
characterization of Franklyn is not without a redeeming feature.   Franklyn does not wish to retaliate for the brutality
endured at the hands of the Indians.   Expostulating "the
golden rule," Franklyn rebukes, "Doing like they do, don't
make it right."[9]   This statement is consistent with the find-
ings of Burke relative to Negro film characterization between
1946 and 1961:

> ...it is clear that the central fact about these
> films is their long-term commitment to the gentling
> of the Negro.   Now, this is an odd development,
> seemingly uncalled for....[10]

Another Negro characterization in a western movie
during 1964 occurred in a film of minimal importance, He
Rides Tall.   Low budget films, such as this one, made for
double-feature distribution, occasionally serve as a showcase
for unrecognized talent.   Howard Thompson concluded his

negative review of He Rides Tall with praise for the portrayal of Dr. Sam:

> ...and a fine Negro actor named Joel Fluellen
> steals every one of his scenes as a brave old doc-
> tor.   In a low-wheeling movie, only Mr. Fluellen
> rides tall. [11]

Fluellen's movie "bit" was merely one of many such
brief appearances made by black performers in motion pictures issued during 1964.   Bringing a bit of color to the military in a Robert Mitchum movie entitled Man in the Middle
was Errol John as Sergeant Jackson.   Well in advance of his
success in the popular television series "Mission Impossible,"
Greg Morris integrated hospital scenes in The New Interns.
As in real life, the "show Negro" was every bit as useful to
films.

Janus Films brought the cast of "The Premise," a
highly successful cabaret entertainment, to the screen in The
Troublemaker.   The movie casts black actors Godfrey Cambridge and Al Freeman, Jr. as a fire inspector and an intern, respectively.   Cambridge, a master of dialect, attempts ethnic satire as the Fire Department employee who
happens to speak with an Irish brogue.

Just one year after his proud venture with Gone Are
the Days, Ossie Davis undertook a small role in Shock Treatment.   Capshaw (Davis) is a mental patient in the same hospital in which he once worked as a medical technician.   In
his more rational moments, Capshaw directs other patients
about with great benevolence.   Each Thursday, he is strait-
jacketed and sent for shock therapy.   In one agonizing scene,
he pleads, "No more shock, no more shock!" [12]   Not even
superficial attention is given to the motivation behind this
non-racial characterization.   In the same film, Pauline Myers,

a black character-actress, is seen as Dr. Walden, a staff
psychiatrist.   One scene shows her utilizing the technique of
hypnosis with a patient.

One must note the appearance of James Earl Jones,
black stage actor, in the 1964 motion picture success, Dr.
Strangelove, Or: How I Learned to Stop Worrying and Love
the Bomb.   The film was a caustic satire on the American
and Soviet nuclear security systems.   The role of Lothar
Zogg, air force bombardier, required little acting ability.
Most of the lines Jones spoke were of the "Bomb door negative, lights red" variety.   Since no reference is made to the
ethnic origin of the character, it is curious that a Negro was
sought for the role.   Jones recalls:

> I was working for Joe Papp in Central Park when
> a producer came to sign George C. Scott for Dr.
> Strangelove.   He looked at me and said 'I'll take
> you, too.   I need a Negro bombardier in that flight
> crew. '[13]

The derogatory names given to all the characters in the film
shed light upon the apparent contradiction.   In a cast of
proper nouns including Major T. J. "King" Kong, Gen. Jack
D. Ripper, and Capt. Mandrake, it is not strange finding a
Lt. Lothar Zogg.   One need only acknowledge an association
between the last two characters to understand the casting of
a Negro as Lothar.   In the Phil Davis syndicated comic strip
Mandrake the Magician, there is a burly and rather taciturn
black character named Lothar.   Thus, we have an esoteric
Kubrick nuance.   Five years later, Jones was to be signed
by Twentieth Century Fox to repeat his stage characterization in The Great White Hope, based upon the life of black
heavyweight champion, Jack Johnson.

A farcical spoof of the Robin Hood legend was the

source of another motion picture appearance of Sammy Davis,
Jr.   Produced in the same slapstick vein as Sergeants 3
(1962), Robin and the 7 Hoods was set in Chicago during the
prohibition era.   Robbo (Frank Sinatra), a night club owner,
orders Will (Davis), his assistant, to dispose of a large sum
of ill-gotten cash.   Will presents it to an orphans' home,
thereby gaining for Robbo the reputation of philanthropist.
Dancing, singing, clowning, romancing, combined with shooting of machine guns, offered frequent distraction from a plot
strained by the loose relationship to the Robin Hood tale.
The role of Will was more a vehicle for the varied talents
of Sammy Davis, Jr. than a straight Negro portrayal.   In a
musical production number, Will swings from a chandelier,
dances atop a bar, and generally wrecks a gambling den with
a submachine gun, while singing, "I like the fun, of reach-
ing for a gun, and going, Bang! Bang!"   Philip French, referring to violence in this particular film, says, "This is the
true spirit of the unselfconscious groundlings breaking through
the rational carapace of our nervous times."[14]   Will is not
a Negro portrayal nor is he even Sammy Davis, Jr., the
entertainer, as he performs before black audiences.   Will is
Reddick's "the uninhibited expressionist" or what Bernard
Wolfe describes as follows:

> ...what we take, in the singing and dancing Negro,
> for his own self-portrait may very well be a com-
> posite portrait which the white world has slapped
> together haphazardly out of its own emotional left-
> overs and flung over the Negro.   We may be cre-
> ating via the Negro's musculature and larynx, what
> we could not create in our own persons.   So that
> the 'happifying' Negro ecstatic we pursue so hotly
> may be a lot closer to us than we think; he may
> be our own phantom self--in blackface. [15]

Paramount Pictures made the popular Harold Robbins

novel, The Carpetbaggers, as a motion picture with Archie
Moore in the minor role of Jedediah. Jedediah has been a
trusty servant to two generations of the wealthy Cord family.
Once again, as with Henry in Toys in the Attic (1963), a
servant possesses a secret which has been concealed from
all the primary characters in the story. Finally Jedediah
reveals Jonas Cord's fear of insanity to his lovely bride,
Monica Cord. Jedediah has no life of his own apart from his
employers. He is sympathetic, obedient and selfless. As
admirable as these characteristics may be, they tend to in-
spire resentment when seen in "the devoted servant" context.
Dale suggests:

> ...the depicting of a Negro as a kindly, thoughtful
> servant may shift attitudes toward the more favor-
> able side of the scale, yet be objected to by Ne-
> groes who feel that the constant showing of the Ne-
> gro as a menial servant is prejudicial to their
> race. [16]

Black Like Me, based upon John Howard Griffin's ac-
count of his masquerade as a Negro in the South, included
several roles for black actors. Unfortunately, most of these
were types rather than full-drawn characterizations. Judith
Crist called the film's characters "super stereotypes."
First, it is incredible that the Negroes encountered by John
Finley Horton (Griffin's name in the movie) would so readily
accept him as a Negro. The poor performance and inadequate make-up of James Whitmore in this part could not be
taken seriously. In a boarding house, in a cafeteria, on a
bus, on the street, even in a public shower room, an assortment of blacks are paraded before us. Each does his "bit"
and departs; each is equally unmemorable. [17] However, two
portrayals do have a certain breath of realism. Early in
his travels, Horton meets a shoeshine merchant named Burt

Wilson (Richard Ward). Wilson indoctrinates Horton on the
prerequisites for survival as a Negro in the South:

>WILSON: For instance, man comes up and say,
>   'I'm here writing an article on race rela-
>   tions,' what you say?
>
>HORTON: Well, anything I can tell you sir, I'd be
>   only too glad to help.
>
>WILSON: You're through right now.
>
>HORTON: I must have sounded kind of stupid.
>
>WILSON: (Laughing) Yeah, kind of...
>
>HORTON: There's a lot of angles to this business.
>   It ain't simple. You got a lot to learn.
>   This man comes up and say, 'Hurry up boy.
>   I ain't got no time.' What you say? Then
>   this other man comes up and say, 'Damn
>   niggers! You can't trust none of them.'
>   What you do? Oh, there's plenty of that.
>   Man, you've got so much to learn. You
>   got to act different. You got to talk differ-
>   ent. You even got to think different.
>
>HORTON: I can see that.
>
>WILSON: Anything you wants to know. You just
>   ask me. [18]

Burt Wilson is a Negro, about whom James Baldwin and other black authors have written. Skillfully, he plays the role
in which society has cast him, all the while secretly hating
the white man for it.

   Black Like Me recognized the arrival of the black
militant in American motion pictures. In a film laden with
trite characterizations, it was something of a surprise to
discover Al Freeman, Jr.'s portrayal of Tom Newcomb. He
is the son of elderly retired Frank Newcomb (P. J. Sidney),
with whom Horton lives for a brief period. The junior and

the elder Newcomb make for real contrast.   Frank Newcomb
is a kind dignified gentle man, resigned to the racial injustices of life.   Tom Newcomb, on the other hand, is an angry
young man, impatient for his just due.   Their conflict is evident in the following scene:

> FRANK: ... in a white man's country.   They ain't
> nothing we can do about it.   If you don't
> understand that, you don't understand noth-
> ing.   I know how Tom feels.   I know how
> come he talk with bitterness.   Tom knows
> though that that ain't no way to talk.   He
> been taught different.   Tom, the man try-
> ing to help.
>
> TOM: We don't need his help! What we want we'll
> get by our own strength. [19]

In the year 1964, Tom is the more interesting character of
the two.   He is a college student and an activist in the civil
rights movement.   Appearing in only one rather lengthy
scene, he challenges the white journalist:

> TOM: If it's necessary to go to jail, you go to
> jail.
>
> HORTON: You know I must tell you that I admire
> the courage of you people very much.
>
> TOM: Yeah, I hear you been interviewing every-
> body.   You been making a lot of money on
> all those stories you've been writing about
> us brave people?
>
> HORTON: I want people to understand what you're
> doing here and I make a living.
>
> TOM: You got a lot of nerve going into people's
> homes pretending you're folks.
>
> HORTON: Will you let me explain to you?
>
> TOM: Sneaking in here all painted up.

HORTON: Will you let me explain?

TOM: The other week when they hauled us all in,
         there wasn't one white man, woman or
         child from this town opened his mouth in
         support. Put twenty-nine of us in jail for
         disturbing the peace, what peace? You
         know what it would have meant for one
         white man to support us at that time and
         I don't mean just talk?[20]

In these lines and in another portion of dialogue, mentioning
school integration in Texas, the script permits a black character to call attention to the climate of social change, referred to in the opening paragraphs of this book.

It is not uncommon to find certain persons repeatedly involved in the writing, producing or directing of motion pictures
which contained portrayals of the black man. Shirley Clarke,
who directed The Connection (1962), is such a person. She
followed this with a film adaptation of Warren Miller's novel,
The Cool World. Most of the characters in the film were performed by non-actors, recruited by Mrs. Clarke in the interests
of realism. The Cool World attempts to expose the seamier
side of black ghetto life. The adolescent group is its particular frame of reference. Duke Custis, the anti-hero, has
as his goal the personal acquisition of a "piece," vernacular
for gun. Shortly after the film opens, Duke replaces "Blood"
(Clarence Williams, III) as gang leader of the Royal Pythons.
Pitifully addicted to heroin, "Blood" is no longer respected
by the members of the gang. The young black characters in
the film are depicted drinking cheap wine, pushing dope and
engaging in communal sex. At the finale, Duke is arrested
for killing Angel, member of a rival gang, as spectators
say, "There goes Duke Custis, a cool killer." Carl Lee,
co-author of the screen play with Mrs. Clarke, plays Priest.

His is one of the few adult portrayals in The Cool World.
Priest is a full-fledged gangster, peddler of guns and vice.
With his sports car and his white mistress, he sets the standard for the young delinquents like Duke.   With the exception
of Carl Lee, Gloria Foster, Georgia Burke and one or two
others, the members of the cast speak in a clipped slang
manner that tends to be unintelligible.   Mrs. Clarke's semi-
documentary style is effective but it does not compensate for
superficial characterizations.   Archer Winston wrote:

> It is when she comes to the fleshing of a story
> in fiction, the treatment of character and its
> deeper understanding in terms of words and thoughts
> that she shows her weakness.
>
> A more serious weakness in Mrs. Clarke's ap-
> proach to the fiction film is her inability to draw
> anything like a strong performance from her char-
> acters.   She usually manages to avoid the patently
> artificial, but not the wooden. [21]

We are told little of the initial motivation of the characters.
For example, why has Luanne (Yolanda Rodriguez), girl
friend of the gang, elected a life of prostitution?   We do approach an understanding of the girl in one poignant scene
filmed in Coney Island.   Luanne marvels at the miracle of
an ocean which to her amazement is just a subway ride
away from her slum environment.

Lawrence Reddick's list of Negro stereotypes is
prominently displayed in The Cool World: Priest is "the vicious criminal"; Mrs. Custis (Gloria Foster) is "the unhappy
non-white." Abandoned by Duke's father, long ago, her subsequent romantic attachments have given Duke a series of
transient "fathers." They have been so numerous that she
cannot remember which "father" took Duke, as a child, to
the zoo.   Explaining why Duke's father disappeared, Mrs.

Custis generalizes about black male fear of responsibility,
"Men think all day about what they're coming home to and
one day they just don't come home." Mrs. Custis is actually more than "the unhappy non-white," she is angry at her
life of drudgery, her inadequate slum apartment, her son's
course of delinquency and her inability to find a strong male
provider. Mrs. Custis does not have even the opiate left
to Duke's grandmother. Grandma Custis (Georgia Burke),
a zealous religious believer, turns to God in times of stress.
Indulging in a bit of ethnic chauvinism, grandma Custis insists that Jesus Christ was a black man.

When we turn to the characterizations of the young
people, only two can be considered free from stereotype.
Hardy, one of Duke's non-gang friends, spends time in the
local playground instructing small children in ballplaying.
Hardy aspires to a college athletic scholarship as his route
to success. Douglas, "Blood's" brother, is seen briefly,
leaving the library with books. Douglas appears to be tormented by the knowlege that "Blood" is a hopeless addict.
On the other hand, "Blood" reminds Douglas that his schol-
arly pursuits would not have been possible within the environs of the ghetto, without his ("Blood's") protection. All
the other adolescents are cut from the same fabric in true
stereotypical fashion. "Blood," Duke, Rod and the other teen
gang members share the characteristics of "the social delinquent," "the petty thief," "the sexual superman," and "the
razor and knife toter." Going beyond these shortcomings,
Stanley Kauffmann searched for a broader delineation of
characters:

> ...if one prime element is missed, it is some
> hint of fundamental kinship with other adolescent

> rebels. The world is becoming increasingly aware
> of increasing violence in teenagers generally. The
> racial injustice that produces Negro delinquents is
> only one aspect of the inadequacies in us that are
> producing all adolescent delinquents.[22]

As well-intentioned as those associated with this film may
have been, the presentation of omni-negative Negro portrayals
in a single setting within the black ghetto can only be a dis-
service to those it most wanted to help. Loften Mitchell
could have been speaking about The Cool World when he
wrote:

> In the nineteen-sixties Harlem is projected by well-
> intentioned white and Negro artists as a slum,
> crowded with winos, addicts, pushers, muggers,
> thugs and impoverished, angry, depraved, rioting
> Negroes. Harlem certainly has more than its share
> of these, but it also has doctors, lawyers, artists,
> writers, cultural groups and ordinary working
> people.[23]

One Potato, Two Potato was the first American motion picture to deal with the theme of interracial marriage
between a black man and a white woman. Essentially, it is
a simple tale about ordinary people, some white, some black.
Julie (Barbara Barrie) has divorced Joe (Richard Mulligan),
her white husband, on the grounds of desertion. In order to
support herself and her little girl, Julie takes a job in a
factory where she meets a Negro, Frank (Bernie Hamilton).
Mutual admiration and compatibility evolve into love and the
couple decide to marry, mindful of possible problems ahead.
They go to live on a farm with Frank's parents. When Joe
returns and discovers that Julie's new husband is a Negro,
he sues for custody of his daughter. Then, out of spite and
racial resentment, he attempts to seduce Julie, unsuccessfully. Fearful of increasing the odds against their custody case,

Frank does nothing to redress this grievance. "They won't
let me be a man," he cries. Finally, the court rules
against the interracial couple, awarding the child to her white
father. The judge bases his decision on the presumptive best
interest of the child in present day society.

The three Negro roles in the motion picture are done
with integrity and sensitivity. The inner turmoil and conflict
confronting Frank are told with honesty. At first, he is reluctant to face a marriage with Julie:

> FRANK: You know what's between us? Hate,
>   riots, lynching, prejudice. It won't work.
>
> JULIE: Somebody's got to take a chance to find
>   out if it'll work. [24]

The viewer is not likely to consider this an overreaction on
Frank's part. An earlier unpleasant scene in which a policeman assumes Julie is a "street-walker" because she is accompanied by Frank more than justifies Frank's attitude. Only once does the customary stability of Frank give way to extreme rage. This occurs when he learns of the attempted
seduction of Julie, prompted basically by contempt for Julie's
alliance with him, a black man. The love scene showing
Frank and Julie kissing is done tastefully and without hint of
sensationalism. Frank's abandonment of his friends, following his marriage, suggests the defensive mechanisms at work
within him. As a college graduate, owner of an automobile
and white-collar employee in the personnel field, Frank is
anything but a Negro stereotype.

The depiction of Frank's parents, William Richards
(Robert Earl Jones, father of James Earl Jones) and Martha
Richards (Vinnette Carroll), lends another touch of reality to
the story. In a demonstration of black racial pride, unprece-

dented in motion pictures, they both reject their son's white
bride, initially. Martha capitulates first but William holds
out until the birth of his grandson, born out of the union of
Frank and Julie. The father is "true to life" when he ad-
vises Frank to protect his wife and family by running away
to another state rather than accept injustice. In reality,
some states, including Vermont and Montana, have ruled in
favor of the interracial couple in child custody cases.[25]
While the Negro press looked upon One Potato, Two Potato
with favor,[26] some white film critics accused the film of
manipulations and melodramatics.[27] From a white perspec-
tive, the prejudice depicted in this film might appear as exaggeration. However, surely it was not exaggeration that
distressed Barbara Barrie's Texas mother when she learned
that her actress-daughter would kiss a black actor in the motion picture.[28] One can only conjecture what her response
might have been were her daughter living, rather than acting, the part of Julie. Perhaps it is Barbara Barrie, herself, who gives the best explanation for the realism and
spontaneity of the characterizations in One Potato, Two Potato. She states, "As far as I know, there is no 'script' of
the film, as we kind of improvised as we went along."[29]

Some of the most vital portrayals of the Negro ever to
grace a motion picture screen occurred in Nothing But a Man,
made by independent film-makers Robert Young and Michael
Roemer. It is the simple story of a man and his efforts to earn
a living, support his family and exist with a bit of dignity. This
basic plot is complicated by the fact that the man in question,
Duff Anderson, is black and will not abide by the traditionally inferior role assigned him in today's Alabama. Duff will either
run away or fight back, but he will not be a "nigger." As the
film opens, Duff (Ivan Dixon) is a footloose, carefree railroad

section hand. He meets and falls in love with Josie (Abbey Lincoln), school teacher and daughter of a preacher. The generation gap between Duff and Reverend Dawson (Stanley Greene) is articulated here:

> REV: It's hard to know how to talk to the white folks these days.
>
> DUFF: Yeah, well I guess it ain't never been easy.
>
> REV: These are changing times. Sit down, son.
>
> DUFF: Thanks.
>
> REV: Well, it looks like we'll be getting our new school.
>
> DUFF: How come you ain't sending them all to the same school?
>
> REV: Well we've got to go easy. We haven't had any trouble in town for eight years and we're not going to have any now.
>
> DUFF: Can't live without trouble can you? [30]

These two characters have some of the most provocative dialogue in the film. It is a relationship of opposites. Reverend Dawson has made his "Uncle Tom" accommodation to a racist society. Duff rejects psychological and economic castration, at any price. This is clear in a later confrontation:

> REV: Use a little psychology. Make em think you're going along and get what you want.
>
> DUFF: It ain't in me.
>
> REV: You can be cocky now boy but it won't last. You won't make it. I just feel sorry for Josie. I knew it wouldn't work out.
>
> DUFF: Well at least she ain't married to no white man's "nigger." You been stoopin' so long,

> Reverend, that you don't even know how
> to stand up straight no more.   You just
> half a man. [31]

Before his marriage to Josie, Duff visits his father,
Will Anderson (Julius Harris), an ill and embittered man,
old before his time.   Despising his lot as an unemployed,
uneducated Negro, Will has taken refuge in alcohol and in the
arms of his attractive mistress, Lee (Gloria Foster).   Duff
also visits his little son, who is receiving minimal care in
a slum section of another city.   We see the boy as a physical and emotional victim of his illegitimate birth.   Thus,
Duff has a vision of "things past" and of "things yet to
come."

After marriage, Duff and Josie have a temporary happiness, soon marred by Duff's unemployment.   His white
employer has fired him for attempting to organize fellow-
blacks in protest against unfair working conditions.   When
Josie offers to get a job, Duff's masculinity is insulted anew.
In a penetrating scene, Duff approaches Josie under the dryer
in a beauty salon.   She tells him to take the money he needs
from her handbag.   Josie radiates a quiet strength and compassion.   Their scenes together are touching:

> DUFF: Maybe we better get out of here.
>
> JOSIE: You can always do that, Duff.
>
> JOSIE: I don't know, I guess I'm not afraid of
>   them.
>
> DUFF: How come you were scared that night in
>   the car?
>
> JOSIE: Just scared of getting hurt.   They can't
>   touch me inside.
>
> DUFF: Like hell they can't.   They can reach right

> in with their damn white hands and turn
> you off and on.
>
> JOSIE: Not if you see them for what they really
> are, Duff. [32]

The death of Will Anderson seems to bring an awakening for
Duff.   He collects his illegitimate son and returns to Josie,
from whom he has separated in a moment of despair.

All the characterizations in Nothing But a Man ring
true.   A death of spirit is mirrored in the eyes of Will.   A
glow of deep warmth and affection for Will is reflected in the
eyes of Lee, his mistress.   Reverend and Mrs. Dawson
maintain the proper amount of aloofness, successfully indi-
cating their fear of militancy.   Josie demonstrates a soft-
spoken courage.   Although she has been over-protected by
her parents, she will chance a life with Duff.   Early in the
film, Josie says, "Look Duff, most of the men I know,
they're kind of sad.   When I met you the other day, I had
the feeling that you're different.   That's why I went out with
you.   I thought we might have something to say to each other." [33]   Duff is indeed different.   Wyatt Tee Walker com-
pares him to Malcolm X:

> The current low-budget movie, Nothing But a Man,
> is the story of another Malcolm, fictitious yet very
> real, who can be found all over this land.   Dove
> [sic] Anderson, the main character, wasn't looking
> for trouble or running away from it either.   His
> unverbalized goal in this magnificent picture was to
> be 'nothing but a man.'   That's what Malcolm X
> was all about.   He was the symbol of Negro males
> who, though groping, have not yet found the answer
> to how they can be 'nothing but a man,' which is,
> really more than enough. [34]

Robert Young, producer of the film, admits sending
the script to Sidney Poitier, who turned it down. [35]   The

presence of such a luminary in the role of Duff might have
detracted from the characterization, which would have been
unfortunate for the film.

On balance, 1964 was a year of fewer stereotypes and
more realistic portrayals. The last two motion pictures discussed in this chapter, One Potato, Two Potato and Nothing
But a Man, were both low budget enterprises, the undertakings of independent producers, and stories created specifically for the motion picture medium. Both films received international acclaim in one way or nother.

Notes

1. Britannica Book of the Year, 1965, (Chicago:
    Encyclopaedia Britannica, 1965), pp. 242-245.

2. Ebony, The Negro Handbook, (Chicago: Johnson
    Publishing Co., 1966), pp. 340, 372.

3. Carolyn H. Ewers, Sidney Poitier: The Long
    Journey, (New York: The New American Li-
    brary, 1969), p. 116.

4. The Long Ships (Columbia Pictures, 1964).

5. Ibid.

6. Ibid.

7. Clifford Mason, "Why Does White America Love
    Sidney Poitier So?," The New York Times,
    September 10, 1967, p. 21.

8. "From Pigskin to Redskins," Life, September 18,
    1964, p. 67.

9. Rio Conchos (Twentieth Century Fox, 1964).

10. William L. Burke, "The Presentation of the Amer-
    ican Negro in Hollywood Films, 1946-1961:
    Analysis of a Selected Sample of Feature Films,"

(Unpublished Ph. D. dissertation, Northwestern University, 1965), p. 321.

11. The New York Times, February 27, 1964, p. 28.

12. Shock Treatment (Twentieth Century Fox, 1964).

13. Robert Wahls, "Footlights," Daily News, September 8, 1968, p. S2.

14. Philip French, "Violence in the Cinema," in Sight, Sound and Society: Motion Pictures and Television in America, ed. by David Manning White and Richard Averson, (Boston, Beacon Press, 1968), p. 321.

15. Bernard Wolfe, "Ecstatic in Blackface, The Negro As a Song-and-Dance Man," in The Scene Before You: A New Approach to American Culture, ed. by Chandler Brossard, (New York: Rinehart, 1955), p. 56.

16. Edgar Dale, The Content of Motion Pictures (New York: The Macmillan Co., 1935), p. 61.

17. Raymond St. Jacques, a Negro actor who achieved stardom in subsequent motion pictures, made his film debut in a "bit" part in Black Like Me. His substantive portrayals will be discussed in later chapters.

18. Black Like Me (Walter Reade Sterling, 1964).

19. Ibid.

20. Ibid.

21. Archer Winsten, "Reviewing Stand," New York Post, April 21, 1964, p. 22.

22. Stanley Kauffmann, A World on Film, Criticism and Comment (New York: Harper & Row, 1966), p. 166.

23. Loften Mitchell, Black Drama: The Story of the American Negro in the Theatre (New York: Hawthorn Books, Inc., 1967), p. 3.

24. One Potato, Two Potato (A Cinema V Distributing,
        Inc., 1964).

25. Newsweek, August 3, 1964, p. 72.

26. Singer A. Buchanan, "A Study of the Attitudes of
        the Writers of the Negro Press Toward the De-
        piction of the Negro in Plays and Films: 1930-
        1965," (Unpublished Ph.D. dissertation, The
        University of Michigan, 1968), p. 150.

27. Kauffmann, op. cit., p. 168.

28. Frances Herridge, "Movie Scene," New York Post,
        July 21, 1964, p. 17.

29. Letter from Barbara Barrie Harnick, January 4,
        1969.

30. Nothing But a Man (A Cinema V Distributing, Inc.,
        1964).

31. Ibid.

32. Ibid.

33. Ibid.

34. Wyatt Tee Walker, "Nothing But a Man," in Mal-
        colm X: The Man and His Time, ed. by John
        Henrik Clarke, (New York: Macmillan, 1969),
        pp. 67-68.

35. William Peper, "The Peper Mill," New York
        World Telegram & Sun, April 3, 1965, p. 20.

Chapter 9

1965

In Watts, a Negro-populated suburb of Los Angeles, six days of fighting, burning and looting in August left 35 dead. A commission appointed by California Governor Edmund G. Brown to investigate the causes of the disturbance reported that "what happened was an explosion--a formless, quite senseless, all but hopeless violent protest" by ghetto Negroes. Malcolm X was assassinated in New York. Carl T. Rowan, a Negro, served as Director of the United States Information Agency, which furnishes countries all over the globe with news and description of life in the United States. Alabama state troopers used tear gas, night sticks and whips on Negroes to halt a march from Selma to Montgomery in support of voting rights. Two weeks later, Dr. Martin Luther King led another march which was not thwarted. Protecting the participants was a federal court order barring state and local police harassment, backed up by an escort of federal agents. A voting rights act was passed, prescribing legal action against any poll tax. Furthermore the legislation suspended all literacy, knowledge and character tests for voters in states where less than 50 per cent of the voting-age population was registered.[1]

Only one year after The Cool World and Nothing But a Man, not a single American motion picture in 1965 was primarily concerned with the depiction of Negroes and Negro life. The matter of race was coincidental to most of the

Negro film portrayals during the year.

Nine of the 1965 film portrayals of blacks could be included in that category of characterization which William
Burke labels as "background":

> Here there exists a preponderate subordination of
> characters cast in visually and/or verbally differ-
> entiated roles (to exclude the normal functions of
> chorus, street backgrounds, etc.) in matters of
> costume, personality and character development,
> film angles, relegation to rear planes of action,
> etc. The character statement here is simply weak,
> or non-existent. [2]

Estelle Helmsley portrays Catherine in Baby, The
Rain Must Fall which was based on Horton Foote's play "The
Traveling Lady." As Sgt. Elmer K. Coxe, Roy Glenn is
caught up in the larcenous machinations of James Coburn as
anti-hero Eli Kotch in Dead Heat on a Merry Go-Round.
Rafer Johnson plays one of the doomed marines on an island
in the Pacific during world War II in None But the Brave.
Each of these is virtually a "don't blink your eyes or you'll
miss them" appearance.

Rex Ingram supplies the "background" for Metro Goldwyn Mayer's Your Cheatin' Heart, a biographical film about
the late Hank Williams, a once popular singer of country music. Ingram plays Teetot, a shabbily dressed old man, who
befriends and protects the young orphaned Hank. While
strumming his guitar, Teetot introduces the boy to the rudi-
ments of music, counseling him about life as well. Quite
suddenly, old Teetot keels over and dies. The saddened
Hank is inconsolable. The entire episode takes place in a
prologue to the motion picture, even before the credits are
projected. In his dying loyalty to Hank, Teetot is a male
mammy or certainly Reddick's "the devoted servant." Obvi-

ously unschooled, Teetot's proficiency with the guitar might
be attributable to his being "the natural-born musician."

The late Nat "King" Cole was nothing more than window dressing for the technicolor western parody entitled Cat
Ballou.   Cole and Stubby Kaye are the "shouters," who sing
"The Ballad of Cat Ballou," providing a running musical commentary on the action of the film.   Plucking their banjos,
costumed in western apparel, the two balladeers appear inter-
mittently throughout the movie.   They are in the film but not
a part of it.   The duo, one white, one black, punctuates
each episode in a sort of Greek chorus fashion.   Cole's entire characterization, if we dare call it that, is not to be
taken seriously.   Pauline Kael, film critic, notes:

> There are even two minstrels.   Wasn't Cole enough?
> Is it perhaps that Stubby Kaye makes it cuter?   A
> black man and a fat man--so nobody can fail to re-
> alize that the ballad singing is 'for fun.'[3]

Another Negro musician, Cab Calloway, accepted a
"background" role in the Metro Goldwyn Mayer technicolor
production, The Cincinnati Kid, starring Steve McQueen.   The
screenplay by Ring Lardner, Jr. and Terry Southern was
based upon Richard Jessup's novel about a stud poker mara-
thon in New Orleans.   The big game initially involved many
gamblers, each one dropping out as the story evolves.   In
his portrayal of Yeller, an appellation in implicit acknowl-
edgment of the actor's light complexion, Calloway sits at the
gambling table and becomes for all practical purposes, a part
of the scene.   This is Burke's "background" character once
more.

James Edwards, who distinguished himself as the
troubled black soldier in Home of the Brave, merely decorates the colorful setting of The Sandpiper.   In the film,

Laura Reynolds (Elizabeth Taylor), a non-conformist painter, has a coterie of assorted Bohemian types, among them, Larry Brant (Edwards). Brant displays a mustache, a beard and beatnik clothes. He participates, in Burke's "background" sense, integrating socially oriented scenes filmed inside Laura's home, on the Big Sur Beach and in a night club. In the latter, Larry is shown seated at a table, sipping drinks with Laura and Hewitt (Richard Burton), the film's co-stars. Throughout the movie, the dialogue assigned to Larry is inconsequential. Judith Crist explains the portrayal by saying that James Edwards is "around to show how earthy and democratic the beat art world is."[4]

The Columbia Pictures film, Major Dundee, was a standard western drama with a Negro added for representation. Brock Peters, who performed a pivotal role in To Kill a Mockingbird (1963), was relegated to the background of this epic. He is seen as Aesop,[5] a Negro trooper in an all-white U.S. cavalry detachment. Essentially, this is the 1965 vintage of the role that Jim Brown played in Rio Conchos (1964), without Brown's calisthenics. This time out, the plot is concerned with the rescue of white children from the hands of the stereotypically murderous Apaches. Aesop speaks few lines, follows directions and remains respectfully in the background.

This rather comprehensive discussion of the categorical "background" presentation of the Negro in films for 1965 would be remiss if mention were not made of the fleeting appearance of Sidney Poitier in the motion picture spectacular, The Greatest Story Ever Told, derived from the life of Jesus Christ. Commenting on the role, Bosley Crowther states:

> Sidney Poitier's Simon of Cyrene, the African-Jew
> who helps carry the cross, is the only Negro con-

spicuous in the picture and seems a last minute
symbolization of racial brotherhood. [6]

Synanon, one of the two 1965 films in this work to
take a look at a current social problem, included two Negro
characterizations.   The motion picture's setting is Synanon
House at Santa Monica, California, a place to which drug addicts voluntarily commit themselves for a program of with-
drawal and rehabilitation.   Negro songstress Eartha Kitt enacts a non-singing dramatic role as Betty Coleman.   As a
prostitute during her own period of addiction, Betty has experienced complete degradation, a life about which she testi-
fies in the film.   One of Betty's more prominent scenes happens at an opening orientation meeting when she relates her
case history, telling the new guests how redemptive Synanon
had been for her.   She has now become a trusted adminis-
trative assistant to Charles Dederich, founder of the establishment.

The second and less conspicuous Negro portrayal in
Synanon is the role of Pete, played by Bernie Hamilton, the
black hero of One Potato, Two Potato (1964).   Pete comes
to the fore only when his surreptitious drinking of cough syrup is discovered by a dissolute white addict.   Once his temporary lapse is made public, Pete is restored to the proper
regimen.   In a movie where all the characters possess some
sort of flaw or weakness, Betty Coleman and Pete are presented humanely as sympathetic figures.   However, no intensive examination of the earlier motivation of either character is attempted by the film's superficial treatment.   George
Amberg defines this sort of unrealistic realism in the following way:

> Realistic motion pictures, fulfilling those particu-
> lar conditions to perfection, are rarely distinguished

by originality and vision. The more they resemble
one another, the more successful they are. They
rely on conventional behavior patterns, familiar
character prototypes, and stereotyped wish-situa-
tions, all of which allow a high degree of identification with the screen events and situations. This
is the essential purpose. This, in the most personal guise, is the public's definition of realism,
although the implications are not consciously realized. A shell of caution surrounds the core of ex-
citation. For good or bad reasons, depending on
the motivation, films of this genre avoid penetration in depth in favor of expansion on the surface.
Conveyed with the tremendous persuasive power of
the moving magnified image, even these films became frightfully 'real' at times. Not that they are
verifiably real; they are merely plausible idealiza-
tions of reality, 'as good as real.'[7]

The Pawnbroker, another film of social concern, was

criticized on exactly the grounds expounded by Amberg: the

avoidance of penetration in depth in favor of surface expan-

sion. Several familiar character prototypes which Amberg

mentions are included in The Pawnbroker, and some are

played by blacks for a change. Thelma Oliver imbues some

freshness into her role as Mabel, the generous whore. She

will do anything for Ortiz, her Puerto Rican lover, who is

a young apprentice to Nazerman, the pawnbroker. Mabel

even unbares her breast in an attempted seduction of the

pawnbroker, hoping to obtain cash for Ortiz. Apparently

lacking a sense of ethnic identity, the voluptuous young wom-

an disguises her natural hair with a silken wig. Mabel is

not without a basic intelligence. Cautioning Ortiz against his

young hoodlum associates, she says, "Nothing they do for you

won't hurt you."[8]

Brock Peters gives a less clearly defined portrayal

as Rodriguez, a ruthless racketeer. Similar to Priest in

The Cool World (1964), Rodriguez deals in vice, extortion and

1965   111

prostitution, running the brothel in which Mabel works. Despite his immorality, Rodriguez is a social snob. He tells
Nazerman:

> RODRIGUEZ: I can't tell you, Nazerman, how
> I've looked forward to this. The people
> I come in contact with, they're dumb
> heads. You've got background, the real
> thing. Me, I never had a regular educa-
> tion but I've got a feel for things, but you,
> you're a welcome change of pace for me. [9]

This preliminary spirit of congeniality terminates abruptly
when Nazerman fails to reciprocate. In a scene unbound by
the customary relationship between the races, it is the black
Rodriguez who rebukes the white Nazerman:

> RODRIGUEZ: You don't know it but the lecture is
> over. Now you're going to listen to me.
> Where do you think the money you've been
> living on comes from, professor, money
> you pay for an old Jew's keep, money you
> give Tessie, money you pay for a nice fat
> house on Long Island and the nice fat fam-
> ily you support there?--Oh, I know all
> about you. [10]

It is plausible for Rodriguez to challenge the white pawnbroker's principles in this way, since he, Rodriguez, uses
his illicit income openly and without subterfuge. Throughout
the film he is seen as a stylish dresser but his standard of
living is most evident in a scene played in his home. Sit-
ting in his attractively decorated apartment, wearing a loung-
ing robe, Rodriguez is the recipient of domestic service performed by a young male Caucasian assistant. Here, director Sidney Lumet, subtly suggests a homosexual relationship
between the two men. [11] This notion, on an innuendo level,
only adds enigma to the entire characterization.

Actor Juano Hernandez contributes a small but mem-

orable characterization to the motion picture. He is seen
as one of Nazerman's more pathetic customers. Mr. Smith
(Hernandez) visits the pawnshop more for conversation than
for a business transaction. The obviously lonely old gentle-
man says, "Mr. Nazerman, a man gets hungry for talk,
good talk."[12] It is an interesting commentary that two
blacks, Rodriguez and Smith, look to the white pawnbroker
for a cultural exchange which, by implication, is not available elsewhere in the ghetto. About Mr. Smith, Pauline
Kael wrote, "The great old Juano Hernandez, as the man
who wants to talk, gives the single most moving performance
I saw in 1965."[13]

In his most professionally prolific year to date, Sidney Poitier was responsible for performing major characterizations in three motion pictures in 1965.

The Bedford Incident was the least important film of
the three in its portrayal of a Negro. The action takes
place aboard the U.S.S. Bedford, a destroyer, cruising in
the North Atlantic within proximity of Greenland. Sidney
Poitier is Ben Munceford, a photographer-journalist on assignment aboard the ship. As Captain Eric Finlander, Poitier's co-star, Richard Widmark has the more solid role.
He is a tyrant of the sea, much in the manner of Herman
Wouk's fictional Captain Queeg. Munceford (Poitier) is
merely the agent used for the progressive revelation of Finlander. Virtually no personal data is provided about Ben,
beyond his occupation, intelligence and perception. One must
question the plausibility of an exacting skipper's passive tol-
erance of Ben Munceford's probing questioning and photograph
taking on a reconnaissance mission such as this one. Clifford Mason, a black writer, sees a credibility gap for other
reasons:

What did we have in 'The Bedford Incident,' ... ?
Poitier as a black correspondent who went around
calling everyone sir. Did anyone ever see Gary
Cooper or Greg Peck call anyone sir when they
played foreign correspondents? And after Richard
Widmark (who starred with Poitier in the film)
barks at him and pushes him around all over the
submarine for almost two hours, the only thing he
gets to do at the end is shout at bad Dicky Widmark. And why do they allow him to shout at Widmark? Because Widmark has just gotten the whole
ship stuck in the path of an onrushing torpedo that
blows them all to heaven the next instant! For
that kind of mistake, Poitier should have at least
been allowed to bust him one in the jaw.

And yet, listening to the things Poitier says, one
wonders if he would have thought it appropriate. [14]

If one views with a sense of humor the role of Alan

Newell, university psychology student in The Slender Thread,

it represents an anachronism in the occupational progress of

Sidney Poitier within films. He had already played a psy-

chiatrist in Pressure Point (1962). Alan is a part-time vol-

unteer at the Crisis Clinic in Seattle, Washington. For all

but a few minutes of the film's running time, he sustains a

telephone conversation with Inga Dyson (Anne Bancroft), who

has attempted suicide. Alan's goal is to keep Inga on the

line until she can be located and saved from death. At no

time in their rather lengthy telephone exchange does Alan re-

veal his racial identity to Inga, although it is intimated in

the following:

>   ALAN: I've been taught some lessons I don't need,
>   understand? Good people I do [need].
>   You've watched the walls close in on you?
>   Me too. You've been ignored or studied
>   out of the corners of people's eyes? Me
>   too. You've been suffered and tolerated?
>   Me too. O.K.? Times are bad, things

> stink, the world's a cinder in your eye but
> what is the alternative? Now I ask you,
> Inga, what in God's name is the alterna-
> tive? [15]

His status as a black man definitely contributes to his im-
patience with Inga:

> ALAN: You can't live with yourself because you
> made a mistake. What the hell gave you
> the right to expect your right? Who the
> hell are you, Miss America? She dances,
> she smiles, she's nothing. Well, you got
> a little messed up, so welcome to the
> club! [16]

The fact that Alan is black has no stated significance on the
plot but it does heighten the dramatic impact of the film. As
Pauline Kael noted:

> The Slender Thread never deals with the irony that
> the audience is constantly soaking in: that the man
> at the end of the telephone wire is a Negro. So
> much more graceful, so much easier to stay on a
> slender thread and not risk crossing wires. [17]

One can only speculate about Alan's motives in rejecting an
offer, at the end, to meet face to face with the woman whose
life he saved. Is it prompted by modesty, indifference, or
a desire to escape racial confrontation?

One can easily understand why Sidney Poitier said,
"I was at my wits' end when I finished A Patch of Blue." [18]
The plot of that particular motion picture required him to
conceal his racial identity and to deny his sexuality, a rather
high price to pay for popular success in films. A chance
meeting in a park advances a friendship between Gordon
Ralfe (Poitier), a sensitive black man, and Selena D'Arcey
(Elizabeth Hartmann), a blind white girl. Their relationship
derives impetus from Gordon's desire to help Selena to at-

tain a better life.   The part of Mark Ralfe, enacted by Ivan
Dixon, protagonist of <u>Nothing But a Man</u> (1964), bears a
closer resemblance to black reality than does the characterization of Gordon.   Mark cannot comprehend his brother's selfless interest in Selena:

> MARK: You figuring on educating the white girl?
> Man, that's not your job.   Let Whitey edu-
> cate his own women.   They've never given
> us anything but a hard time.
>
> GORDON: Let's not get into a political argument.
> This is a personal matter.
>
> MARK: It's personal hmm...
>
> GORDON: What do you mean by that?
>
> MARK: Nobody takes this kind of interest in a
> girl if there isn't something in it.
>
> GORDON: You're out of your shtik.
>
> MARK: Yeah?   All right, then tell her, tell her
> she can never really mean anything to
> you.
>
> GORDON: On race and politics we don't agree, so
> let's drop this.
>
> MARK: Tell her that she doesn't fit in here.   If
> she could see, she'd know that already.
>
> GORDON: I said drop it.   I'll handle things may
> way.
>
> MARK: Well this isn't your way.   It's always
> been facts with you.   No half truths.
> You rammed that down my throat often
> enough.   Now you do out there and tell
> her the score, man, |or| I will. [19]

Mark is a medical intern, an achievement owed in part to
implied sacrifices made by Gordon.   Mark loves his brother,

even admiring him until the folly of Selena.   Sharing Mark's
views on this score, Clifford Mason says:

> ...'A Patch of Blue' was probably the most ridicu-
> lous film Poitier ever made.   He's a newspaper
> reporter who befriends a blind white girl from the
> slums, a girl whom he doesn't even make love to.
> He gets her away from her whoring mother and
> sends her off to a home for the blind, and the little
> symbolism at the end with the music box makes it
> clear that they'll never see each other again.   And
> why does he go to the park day after day and sit
> with her and string her beads and buy her lunch?
> Because he's running his private branch of the
> ASPCA, the Black Society for the Prevention of
> Cruelty to Blind White Girls, the BSPCBWG?[20]

This charitableness is easier to understand than other
aspects of Gordon's behavior.   If it seems unreasonable for
Gordon to announce that he is black in his introductory remarks to Selena, it seems just as unreasonable for him to
avoid telling her in some of their later conversations such
as this one:

> SELENA: She used to come up to the room and
> play with me.   We had a lot of fun to-
> gether.   Me and Pearl, we was great
> friends.
>
> GORDON: Not any more?
>
> SELENA: No!   Roseann, she put a stop to it.
>
> GORDON: What for?
>
> SELENA: She came home early one day and raised
> hell.
>
> GORDON: What were you up to?
>
> SELENA: Nothing much.   She got mad cause Pearl
> was colored, you know, black.   She said
> I could never have a black friend.

GORDON: Did you ask her why?

SELENA: When Roseann gets going you don't bother
about why, just keep out of her way.
Pity, Pearl was colored. Anyhow she
never came again. [21]

It would have seemed natural, at this point, for Gordon to
tell Selena that he, like Pearl, is black. Fear of rejection
seems an unlikely motivation, since Gordon has become
friend, confidant, teacher, benefactor and even idol to Selena.
Yet we are constantly reminded that the matter of race is
seldom out of Gordon's thoughts. When Selena says, "I do
love you," Gordon replies, "Stop it, you hardly know me," [22]
a response more properly made by a blushing ingénue. Nothing that Selena could say or do would make Gordon respond
as a sexually aware adult male in a script that precludes interracial romance. Although Gordon does not know it, Selena has been told that he is black. As he is about to tell
Selena the truth in the last scene of the film, Gordon makes
one final expression of self-derogation:

GORDON: Now you listen to me for a minute.
There's something I want to tell you
about me.

SELENA: I know everything I need to know about
you. I love you. I know you're good
and kind. I know you're colored...

GORDON: What?

SELENA: ... and I think you're beautiful.

GORDON: Beautiful? Most people would say the
opposite.

SELENA: Well that's because they don't know you.

GORDON: It's time to say goodbye Selena.

SELENA: Gordon, do I really have to go?

GORDON: Yes, for a while. [23]

Gordon has been brainwashed by white aesthetic standards. Black is not beautiful to him, ergo, he cannot be beautiful to Selena. Having rendered his act of beneficence, which Clifford Mason abhors, [24] the portrayal of Gordon is finished. Contrary to his brother's suspicions, Gordon seeks nothing for himself from this association with Selena. William Burke observed this phenomenon in his investigation of Hollywood films prior to 1962:

> ... considerable evidence exists to suggest that, over time, [sic] the Negro (especially the young Negro male) is increasingly structured into the image of the supremely 'good person.'[25]

Thus, black actors in American motion pictures in 1965 appeared largely in a "background" capacity. With possibly a single exception, it did not matter that the roles were performed by blacks. In A Patch of Blue, where the character's being black was relevant to the drama, the subject was not dealt with in a mature fashion.

Notes

1. The World Almanac and Book of Facts, 1966, (New York: New York World-Telegram and The Sun, 1966), pp. 53, 57, 60 and 80.

2. William L. Burke, "The Presentation of the American Negro in Hollywood Films, 1946-1961: Analysis of a Selected Sample of Feature Films," (Unpublished Ph. D. dissertation, Northwestern University, 1965), p. 146.

3. Pauline Kael, Kiss Kiss Bang Bang, (Boston: Little, Brown, 1968), p. 30.

4. Judith Crist, The Private Eye, The Cowboy and
    The Very Naked Girl: Movies From Cleo to
    Clyde, (New York: Holt, Rinehart and Winston,
    1968), p. 129.

5. Ludicrous names for the Negro characters in the
    motion pictures under investigation are a com-
    mon occurrence.

6. The New York Times, February 16, 1965, p. 40.

7. George Amberg, "The Ambivalence of Realism,
    Fragment of an Essay," in The Visual Arts To-
    day, ed. by Gyorgy Kepes, (Middletown, Conn.:
    Wesleyan University Press, 1960), p. 152.

8. The Pawnbroker (Allied Artists, 1965).

9. Ibid.

10. Ibid.

11. Time, April 23, 1965, p. 103.

12. The Pawnbroker (Allied Artists, 1965).

13. Kael, op. cit., p. 161.

14. Clifford Mason, "Why Does White America Love
    Sidney Poitier So?," The New York Times, Sep-
    tember 10, 1967, p. I.

15. The Slender Thread (Paramount Pictures, 1965).

16. Ibid.

17. Kael, op. cit., p. 145.

18. Carolyn H. Ewers, Sidney Poitier: The Long Jour-
    ney, (New York: The New American Library,
    1968), p. 116. (By permission of the Author and
    Henry Morrison, Inc. her Agents)

19. A Patch of Blue (Metro Goldwyn Mayer, 1965).

20. Mason, op. cit., p. 1.

21. A Patch of Blue (Metro Goldwyn Mayer, 1965).

22. Ibid.

23. Ibid.

24. Mason, op. cit.

25. Burke, op. cit., p. 305.

Chapter 10

1966

During the summer months, racial rioting occurred in Chicago, Omaha, Cleveland, Brooklyn, San Francisco and other places throughout the United States. James Meredith, whose admission to the University of Mississippi in 1962 had caused rioting, was ambushed and shot as he led a "pilgrimage" from the Tennessee border to Jackson, the Mississippi state capital. The purpose of the march was to show Mississippi's unregistered Negroes that they no longer had anything to fear. Dr. Martin Luther King (Southern Christian Leadership Conference), Floyd McKissick (Congress of Racial Equality) and Stokely Carmichael (Student Non-Violent Coordinating Committee) formed a larger march to continue the "pilgrimage" of Meredith, who had not been seriously hurt. The national convention of the Congress of Racial Equality in Baltimore adopted resolutions endorsing the concept of "black power." The National Association for the Advancement of Colored People at its annual convention in Los Angeles rejected the "black power" concept. Roy Wilkins, executive director of the organization, termed it anti-white power, separatism, and a reverse Ku Klux Klan.[1] Robert Weaver became the first black cabinet member as Secretary of the Department of Housing and Urban Development.[2] Sammy Davis, Jr., whose autobiography was a current best-seller, attained his own television show but it was terminated after a short run. Bill Cosby became the first black

performer to win an "Emmy" award as best actor of the
year for his role in the I Spy television series.   Accepting
the honor at the National Academy of Television Arts and
Sciences presentation ceremony, Cosby thanked the National
Broadcasting Company for "having guts."[3]

Warner Brothers presented a film version of the National Theatre of Great Britain production of Shakespeare's
Othello with Sir Laurence Olivier in the title role.   The technicolor film, which was made in England, received a limited
release in the United States.   The stage production won un-
stinting acclaim abroad but reaction to the film was not un-
mixed praise.   Relevant to this work were the remarks of
American film critic, Bosley Crowther:

> He plays Othello in blackface! That's right, black-
> face--not the dark-brown stain that even the most
> daring white actors do not nowadays wish to be be-
> yond.   What's more, he caps his shiny blackface
> with a wig of kinky black hair and he has the in-
> sides of his lips smeared and thickened with a
> startling raspberry red.   Several times, in his
> rages or reflections, he rolls his eyes up into his
> head so that the whites gleam like small milk ag-
> ates out of the inky face.
>
> The consequence is that he hits one--the sensitive
> American, anyhow--with the by-now outrageous im-
> pression of a theatrical Negro stereotype.   He does
> not look like a Negro (if that's what he's aiming to
> make the Moor)--not even a West Indian [sic]
> chieftain, which some of the London critics likened
> him to.   He looks like a Rastus or end man in a
> minstrel show.[4]

As in the preceding year, the presence of blacks in
some of the 1966 American movies was mainly in a background function.   Burke states, "This is a particularly useful category, within which the character becomes, for all
practical purposes, a part of the Scene."[5]

Passing through the motion picture, <u>Mr. Buddwing,</u> was Raymond St. Jacques as Hank, a New York City crap shooter, one of a procession of characters encountered by Mr. Buddwing (James Garner), an amnesiac. A long way yet from the stardom he would soon achieve, St. Jacques was required to speak the unlikely line, "Man, when you're born black you never know the smell of luck till it comes sailing down Broadway..."[6] That the only black in the film should be a crap shooter is comment in itself about the nature of that portrayal.

One of the many attractive females fawning over Flint (James Coburn) in <u>Our Man Flint</u> is black actress Ena Hartman, appearing as a WAC.

Juanita Moore, who created a substantial characterization as Annie Johnson in the 1959 remake of <u>Imitation of Life,</u> was consigned to a thankless background role in <u>The Singing Nun.</u> Based upon the life of Soeur Sourire, a Belgian Dominican whose songs won world-wide popularity, the film cast several actresses as nuns, among them Miss Moore. As Sister Mary she contributes little to the development of the plot and her race has no bearing on the part.

One sequence of the Allied Artists film, <u>Terror in the City,</u> involved two touching black portrayals. The boy hero of the story, Brill (Richard Bray), has run away from home to the big city. Among the array of people the white youngster meets before returning home is a black farmer (Robert Earl Jones) and his wife (Ruth Attaway). The couple extend the hospitality of their humble home to Brill for the night. The boy repays their kindness with a false accusation of theft. When he realizes that he is wrong about his hosts, he runs away, hurling at them an unwanted tip. Brill is embarrassed, but he is also wiser. The black couple have taught the white boy the meaning of self-respect.

Woody Strode joined some top Hollywood stars including Burt Lancaster, Lee Marvin and Robert Ryan in The Professionals. The film is a tale of kidnap, chase and escape. The young and beautiful wife of a wealthy American is held captive in a Mexican bandit stronghold. Four soldiers of fortune--"the professionals"--are hired to rescue her, each using his own special skills. One of the four adventurers is a Negro, Jake Sharp (Strode). Jake is a proficient archer who uses his bow and arrows on more than one occasion to extricate the quartet from imminent peril. Jake is alert, skillful, brave and most of all, silent. Unlike the other three "professionals," Jake consistently remains in the "background."

Three appearances by blacks in the supporting role category did amount to more than mere background characterization. The common denominator of the three characterizations was an overriding concern for the welfare of a white person.

Errol John played the complex role of Linc Langley in Assault on a Queen. He is right-hand man to Mark Bretaigne (Frank Sinatra), who operates a charter boat business. Linc assists Mark and his white associates in a fantastic plot to rob the "Queen Mary" in mid-ocean. Linc, a former wireless operator in the British navy, is an intelligent man. Despite his alcoholic problem, he understands himself and the deeper implications of what he is doing. This is evident in the following exchange.

> LINC: We're digging ourselves a grave here.
> Each of us for his own particular reason,
> love, loyalty, greed. The atmosphere is
> stifling. It's becoming extremely difficult
> to breathe.

MARK: You want out, Linc?

LINC: I signed on for the duration. Funny thing
though, ever since I went into long trousers,
I've been running away from myself. I
found a hiding place in a bottle. Where do
I hide after this, Mark?[7]

Linc has become a party to the criminal scheme out of a
sense of personal allegiance to Mark. As Linc explains to
Rosa, another character in the film:

LINC: He [Mark] recreated me. I'd been ill. He
found me lying on the sidewalk one night.
I weighed 104 pounds. Death was waiting
just around the corner. Mark beat him to
it. He picked me up, fed me, shared his
clothes with me and taught me to play Gin.
I owe him very much, Rosa, certainly for
my life.[8]

Although this portrayal has some of the symptoms of Reddick's "the devoted servant," it should not be so classified
because Linc's bondage may be directly traced to admitted
past favors rendered by Mark.

Lester Johnson, a character played by Joel Fluellen
in The Chase, bears a striking resemblance to the character,
Linc Langley. Because of an outstanding obligation to the
white Bubber Reeves (Robert Redford), now an escaped convict, Lester too becomes involved against his better judgment. Bubber's plea for help must be coupled with a re-
minder:

BUBBER: Now look Lester, this time it's big. Now
if I'm running in the luck I'm used to I'm
going to get blamed for a murder I didn't
do. Now, you got to help me.

LESTER: But I can't. I ain't got nothing. Bubber,
go way please.

> BUBBER: No! Now Lester, you owe me a favor.   I
>   took a 'rap' for you once.   You swore
>   you'd pay me back some day.
>
> LESTER: Yeah, I remember. [9]

That the black man is depicted here on a familiar first name
basis with the white man almost belies the fact that the film
is set in as bigoted and parochial a town as one is likely to
meet in the South.   The racial climate of the town is more
clearly revealed when Lester, who has taken a message to
Bubber's wife, is accosted by hostile white men:

> VOICE: What are you doing up there?
>
> LESTER: I was walking by and I just thought may-
>   be Anna was...
>
> SOL: Anna? He says Anna. Maybe he's got the
>   right to ...leave out the Miss before a
>   white girl's name?
>
> LESTER: But Mr. Sol, don't you remember me?
>   I'm Lester Johnson, I just come along...
>
> SOL: Just come along to visit in a white girl's
>   room? You go in that room? Make your-
>   self at home? You make yourself a
>   drink? [10]

The interrogation continues with further foundless accusations.
The men, who are in an ugly mood, try to plant a knife on
Lester.   They are interrupted by the timely arrival of the
sheriff.   Lester is reprieved from a group beating which is
visited upon him later by the same men.   Unlike Tom Robinson in To Kill a Mockingbird (1962), who also faced southern
racial injustice, Lester is not passive in any way.   He resists, even if only verbally, the men who seek to destroy him.

Although the Negro is quite visible in professional athletics, he is not shown in this capacity in motion pictures

with any frequency.   In this respect, the portrayal of Luther
"Boom Boom" Jackson by Ron Rich in The Fortune Cookie
was something of an exception.   Much like Jim Brown once
was in fact, "Boom Boom" is a football star for the Cleveland Browns.   An interest in athletics is not new to the Jackson family for "Boom Boom"'s father is a former light heavyweight boxer who killed a man in the ring.   Interestingly,
this part is played by Archie Moore, actually a light heavyweight boxing champion from 1953-1963.[11]   The money that
"Boom Boom" earns in football pays for a bowling lanes/-
cocktail lounge, which Mr. Jackson now manages for him.
"Boom Boom" has a penchant for cooking but "soul food"
(collard greens, peas and rice, corn bread, watermelon,
etc.), with which the Negro is traditionally linked, is not on
"Boom Boom"'s menu.   Instead he specializes in chicken
paprika, red cabbage and apricot dumpling.   It seems his
mother worked as a cook in a Hungarian restaurant.   In ac-
cordance with the tenets of athletic training, "Boom Boom"
is a clean-cut, non-drinking, all American type.   "I never
hurt anybody in my life, not even when they play dirty," says
"Boom Boom."[12]   The athlete's entire life is altered after
he accidentally knocks down Harry Hinkle (Jack Lemmon), a
TV camera man, during a game.   Harry, persuaded by his
conspiring brother-in-law, Willie Gingrich (Walter Matthau),
feigns serious injury in a hoax to collect an insurance settle-
ment.   Neglecting the football field, a remorseful "Boom
Boom" devotes his time and energy to Harry.   This brings
"Boom Boom" into contact with Sandy, Harry's estranged
wife, who makes a recognizable image-response to the Negro:

> BOOM BOOM: Let me take these [bags].   Mr.
> Gingrich sent me to pick you up.

> SANDY: Oh? Has he got a chauffeur now?
>
> BOOM BOOM: I'm a friend of Harry's.
>
> BOOM BOOM: Where do you want these [bags], in the bedroom?
>
> SANDY: Well I certainly don't want them in the kitchen. [13]

None of these thoughtless remarks bother the good natured football player. "Boom Boom" appears insensitive to the nuances of racial bigotry. However, the film does make incidental reference to the Negro revolution. In a scene between Harry and Sandy, the television channel they are watching reports a riot in Cleveland, the setting of the story. In another scene, Perkie, an insurance claims investigator, deliberately baits the fair-minded Harry:

> PERKIE: Our black brothers, they've been getting a little out of hand lately, just too damn cocky, you know what I mean? Look, I'm all for equal. Yeah, but what gets me is I'm driving an old Chevy. When I see a coon riding around in a white Cadillac... (At this point Harry rises from his wheel chair and socks Perkie, revealing the ruse.)[14]

Harry's delayed action in favor of honesty is responsible for the ultimate regeneration of "Boom Boom," who, still guilt-ridden, has resorted to alcohol, been arrested in a brawl and been suspended from the team. The portrayal of "Boom Boom" Jackson is a composite of three Reddick stereotypes, "the devoted servant," "the superior athlete" and "the mental inferior." He is the latter because he is the only character in the film who does not even suspect that Harry has perpetrated a trick.

Sidney Poitier and Ralph Nelson, star and director,

respectively, of <u>Lilies of the Field</u> (1963) were reunited in a
technicolor movie entitled <u>Duel at Diablo.</u> For a star of
Poitier's magnitude, the role would have been less meaning-
ful had it not been a departure from previous attempts to
portray the Negro as a part of the western scene. Poitier's
role as Toller, a former cavalry sergeant, is flashy, heroic
and smart. Where other blacks in this kind of film have
been preoccupied with the fortunes of whites, Toller is primarily concerned with Toller, as in the following:

> TOLLER: Look, the army owes me for forty
> horses, I spent the last four months hunt-
> ing and breaking. I'm planning on invest-
> ing my stakes in a nice profitable gambling
> saloon. My contract with the army calls
> for the delivery of fresh mounts to McAl-
> lister and I delivered them. The men I
> hired to help catch those mustangs are
> paid off and gone. The clothes I lived in
> for four months I burned and I didn't buy
> this new outfit to meet no trail dusting.
> Now look, you gave me this off the bottom
> of the deck. This is a swindle!
>
> McALLISTER: Now look...
>
> TOLLER: Shut up, McAllister. You don't scare
> me none and you sure can't pull no rank
> on me. [15]

Neither Jonah in <u>Sergeants 3</u> (1962) nor Franklyn in <u>Rio Con-</u>
<u>chos</u> (1964) would have dared to utter these words to a white
officer. But there is no bravado here; Toller supports his
brash words with courageous deeds. He is depicted as a
fast gun-draw and a seasoned fighter. In Clifford Mason's
opinion, none of this exonerated Poitier's acceptance of a
secondary role:

> In 'Duel at Diablo' he did little more than hold
> James Garner's hat, and this after he had won the

> Academy Award.   What white romantic actor would
> take a part like that?   He gets to kill a few Indi-
> ans, but Garner gets the girl and does all the real
> fighting.   Poitier was simply dressed up in a fancy
> suit, with a cigar stuck in his mouth and a new
> felt hat on his head. [16]

Mason seems to have missed Toller's active participation in
the real fighting, but there is validity to his remark about
the girl.   There is not the slightest hint of romance for Toller, black or white, not even a dance hall girl in the casino
he frequents.   Archer Winsten finds reason for optimism:

> One of the heroes is Sidney Poitier, a Negro, who
> had been a sergeant in the cavalry and appears as
> a finely dressed gambler, gunman and supporter of
> the downtrodden.   He rights wrongs in the way that
> the Lone Ranger used to do, and this is new be-
> cause Negroes have been conspicuous in westerns
> by their absence, and conspicuous in other pictures
> as being on the receiving end of wrongs. [17]

In the portrayal of blacks in American motion pictures,
the year 1966 should be remembered as one in which blacks
were involved in the production aspects of a major film, A
Man Called Adam.   Ike Jones, a Negro, co-produced the film
for Sammy Davis, Jr.'s Trace-Mark productions.   Mr. Davis
starred as trumpet player Adam Johnson, a man of extraordinary complexity.   Adam's intoxication has caused the death
of his wife and child and the blindness of a fellow-musician
in an automobile accident.   Added to his grief over this tragic incident is a burning resentment of racial discrimination.
One gets the impression that the music Adam plays (actually
played by Nat "Cannonball" Adderly) is much needed therapy
for him.   Then Claudia Ferguson (Cicely Tyson) enters his
life.   With her closely cropped hair and coffee complexion,
Miss Tyson displayed a truly Afro-American type of beauty,
quite different from the Caucasian standard common to other

black actresses who have achieved leading role status in
American films.

Claudia is an activist in the civil rights movement,
with a police record to prove it.   The romance between Adam
and Claudia is doomed from the start.   She wants him to
control his temper and his drinking.   Adam tries but it is
not within his tempestuous make-up.   In a sample of the
film's stilted dialogue, he says, "Easy don't make it no
more."[18]   Louis "Satchmo" Armstrong makes more than his
customary guest appearance in this one.   He plays Willie
"Sweet Daddy" Ferguson, Claudia's grandfather, long past his
prime as a musician.   Black actor-playwright Ossie Davis
fills the role of Adam's best friend, Nelson Davis.   This
portrayal required only that he look compassionate and loyal.
All these characterizations notwithstanding, only the composite
Adam Johnson-Sammy Davis, Jr. portrayal assumes any reality.   It is difficult to separate the two, as Davis admits:

> As far as I'm concerned, this is my first picture...
> I'm grateful for 'Anna Lucasta,' the three Sinatra
> pictures and 'Porgy and Bess,'--but this one, this
> one is about a man, a musician as it happens,
> who's dying because of his inability to communicate.
> He only happens to be a Negro.   In a way, there's
> a lot of me in him.   I insisted on that in the writ-
> ing.   And I insisted, too, that he should die in the
> end.   Why?   So the people close to him--Cicely
> and Ossie--would perhaps have a better knowledge
> of life for the way he's lived his.[19]

When the movie is finished, we are no closer to understanding the self-destructive forces within Adam.   Other
men have recovered from personal tragedy.   Other men, too,
have survived racial abuse.   Why Adam cannot be one of
these is never clarified.   Then, too, there are certain con-
tradictions which detract from the veracity of the characteri-

Home of the Brave, an early Stanley Kramer production about the Negro problem, starred James Edwards, seen here with Lloyd Bridges.   (Photo by permission of Stanley Kramer)

zation. For example, Adam impulsively resists a white policeman's infringement upon his civil liberty but later stands
by while a white friend is unmercifully beaten by racists.
Claudia's insistence on a non-violent Adam cannot suffice as
an explanation, for it would have to apply in both instances.
A further inconsistency involves Adam's booking agent, Manny
(Peter Lawford). In one scene, Adam threatens the callous
Manny with a broken bottle, but in another scene, he literally crawls in humiliation to the now vindictive agent. The au-
thentic "on location" filming at Small's Paradise, a Harlem
night spot, and other places in and around New York, as well
as a scene inside a segregated theatre in the South, fails to
save the motion picture. It seems a pity that the other black
portrayals in the film serve only as mirrors upon which the
tormented personality of Adam Johnson can be reflected.
This is particularly true of Claudia Ferguson, whose unde-
veloped characterization offered great promise. The attempt
by blacks to tell their own story is commendable. It is the
excessive ambition of A Man Called Adam that is its ruina-
tion. As one film critic sees it:

> You know you're in for less than perfection...with
> Sammy Davis, Jr., who can do just about every-
> thing in the entertainment dodge except play a
> trumpet or Hamlet, playing a Hamletesque trumpet-
> er in A Man Called Adam.[20]

One additional film provides a valid instrument for
measuring the status of blacks in films during the year.
Shago Martin, an important black character in Norman Mailer's novel, An American Dream, is omitted from the 1966
film of the same title.[21] The interracial affair between
Shago and the white heroine, Cherry (portrayed by Janet
Leigh in the movie) is obviously eliminated as well.

Blacks were depicted in non-traditional ways in some
of the motion pictures released during 1966. A black artist
was involved in the production aspect of at least one major
motion picture during the year. The total number of portrayals remained approximately the same as the immediately
preceding years.

Notes

1. The World Almanac and Book of Facts, 1967,
    (New York: New York World-Telegram and The
    Sun, 1967), p. 76, 80-83.

2. The World Almanac and Book of Facts, 1969,
    (New York: Newspaper Enterprise Association,
    Inc., 1969), p. 47.

3. Ebony, The Negro Handbook (Chicago: Johnson
    Publishing Co., 1966), p. 362.

4. Bosley Crowther, "The Screen: Minstrel Show
    'Othello'," The New York Times, February 2,
    1966, p. 24.

5. William L. Burke, "The Presentation of the Amer-
    ican Negro in Hollywood Films, 1946-1961:
    Analysis of a Selected Sample of Feature Films,"
    (Unpublished Ph.D. dissertation, Northwestern
    University, 1965), pp. 147-148.

6. Mr. Buddwing (Metro Goldwyn Mayer, 1966).

7. Assault on a Queen (Paramount Pictures, 1966).

8. Ibid.

9. The Chase (Columbia Pictures, 1966).

10. Ibid.

11. The World Almanac and Book of Facts, 1967,
    (New York: New York World-Telegram and The
    Sun, 1967), p. 886.

12. The Fortune Cookie (United Artists, 1966).

13. Ibid.

14. Ibid.

15. Duel at Diablo (United Artists, 1966).

16. Clifford Mason, "Why Does White America Love
     Sidney Poitier So?," The New York Times,
     September 10, 1967, p. 1.

17. Archer Winsten, "Reviewing Stand," New York Post,
     June 16, 1966, p. 58.

18. A Man Called Adam (Embassy Pictures, 1966).

19. Howard Thompson, "Golden Boy Turns to the Trum-
     pet for Film," The New York Times, November
     26, 1965, p. 44.

20. Judith Crist, The Private Eye, The Cowboy and
     The Very Naked Girl, (New York: Holt, Rine-
     hart and Winston, 1968), p. 209.

21. Norman Mailer, An American Dream, (New York:
     Dial, 1965).

Al Freeman, Jr. starred with Shirley Knight in Dutchman. (Photo courtesy Walter Reade Organization, Inc.)

Chapter 11

1967

Rioting by blacks took place in Detroit, Newark, Milwaukee, Cincinnati and other cities across the United States. The U. S. Civil Rights Commission stated that compensatory programs in ghetto schools were largely ineffective and urged Congress to pass legislation requiring racial balance in all public schools. Adam Clayton Powell, excluded from his seat in the U. S. House of Representatives on the charge of misusing public finds, filed suit, claiming his removal was unconstitutional. Meanwhile, in a special election, the 18th Congressional District (Harlem) voted Powell in again by a 6-1 margin, although he had not campaigned. Powell was still not permitted to return. Muhammad Ali (Cassius Clay) was deposed as heavyweight champion of the world by the World Boxing Association and by the New York State Athletic Commission when he refused to be drafted into the U. S. Armed Forces on religious grounds. H. Rap Brown became chairman of the Student Nonviolent Coordinating Committee following the resignation of Stokely Carmichael. Meanwhile, Carmichael addressed black audiences throughout the country, inciting them to resort to violence in attainment of their goals. A "black power" conference in Newark closed with delegate approval of resolutions aimed at establishment of a course of separatism for black Americans. Despite a rejection of the white power structure by some blacks, there was evidence of personal achievement, as usual, by individual

137

Negroes.   Thurgood Marshall became the first black associate justice in the history of the U.S. Supreme Court.   Carl
B. Stokes was the first Negro to be elected mayor of a major city, Cleveland, Ohio.   Other blacks elected to the may-
oralty were Richard G. Hatcher in Gary, Indiana and Walter
E. Washington in Washington, D. C. [1]

   In 1967, the number of portrayals by blacks in American motion pictures increased slightly over the preceding
year.   Characterizations generally tended to have more rele-
vancy to the plots of the films in which they occurred.   Of
the four portrayals subject to categorization as "background,"
three were in comic roles.

   Godfrey Cambridge and Richard Pryor, the latter in
his motion picture debut, play small nonsensical parts in
The Busy Body.   Cambridge is Mike, one of a pair of gang-
land errand boys.   Marty Ingels, a white comedian, is Willie, his partner.   Pleased with his role in the movie, Cambridge said:

> I don't want to be white, you know.   I just say,
> 'Isn't it a joy that Marty and I can each bring our
> own richnesses to this picture?'   We have a scene
> where we're both looking over a fence into a grave-
> yard.   Once, in any scene like that, the Negro
> was the only one afraid, but this time Marty's
> afraid, too. [2]

However, certain stereotypical distinctions between blacks
and whites permeate the film.   In humorous exchanges between the two men, the script intimates that the white man
is intellectually superior to the black man, even at the gangster level.   When Mike says, "trying to allocate us," Willie
corrects him with, "you mean locate us."   On the right side
of the law, Richard Pryor plays Whittaker, a black lieuten-
ant of an integrated police force.   Even the amusing aspects

of his role border upon stereotype. For example, when
Whittaker continues talking on a telephone, oblivious of the
corpse with a knife in its back which is propped up next to
him, he is playing "the mental inferior."[3]

Geoffrey Holder, a black ballet dancer, has the laugh-
producing name of Willie Shakespeare in Dr. Dolittle. As
the native ruler of a mythical floating island, Willie boasts
that he and his subjects speak seven languages including English.

Such linguistic excellence would be unlikely indeed in
the troubled New York City public school that Up the Down
Staircase depicts. As a concerned parent of a black pupil,
Vinnette Carroll has one moving scene with her son's teacher
in this film.

Hotel, the motion picture version of Arthur Hailey's
novel, is really a series of vignettes about the people who
arrive at and depart from a fashionable hotel in New Orleans.
Attempting to register at the Hotel, Dr. Adams (Davis Ro-
berts) and his wife, a respectable looking black couple, are
turned away politely with the excuse that no accommodations
are available. The couple go elsewhere but inform the press
of this discriminatory act. Subsequent developments reveal
that the couple were actually agitators hired by O'Keefe (Kevin McCarthy), a business competitor of the Hotel's owner.
O'Keefe hoped that unfavorable publicity over the racial incident would damage a pending sale of the Hotel. In making
provocateurs of Dr. Adams and his wife, the script, intentionally or otherwise, minimizes the inhumanity of the bias
perpetrated against them. Commenting on this episode, Bosley Crowther states:

> ...it shows rather forcefully how the issue of civil
> rights might be maneuvered to cynical and corrupt

purposes. And it brings into illustrative focus, for
the first time in a Hollywood film that I recall, the
helpfulness of the National Association for the Advancement of Colored People in a case of deliberate
fraud. [4]

Herbert Hill, labor secretary for the N.A.A.C.P.,
contended that a major Negro character in the novel was written
out of the motion picture. [4a]

Black discrimination against whites occurs in The Comedians, a film made from Graham Greene's novel about political
life in the dictatorship of Haiti. Black portrayals included Magiot (James Earl Jones), a rebel doctor; Petit Pierre (Roscoe Lee
Browne), a garrulous gossip columnist; Marie Therese (Cicely
Tyson), a friendly prostitute; Henri Philipot (George Stanford
Brown), a young patriot; Madam Philipot (Gloria Foster), widow
of an official eliminated by the government; and Captain Concasseur (Raymond St. Jacques), a merciless police officer. All are
native Haitians. Perhaps this gamut precluded the progressive
development of any single characterization. Rather succinct dialogue gives instant insight into the nature and goals of each character. Speaking about Caucasians, Captain Concasseur says,
"I'm offended by the color. Like a toad's belly, but we accept
some of you, if you are useful to the state." Referring to the
Ton-Ton Macoute, the president's special police, the widow Philipot says, "Look at them, the cowards, they call themselves
brave but they are afraid of him, [her husband] even though he is
dead." Bidding farewell to two white American tourists, Petit
Pierre says, "But 'parting is a little death,' one of our poets
said. We make friends; you go away. So seldom in Port-au-
Prince we see our friends return." Just from these isolated
lines, we know that Concasseur is a black racist; Madam Philipot
is a courageous woman and Petit Pierre is a hypocritical charm-
er. So it is with all the portrayals in the film. Where dia-

logue is insufficiently telling, other devices are used. The special police are made to appear more sinister through the wearing of dark glasses. A Prostitute, Marie Therese, must laugh incessantly to demonstrate her earthiness. Magiot must underplay as proof of his seriousness. [5]

The difference in the reactions to the film by a black and a white writer provides an interesting contrast. Lindsay Patterson, editor of Anthology of the American Negro in the Theatre, called The Comedians "a landmark in movie history." He added:

> It was the first time that a varied character scale of black people were grouped in one setting as honest-to-goodness, everyday, ordinary, intelligent, fallible human beings, existing or trying to exist as any other people would under similar circumstances. [6]

Bosley Crowther, newspaper film critic, was of another opinion:

> By far the most agitating aspect of the film...is the sinister image it presents of a rigid reign of terror in a Caribbean country under a black dictatorship--and thus, by a quick association out of our own recent experiences, an image of the fearful implications of burgeoning 'black power.' [7]

In an escapist adventure film such as The Dirty Dozen, blacks and whites alike could applaud the heroics of Jim Brown as Robert T. Jefferson. He is one of twelve American criminals recruited from prison to infiltrate Nazi-held territory in World War II and blow up a chateau. The other characters never let Jefferson forget that he is the only black around. Early in the movie, a prison guard tells Jefferson, "Hey midnight! Be a real good boy and maybe I'll let you eat with the white folks tomorrow." Maggot, the psychopath of the "dozen" says, "Hey guard, do we have to eat with niggers?" When Jefferson attempts to stop Franco, one of

the "dozen," from deserting, Franco says, "What is this anyway?   Uncle Tom week?"   Jefferson is not a stranger to
bigotry.   Asked why he has been sentenced to death by hang-
ing, Jefferson replies, "You know why or maybe you think I
should let those cracker bastards go right ahead and castrate
me."

If murder is only implicit in Jefferson's background,
it becomes an actuality toward the end of the movie.   He
shoots and kills Maggot (Telly Savalas) after the latter has
brutally murdered a German woman and thereby endangered
the mission of the "dirty dozen."   In the last minute of the
movie, Jefferson has twenty seconds in which to drop hand
grenades into a cellar air raid shelter where Nazi senior officers are hiding.   Although this feat is accomplished speedi-
ly, in the process Jefferson is shot to death by a Nazi
sniper. [8]   If the "No, no!!" shouted at this point by black
movie-goers at the Adams Theatre in Newark is any indication, Jim Brown is truly an identity symbol to black males.
Renata Adler has another notion:

> What is extraordinary about Brown's grenade run,
> aside from the way it is timed in the film's own
> terms, is that it seems to work so well for audi-
> ences just because they know who James Brown
> really is.   It is not as an actor that he makes his
> run with those grenades; it is as a great Negro
> football star and a man with a public career. [9]

In still another film, The President's Analyst, a satire, violence is associated with a black.   In the opening
scene, Godfrey Cambridge as Don Masters is seen pushing
a dress cart through Manhattan's garment district.   Quite
suddenly, he whips out a knife and stabs a man to death.   A
few moments later, in the office of his psychoanalyst, Dr.
Sidney Schaefer (James Coburn), Don confesses the act.   Dur-

ing the ensuing questioning by his psychiatrist, Don reveals
a secret trauma from his past.   In his early days in kinder-
garten, Don noticed some white children laughing and yelling,
"Run, run, here comes the nigger." In his naïveté, Don
joined them, playfully yelling the same racial epithet.   Don's
older brother, who was in the third grade, found him and explained the insult.   Instead of becoming angry at the white
children, Don has hated his brother ever since the moment
of harsh revelation.   Bringing Dr. Schaefer and the audience
up to date, Don discloses his identity as a C. E. A. agent for
Uncle Sam.   The man he has slain was an Albanian double
agent, a threat to American security.   In Don's psyche, it
is not the Albanian spy but his brother he has killed.   We
have observed Don as "the razor and knife 'toter' " earlier
but "the savage African" emerges incognito:

> DON: It bothers me sometimes because I don't
> feel guilty about it.   Don't you think that's
> psychotic behavior?
>
> DR. SCHAEFER: No I don't.   It explains your
> utter lack of hostility.   You can vent your
> aggressive feelings by actually killing
> people.   It's a sensational solution to the
> hostility problem. [10]

Violence, this time by whites, was the theme of The
Incident, a film directed by Larry Peerce, who also directed
One Potato, Two Potato (1964).   One car of a subway train
headed from Bronx to Manhattan late at night is seized by
two white hoodlums.   Arnold Robinson (Brock Peters) and his
wife, Joan (Ruby Dee), are two blacks among a dozen or
more white passengers who are terrorized by the duo.   Brief
sequences introduce each of the characters before they board
the train.   The fearsome ride bares the frustrations, personal problems and ambitions of each.   Arnold and Joan have

just left a civil rights meeting where the strategy of peace-
ful demonstration has been advocated.   The Robinsons dis-
agree on the racial issue.   He is impatient and would fight
for Negro rights; she espouses a more passive approach.
Although Arnold boasts "I ain't non-violent," he cowers under
the pressure of the nightmarish incident.   Film journalist
Frances Herridge observed:

> ...Brock Peters, as a Black-Power Negro, steam-
> ing over his wife's...tolerance of Whities....The
> militant Negro, for example, delighted to see the
> Whites pushed around, goes to jelly when his turn
> comes. [11]

Another 1967 film to have a subway car as its setting
was Dutchman, a film adaptation of the powerful off-Broadway stage play by black playwright LeRoi Jones.   Lula (Shirley Knight), a psychotic white girl, tries to seduce Clay, a
young black male, as the subway proceeds from station to
station.   Gradually, Lula baits and goads Clay.   She ridi-
cules his three-button suit conventionality, his interest in
Baudelaire and his middle-class "white Negro" responses.
From the start, Lula attempts the sexual seduction of Clay.
Finally, Clay can restrain himself no longer and he erupts,
spewing the harsh philosophy of Jones.   Al Freeman Jr.,
cited previously for Black Like Me, enacts this role.   Early
in his diatribe, Clay says:

> CLAY: ...Let me be who I feel like being.   Uncle
>   Tom.   Thomas.   Whoever.   It's none of
>   your business.   You don't know anything
>   except what's there for you to see.   An
>   act.   Lies.   Device.   Not the pure heart,
>   the pumping black heart.   You don't ever
>   know that.   And I sit here, in this but-
>   toned-up suit, to keep myself from cutting
>   your throats. [12]

With these words, Jones introduces the idea that there is a
concealed black within every Negro. If released, as a genii
from a bottle, he will menace the white society to which he
appears to conform. One has to recognize the polemical nature of a script that has a twenty-year-old speak as follows:

> CLAY: Don't make the mistake, through some ir-
> responsible surge of Christian charity of
> talking too much about the advantages of
> Western rationalism, or the great intellec-
> tual legacy of the white man, or maybe
> they'll begin to listen. And then, maybe
> one day, you'll find they actually do under-
> stand exactly what you are talking about,
> all these fantasy people. All these blues
> people. And on that day, as sure as shit,
> when you really believe you can 'accept'
> them into your fold, as half-white trusties
> late of the subject peoples. With no more
> blues, except the very old ones, and not a
> watermelon in sight, the great missionary
> heart will have triumphed, and all of these
> ex-coons will be stand-up Western men,
> with eyes for clean hard useful lives, sober,
> pious, and sane, and they'll murder you.
> They'll murder you, and have very ration-
> al explanations. Very much like your
> own. [13]

When Clay completes his denunciation, Lula stabs him to
death. The act of Clay's murder symbolizes the ways in
which some whites bring about the death of some blacks, eco-
nomically and socially, if not physically. The film ends as
Lula stalks new prey, another young Negro who has boarded
the train. We can only wonder if he will be as vulnerable
as Clay. LeRoi Jones has been criticized for terminating his
play with the destruction of the black man, a peculiar custom
dating back to William Shakespeare's Othello.

> The stereotype of the Negro drama is the unhappy
> ending--spiritually and physically defeated, lynched,

> dead--gotten rid of to the relief of the dramatist
> and the audience, in time for a late supper. [14]

Crediting those responsible for Dutchman with integrity in attempting the transition from stage to film, Judith Crist blamed the reality of the medium for any failure of the film. She also found Clay "gullible rather than vulnerable" and "his outburst...easy to reject intellectually."[15] Crist made no comment concerning acceptance or rejection of Clay's tirade on an emotional level.

Shirley Clarke, noted for her direction of The Connection (1962) and The Cool World (1964), focused on the Negro again for Portrait of Jason. The film, a semi-documentary, was actually 105 edited minutes of a twelve-hour interview with a male prostitute. Jason Holiday, whose real name is Aaron Paine, gazes directly at the camera and reminisces about his perverted life. An aspiring entertainer, Jason performs as if he were auditioning, even doing an embarrassing imitation of Mae West. When he is not trying to amuse with remarks such as "I'm a nervous duster," Jason is imparting the tragedy of his particular human condition. Jason is less interesting as a Negro than as a misfit. Evidently neurotic, homosexual, vain, confused, Jason can tell us little about the why of himself because even he does not understand. This is the reason Jason admits, "I'm a pretty frightening cat."[16] If Jason is any stereotype, it is "the uninhibited expressionist."

Another pretty frightening cat, fictitious this time, was Richie "Eagle" Stokes played by Dick Gregory in Sweet Love, Bitter. The film was based upon Night Song, a novel by black author, John A. Williams. Lewis Jacobs, author of The Rise of the American Film, wrote the script with Herbert Danska, who also directed. Both men claimed that

their script was distorted by business associates, who edited
and juxtaposed scenes, altering the intended meaning of the
film. [17] As it was released, the film focused upon the character of Eagle, a Negro saxophonist. The characterization
was inspired by the life of Charlie "Bird" Parker, famed jazz
musician. Similar to the character Sammy Davis, Jr. played
in A Man Called Adam (1966), Eagle is at war with himself
over his inequitable status as a black in a white-dominated
society. He says:

> EAGLE: This is all I know, man. I ain't makin'
> a quarter.... Ain't no spade critics. Most
> spade dee-jays play rock n' roll. Ain't
> but a few spade joints can pay my way--
> Sheet! Paddy boys pick up a horn--go
> boo-bip--and right away, man, they're
> playin' jazz....Now ain't them some apples?
> Do you dig, frig? Understand? It's your
> world. You won't let me make it in it,
> and you can't! Now ain't that a bitch? [18]

Despite these remarks and similar ones, Eagle helps a down-
on-his-luck white college instructor. When this man is restored to his former environs, largely due to Eagle's efforts,
he needlessly and cruelly rejects his black benefactor.
Wearing a beret and speaking jazz jargon, Eagle's life consists of jazz, liquor, sex and drugs. An overdose of heroin
kills him. Once again, the rage, hostility and problems of
a black man are resolved by his death. The portrayal of
Eagle is essentially "the sexual superman," "the unhappy
non-white" and "the natural-born musician."

In the same movie, Robert Hooks[19] depicted the role
of Keel Robinson, Eagle's best friend. Where Eagle has
many women in his life, Keel has found romance with only
one white girl, Della (Diane Varsi). Previously a divinity
student, Keel now operates a coffee house with Della but his

main interest seems to be the care and feeding of Eagle.
This is plainly stated in Keel's early appraisal of the white
man, whom Eagle has befriended.

> KEEL: Everybody has chipped a piece out of Eagle.
> Everybody. I figured you for one of them.
> You know, 'we dig the N. A. A. C. P. , even
> though they have no use for his kind. ...
> They have their function, I guess. Some
> people preserve statues and cave drawings.
> Well--we've got that shabby bean-picker.
> You've heard--when he builds on a blues
> theme: building with such speed and intri-
> cacy that we don't even know it's the blues
> right off? He's our record: The aggres-
> siveness, the self-hate, the pain and, our
> will to go on. End of sermon. [20]

In the sexual department, anyway, Keel destroys one Negro
myth. His hatred of all whites makes him impotent in his
sexual relationship with Della. Under the cirumstance, one
can only conjecture as to why Keel does not seek romance
with a black girl. While Keel is definitely not "the sexual
superman," he, too, is "the unhappy non-white." He is
"The Problem Negro" which Hollis Alpert rejects:

> When I turn on my TV set for the 6 o'clock news
> I meet, through this medium each day, intelligent,
> articulate, and impressive Americans who are Ne-
> gro. ... But I do not meet these people in movies.
> Instead of problems, I meet The Problem, and it's
> always the same, and it's always all but hopeless.
> I doubt that it is... [21]

Visual or verbal references to the civil rights movement and to police brutality against blacks lent a touch of
timeliness to the film, subsequently redistributed under the
title It Won't Rub Off, Baby, a line Eagle speaks in the film.
Herbert Danska tells of a small but striking role, patterned
after Miles Davis, jazz musician, which was completely

edited out of the film.   The role had been performed by
Carl Lee of The Connection (1962) and The Cool World
(1964). [22]

The image of the Negro as a superhero prevailed in
four American motion pictures released in 1967.   The only
one of the four not to have Sidney Poitier as star was Otto
Preminger's production of Hurry Sundown.   Diahann Carroll
is Vivian Thurlow, an attractive school teacher who has re-
turned from New York and an unhappy romance.   Robert
Hooks is Reeve Scott, a robust young black farmer who is
romantically drawn toward Vivian.   Beah Richards is Rose
Scott, Reeve's mother, who has been subservient to whites
all her days.   The generation gap between Reeve and Rose
Scott recalls a similar one between the Newcombs in Black
Like Me (1964).   The Scott family schism goes as follows:

> REEVE: Mama, you're living in a dream.   We
> can't trust no Miss Julie or no other white
> folks to watch out for us.   We gotta start
> watching out for ourselves.

> ROSE: I don't know what they done to you in that
> there army.   Seem like you ain't got a
> kind word to say about nobody since you
> got back.

> REEVE: You go away, you get to take a good long
> look at yourself, your life, everything.
> Ain't so easy after that to fall back into
> old ways. [23]

Present in a background capacity as Vivian's grandfather is
Rex Ingram.   He has virtually nothing to do but he does it
with dignity.   His resonant voice, white hair and goatee con-
jure up an earlier Ingram portrayal of De Lawd in The Green
Pastures (1936).   He is called Professor, although his professional affiliation is with an all-black grade school, rather

From <u>Sweet Love, Bitter</u>... -- Dick Gregory and Robert Hooks.
(Photo courtesy Arnold Engle)

than a college or university. Since it is blacks who address
him in this way, derogatory intent is improbable.

When Rose Scott is betrayed by the young white woman she has served, loved and trusted, a transformation of
character is clearly enunciated:

> ROSE: I was...I was a...I was a white folks' nig-
> ger. I was! I was! You've got to learn
> from my mistakes. You've got to fight!
> You've got to! Passin' out of this life,
> Reeve. In these last minutes, you know
> what I feel most of all? Anger. Yes,
> Anger. And hatred. Not so much at them
> for what they done to me...but at myself
> for letting them...no! Helping them to do
> it. Mmmm...and I grieve...I truly grieve
> ...for this sorry thing that has been my
> life. [24]

Before she dies, Rose hears that her land will be stolen, le-
gally, by greedy whites. Following his mother's death,
Reeve learns that the sheriff is coming to arrest him on fab-
ricated charges. At this point, the superhero emerges. Instead of attempting evasion, Reeve takes his guitar and begins
to warble the theme song, "Hurry Sundown." This unrealistic
reaction to imminent danger is ironical, considering the fact
that a bigot actually shot at Robert Hooks while the story was
being filmed in Baton Rouge, Louisiana. [25] A note of truth is
injected into the Negro characterizations at this point. A
group of black women outsmart the sheriff by playing obsequi-
ous roles. They bribe him with food and drink, disarm him
with pretended friendliness and distract him with femininity.
He departs without Reeve. When Reeve's case finally comes
to court, it is Vivian who dons the cloak of superheroics.
Using subterfuge, she gets a look at the archives which sub-
stantiate Reeve's right of ownership. As if this weren't sufficient, Vivian outtalks an elderly white racist judge. Bosley

Crowther, Judith Crist and Arthur Knight were just a few
of the critics to attack Hurry Sundown as "a massive mish-
mash of stereotyped Southern characters," for its "cartoon
characters and patronage of Negroes" and for its having "un-
derlined everything, nuanced nothing."[26]   Perhaps it is Foster
Hirsch who understands the problem best:

> The reticence toward the Negro is felt throughout
> the film, with the result that the Negro characters
> emerge as bland and uninteresting. It is as if
> Preminger and his writers were afraid to give any
> definitive characters to the Negroes for fear of of-
> fending. So the Negroes remain an unknown quan-
> tity, very distant from the center of action, and
> from our center of attention. The character played
> by Robert Hooks (an incipient Poitier but as yet
> lacking in presence or force) has virtually no per-
> sonality at all. He seems pleasant enough, and (in
> terms of the plot) intent on keeping his land, but
> we are never permitted to find out what he really
> is thinking.[27]

To this criticism, one might add a comment on the nature of
the relationship between Reeve (Hooks) and Vivian (Carroll).
Their cinema romance, appropriate only for repressed superhero and superheroine, is confined to a single kiss with
faces turned away from the camera, and this in a film with
explicit sex between whites.

The South was the setting of In the Heat of the Night,
a film in which Sidney Poitier starred as Virgil Tibbs, a
police detective from Philadelphia, Pa. Visiting his mother
in Mississippi, Tibbs is accused of a murder. He is pushed
around, interrogated and affronted until his credentials are
substantiated. Then he is mocked and patronized. Bill Gillespie (Rod Steiger), the white police chief of Sparta, is incredulous about a Negro as colleague. The black detective
quickly demonstrates his occupational expertise and knowledge

of the latest scientific procedures of criminal investigation.
Soon Gillespie must turn to Tibbs for assistance in solving
the crime:

> GILLESPIE: She wants us to catch the killer. No
> killer, no factory. Well, a lot of jobs for
> a lot of colored people. You follow me?
>
> TIBBS: I'm going home, man...
>
> GILLESPIE: They're your people!
>
> TIBBS: Not mine, yours, you made this scene.
>
> GILLESPIE: What do you want me to do? You
> want me to beg you? Is that what you're
> after?
>
> TIBBS: Look, I've had your town, up to here.
>
> GILLESPIE: Boy, it would give me a whirl of
> satisfaction to horse whip you, Virgil. [28]

Whether from personal conceit or irresistible challenge (the
script never makes this clear), Virgil decides to remain in
Sparta and solve the case. When Virgil says, "I'll find a
hotel," a local Negro laughs and offers Tibbs the hospitality
of his home. The brief sequence is a comment about the
unavailability of public accommodations for non-whites in the
South. Later, Endicott, a white aristocrat, slaps Tibbs
across the face out of resentment at being questioned by a
black. Unintimidated by the alien and anti-black milieu in
which he finds himself, Tibbs retaliates in kind with a slap
across the face of an enraged Endicott, to the astonishment
of an onlooking Negro servant. Even Endicott acknowledges
a slight change in the traditional code of the South, when he
says to Tibbs, "There was a time when I could have had you
shot!" As though this episode was not sufficient proof of
superheroism, Tibbs survives first an ambush by several

racist assailants, and then a mob of hostile and armed white
toughs.   Singling out the sought-after killer from among this
lawless group of whites, Tibbs brings about the triumph of
justice over bigotry.[29]

Beah Richards, Mrs. Scott in Hurry Sundown, made
a brief appearance in this film as Mrs. Bellamy.   In the
course of his investigation, Tibbs talks with her.   Mrs. Bellamy arranges abortions and apparently is capable of fulfilling
a variety of illicit requests.   She provides her services without discrimination, to blacks and whites.   Mrs. Bellamy lives
behind a store in a shanty section on the outskirts of town,
possibly to avoid unwanted confrontation.   Referring to whites,
she says, "They chew you up and spit you out."[30]

However, it is the character of Virgil Tibbs and his
relationship with white Southerners on which the film is cen-
tered.   The script implies a rapport between two antithetical
human beings, one white, one black.   The scene between
them at Gillespie's home is quite unreal.   The foundation of
social intercourse between Tibbs and Gillespie has not been
established nor is it probable.   Yet there Gillespie sits, con-
fiding the loneliness of his life to Tibbs.   Is this another
miracle the black superhero hath wrought?   In the conclud-
ing scene, just before Negro blues singer Ray Charles ren-
ders the title song, the white police chief carries the black
detective's bag and bids him farewell with a "Virgil, you
take care, you hear?"[31]   As incredible as this finale may
seem, it is consistent with the entire portrayal of Virgil
Tibbs which Hirsch synthesized:

> ...Poitier, stalwart, dignified, clean-cut, articu-
> late, walks unscathed through this jungle of deprav-
> ity.   Indeed, his perfect English contrasts pointed-
> ly with the butchered grammar and blurred Southern
> drawl of the white characters.   While the whites

> sweat profusely and wear their clothes sloppily,
> Poitier is invariably well-tailored and immaculate-
> ly groomed. [32]

Interestingly enough, this description of Virgil Tibbs
could apply equally to Sidney Poitier's characterization of
Mark Thackery in To Sir, With Love. One need only substi-
tute "Cockney accent" for "Southern drawl" and the rest of
the statement above needs no alteration. The portrayal of
Thackery was based upon the autobiography of Edward Ricardo Braithwaite, a British Guianan black. Newly arrived
in England and unable to find employment as an engineer, for
which he is qualified, Thackery accepts a teaching appointment in an impoverished district of London. Most of his pupils are rude, slovenly, apathetic and undisciplined. Once
the superhero springs into action, order is created out of
chaos, by his merely treating his adolescent charges like
adults and insisting upon mutual respect. In no time at all,
they become well-groomed, polite and curious. A pretty
white co-ed develops an infatuation for Thackery, which he
properly discourages. Although the book told of a mature
interracial romance between Braithwaite (Thackery) and Gil-
lian Blanchard, she remains only a colleague and platonic
friend in the movie. Clifford Mason calls this "the all-time
Hollywood reversal act. Instead of putting a love interest into a story that had none, they took it out."[33] Actually the
subject of race is practically ignored in the film. Weston
(Geoffrey Bayldon), a cynical white teacher, does cast a few
color-oriented quips in Thackery's direction. The solitary
colored student in Thackery's class is the offspring of a
white father and a black mother. Seals (Anthony Villaroel)
is "the unhappy non-white," evident in the following emotional outburst:

> SEALS: My old man's a proper bastard.
>
> THACKERY: You shouldn't speak like that about
>   your father.
>
> SEALS: I hate him, hate him. White man. Never
>   forgive him for what he did to my mum.
>   Never. Well he married her didn't he?
>   Didn't he? [34]

When Seals' mother dies, the white pupils hesitate to pay
their respects because of familial adherence to Britain's
"colour bar." Their eventual appearance at the funeral is
yet another personal victory for Thackery. Braithwaite's
book detailed an act of racial discrimination committed
against him in an elegant London restaurant, an incident which
had the potential of a dramatically-charged motion picture
scene, had it been included. In the autobiography, this episode influences the progress of the love affair between the
two teachers. [35] As to the elimination of mature romance
from the movie, Hollis Alpert wrote:

> ...Poitier, as the teacher, while insisting upon all
> his elemental rights as a human being, draws a
> firm line in matters of romance. This renuncia-
> tion is meant as one more example of his dedica-
> tion to righteousness, as a reinforcement of his
> essential dignity...it's an easy way out, too, for
> his screen-writers, who become curiously race-
> conscious while seeming to promote both tolerance
> and idealism. [36]

In Guess Who's Coming to Dinner? Sidney Poitier finally achieved film romance as a super-star but it was not the
kind that could refute the criticism of Clifford Mason, Foster Hirsch, Hollis Alpert and others. Wilfred Sheed calls
the movie, "The Old Hollywood knack for misstating a situation so grossly that the problem never arises." Identifying
Poitier as "the problem that never arises," Sheed pinpoints

the theme as "whoever thought that that nice young man was
a Negro?"[37] Dr. John Prentice (Poitier) and his young white
fiancée, Joanna Drayton (Katherine Houghton) arrive in San
Francisco from Hawaii, where they met while both were va-
cationing.   The couple inform both sets of parents of their
plans to wed immediately.   Initially, the four parents are
shocked and less than happy about the prospect.   The entire
plot hinges upon parental approval.   Andrew Greeley called
it "Abie's Irish Rose in blackface."[38]

      Just as in One Potato, Two Potato (1964), the mother(s)
capitulate first, and why shouldn't they?   For the third time
in 1967, Poitier portrayed a superhero.   Dr. John Prentice
is handsome, prosperous and well educated.   His curriculum
vitae includes a magna cum laude graduation from Johns Hopkins, professorship at Yale Medical School, a stint with the
London School of Tropical Medicine, service with the World
Health Organization, the authorship of two technical books and
a lengthy list of monographs, to name only a few accomplish-
ments.   Yet John tells Joanna's parents, "...I fell in love
with your daughter and as incredible as it may seem she fell
in love with me."[31]   In short, John is unrealistic.   His
father (Roy E. Glenn), an outspoken man, is a retired post-
al employee.   Father and son share one of the film's poignant scenes:

> MR. PRENTICE: Have you ever thought what
> people would say about you? Why in six-
> teen or seventeen states, you'd be break-
> ing the law. You'd be criminals. And say
> they changed the law, that don't change
> the way people feel about these things.
> You know, for a man who all his life never
> put a wrong foot anywhere, you're way out
> of line, boy.

> JOHN: You can't tell me when or where I'm out of

line or try to get me to live according to
your rules. You don't know what I am,
dad, you don't know who I am, you don't
know how I feel, what I think and if I tried
to explain the rest of your life, you'd never understand. You are thirty years older
than I am. You and your whole lousy generation believes the way it was for you is
the way it's got to be and not until your
whole generation has lain down and died
will the dead weight of you be off our
backs. You understand? You've got to
get off my back. Dad, dad, you're my
father. I'm your son. I love you. I always have and I always will but you think
of yourself as a colored man. I think of
myself as a man. [40]

Before this catharsis, Mr. Prentice has reminded John of
the untold financial and other sacrifices he has made on his
behalf. Mrs. Prentice (Beah Richards) is depicted as a
modestly-dressed, genteel member of the "black bourgeousie."[41] She keeps her gloves on while drinking sherry with
Joanna's parents. Her reaction to the imminent nuptials is,
"Frankly, it never occurred to me that such a thing might
happen but it wouldn't be true to say that I'm surprised."[42]

The old "mammy" Negro stereotype in modern dress
is an anachronistic addition to Guess Who's Coming to Dinner?, providing comic relief with every utterance. Isabell
Sanford enacts this role of Matilda (Tillie) Banks, domestic
for the Drayton family. Matilda is the epitome of racial
self-contempt. She cannot imagine that any black man could
be worthy of the well-bred white girl for whom she labors.
The "mammy" that Hattie McDaniel portrayed in films of
the thirties never permitted her pro-white sentiment to make
her as anti-black as Matilda in the following:

TILLIE: I got something to say to you, boy. Just
exactly what you trying to pull here?

The attractive Claire (Lena Horne) seems unduly thankful for Frank Patch's (Richard Widmark) affection in <u>Death of a Gunfighter.</u> (Photo courtesy Universal Studios)

PRENTICE: I'm not trying to pull anything.   I was
 looking to find me a wife.

TILLIE: Ain't that just likely?   You wanna answer
 me something?   What kind of doctor you
 supposed to be anyhow?

PRENTICE: Would you believe horse?   (Laughs)

TILLIE: Oh!!!   You make with witticisms and all,
 hah?   Well let me tell you something.   You
 may think you foolin' Miss Joey and her
 folks but you ain't foolin' me for a minute.
 You think I don't see what you are.   You
 one of those smooth talking smart-assed
 niggers, just out for all he can get, with
 your black power and all that other trouble-
 making nonsense and you listen here.   I
 brought up that child from a baby in a
 cradle and ain't nobody gonna harm her
 none while I'm here and as long as you are
 anywhere around this house I'm right here
 watchin'.   You read me, boy?   You raise
 any trouble in here, you just likely to find
 out what 'black power' really means. [43]

In the interest of effective communication, well-edu-
cated blacks have been known to lapse from standard English
when speaking with their less educated black brothers.   Dr.
Prentice's "I was looking to find me a wife," in the above
passage, is an example of this sort of linguistic duality.   In
the original film release, Tillie was asked to guess who else
was coming to dinner and her sarcastic reply was, "I know,
it's the Reverend Martin Luther King."   This line was deleted, following the assassination of the civil rights leader.

Visual confirmation of the romance between John Prentice and Joanna Drayton is restricted to one fleeting kiss,
glimpsed by the audience in a rear view mirror of a taxi in
the opening sequence of the film.   Charles Sanders, a man-
aging editor of Ebony, tells of other love scenes in the movie:

> Actually, he kissed Katherine Houghton a great deal,
> and passionately too,...but all of that footage was
> left on the cutting room floor before the film was
> released for public viewing.   And all of the still
> photographs that show these 'romantic interludes'
> are kept in three press books on the third floor of
> the New York office of Columbia Pictures and are
> marked with bold red Xs and the word HOLD.[44]

In a visit to Columbia Pictures, this author examined
one press book with an M. P. A. A. approval date, 1/18/68.
This was obviously not one of those to which Mason refers.

To remove any further doubt about the status of their
affair, Joanna tells her mother, "Do you mean have we been
to bed together?   I don't mind your asking me that.   We
haven't.   [PAUSE] He wouldn't."   Supporting the contention
that the portrayals are unreal, Renata Adler states:

> The thing is, the years have passed these people by.
> It is a forties confrontation.   In the sixties a black
> doctor's engagement to a white educated girl has
> turned out not to be the context where problems
> exist.
>
> What Hollywood has traditionally done with its fan-
> tasies--given a false picture, a romanticized prece-
> dent, an unreal model for people to measure their
> own lives by--this film does for miscegenation.   It
> is Hollywood's imprimatur and a kind of first.[45]

Stanley Kramer, director of the film, believes that
Guess Who's Coming to Dinner? depicts the problem exactly
as it exists for a particular segment of American society.
According to Kramer, the Draytons would not have been interested in a gas station attendant, white or black.   Therefore John Prentice was characterized as a hallmark of perfection so that the point of the film would be unmistakably
clear.   Any objections to the marriage of John and Joanna
would have to be drawn on racial lines.[46]

Alvin Poussaint, black psychiatrist, relates one reaction to the over-endowment of the black man in American motion pictures:

> In seeking acceptance among whites many blacks
> expend a great deal of internal energy trying to
> prove that they are 'all right.' Sometimes they
> must even show that they are special and highly
> superior Negroes. Black youth resent this type
> of psychological pressure from whites. Sidney
> Poitier in his current movies plays this role of
> the all-perfect, noble Negro. These roles have
> inspired many humorous remarks among Negro
> people. For instance, in his new movie about an
> interracial romance, 'Guess Who's Coming to
> Dinner?' black youth have quipped, 'Is it a bird?
> Is it a plane? No! It's Superspade!'[47]

One can understand that Poitier might reject criticisms of the movie, seeing that it increased his popularity and enhanced his career. Poitier comments on the racial implications of Guess Who's Coming to Dinner?:

> I have no way of determining how important it will
> be in a racial sense. It's awfully complex and we
> are not in the business of addressing ourselves di-
> rectly to, nor exclusively to, the racial issue. In
> this film we are first and foremost, it seems to
> me, interested in presenting entertainment with a
> point of view--entertainment that will first be ac-
> cepted as such, then as a premise, a side of the
> issue.[48]

Notes

1. Britannica Book of the Year, 1968, (Chicago: En-
     cyclopaedia Britannica, 1968), pp. 53-59, 140,
     153, 175 and 666.

2. Joan Barthel, "The Black Power of Godfrey Mac-
     Arthur Cambridge," The New York Times,
     November 20, 1966, p. D13.

3. The Busy Body (Paramount Pictures, 1967).

4. The New York Times, January 20, 1967, p. 27.

4a. Peter Bart, "The Still Invisible Man" The New York
    Times, July 17, 1966, Section II, p. 13.

5. The Comedians (Metro Goldwyn Mayer, 1967).

6. Lindsay Patterson, "To Make the Negro a Living
    Human Being," The New York Times, February
    18, 1968, p. 8D.

7. The New York Times, November 1, 1967, p. 37.

8. The Dirty Dozen (Metro Goldwyn Mayer, 1967).

9. Renata Adler, "The Negro That Movies Overlook,"
    The New York Times, March 3, 1968, p. 1.

10. The President's Analyst (Paramount Pictures, 1967).

11. Frances Herridge, "Movie Scene," New York Post,
    November 6, 1967, p. 82.

12. Dutchman (Gene Persson Enterprises, 1967).

13. Ibid.

14. Langston Hughes, "The Negro and American Enter-
    tainment," in The American Negro Reference
    Book ed. by John P. Davis (Englewood Cliffs,
    New Jersey: Prentice-Hall, 1966), p. 847.

15. Judith Crist, The Private Eye, The Cowboy & The
    Very Naked Girl: Movies from Cleo to Clyde
    (New York: Holt, Rinehart & Winston, 1968),
    p. 230.

16. Portrait of Jason (Film-Makers, 1967).

17. Judith Crist, "The New Movie," World Journal
    Tribune, January 31, 1967, p. 15.

18. Sweet Love, Bitter (Film 2 Associates, 1967).

19. Robert Hooks, in addition to his work as a stage
    actor, co-founded with Douglas Turner Ward,
    the Negro Ensemble Theatre, an off-Broadway
    showcase for black dramatists and performers.

20. <u>Sweet Love, Bitter</u> (Film 2 Associates, 1967).

21. Hollis Alpert, "The Problem," <u>Saturday Review</u>, January 21, 1967, p. 35.

22. Herbert Danska, telephone communication, New York City, March 3, 1969.

23. <u>Hurry Sundown</u> (Paramount Pictures, 1967).

24. <u>Ibid.</u>

25. Rex Reed, "Our Man Flint, Meet Georgy Girl," <u>The New York Times</u>, June 8, 1969, p. D15.

26. <u>Critics' Guide to Movies and Plays</u>, v. 1, no. 5, 1967, p. 25.

27. Foster Hirsch, "Uncle Tom Is Becoming a Super-hero," <u>Readers & Writers</u>, November-January 1968, p. 13.

28. <u>In the Heat of the Night</u> (United Artists, 1967).

29. <u>Ibid.</u>

30. <u>Ibid.</u>

31. <u>Ibid.</u>

32. Hirsch, <u>op. cit.</u>, p. 13.

33. Clifford Mason, "Why Does White America Love Sidney Poitier So?" <u>The New York Times</u>, September 10, 1967, p. 1.

34. <u>To Sir, With Love</u> (Columbia Pictures, 1967).

35. Edward Ricardo Braithwaite, <u>To Sir, With Love</u> (Englewood Cliffs, New Jersey: Prentice-Hall, 1959).

36. Richard Schickel and John Simon, eds., <u>Film 67/68: An Anthology by the National Society of Film Critics</u> (New York: Simon & Schuster, 1968), p. 216.

37. Schickel and Simon, op. cit., p. 223.

38. Andrew M. Greeley, "Black and White Minstrels,"
     The Reporter, March 21, 1968, p. 40.

39. Guess Who's Coming to Dinner? (Columbia Pictures,
     1967).

40. Ibid.

41. Edward Franklin Frazier, Black Bourgeousie (Glen-
     coe, Illinois: The Free Press, 1957).

42. Guess Who's Coming to Dinner? (Columbia Pic-
     tures, 1967).

43. Ibid.

44. Charles L. Sanders, "Sidney Poitier: Man Behind
     the Superstar," Ebony, April 1968, p. 178.

45. Renata Adler, "The Negro That Movies Overlook,"
     The New York Times, March 3, 1968, p. 1.

46. "David Frost Show," W. N. E. W. telecast, August
     28, 1969.

47. Alvin F. Poussaint, "Education and Black-Self Im-
     age," Freedomways: A Quarterly Review of the
     Freedom Movement, vol. 8, no. 4, (Fall 1968),
     p. 337.

48. Roy Newquist, A Special Kind of Magic (Chicago:
     Rand McNally & Co., 1967), p. 122.

Barbara McNair appears as a Catholic nun in <u>Change of Habit</u>.
(Photo courtesy Universal Studios)

Chapter 12

1968

The President's National Advisory Commission on Civil Disorders, headed by Governor Otto Kerner of Illinois, released its report on the riots of the previous summer. A major finding of the Commission was that white racism is the cause of violence and riots by blacks. The report noted that the United States is moving toward two societies, one black, one white--separate and unequal. The Commission called for unprecedented action at every level of government in order to reverse the situation.

A report issued by the Governor's Commission on the 1967 riot in Newark found that excessive and unjustified force had been exercised by the National Guard and police. Dr. Martin Luther King, Nobel Peace Prize winner and leader of the non-violent civil rights movement, was assassinated in Memphis, Tennessee. Poor people's caravans from across the nation converged upon Washington, D. C., where they camped upon an area of land named temporarily Resurrection City, U. S. A. Under the sponsorship of the Southern Christian Leadership Conference, the campaign urged Congress and the Administration to act on behalf of poverty-stricken Americans. Shirley Chisholm, Democrat from Brooklyn, became the first black female to be elected to the U. S. House of Representatives. The Civil Rights Act of 1968 imposed a Federal ban on discrimination in the sale and renting of about 80 per cent of the nation's housing. In

other federal legislation, penalties were prescribed for persons who cross state lines to incite riots. [1]

Two black men were nominees for the highest office
in the land, president of the United States.   Eldridge Cleaver
ran under the auspices of the Peace and Freedom Party and
Dick Gregory ran under the New Party endorsement. [2] The
William Styron best-seller, Confessions of Nat Turner, a
book about the famed black preacher and leader of a slave
rebellion in 1831, received the 1968 Pulitzer prize for fic-
tion. [3]

Blacks set precedents in the performing arts.   Diahann Carroll, seen in Hurry Sundown (1967), became the first
black female to star in a television series.   The National
Broadcasting Company signed her to play the title role in its
comedy-drama, Julia. [4] Sidney Poitier was the number one
movie-star at box offices in the United States and Canada,
according to a survey conducted by Motion Picture Herald,
a weekly trade publication. [5]

The Motion Picture Association of America promul-
gated a new code and system of self-regulation, applicable to
production, to advertising and to titles of motion pictures.
Under the new program, motion pictures to be exhibited in
the United States would be submitted for code approval and
rating or for rating only.   A "G" rating is suggested for general audiences.   An "R" rating denies admission to persons
under 17 unless accompanied by parent or adult guardian.
An "X" rating excludes admission to persons under 17.   The
Standards for Production states: "Words or symbols con-
temptuous of racial, religious or national groups shall not be
used so as to incite bigotry or hatred." [6]

Five Card Stud, a "western" movie tale of revenge,
cast Yaphet Kotto as Little George, the bartender.   Most

films of this type traditionally include saloon scenes but rarely, if ever, have the bartenders been black.   Little George
joins the ranks of film Negroes who are privy to secrets
pertinent to the plots of the films in which they appear.   His
willingness to warn the hero about possible danger leads to
Little George's own murder.

William Marshall performed in two American motion
pictures released in 1968.   That both small roles possessed
a certain dignity is no coincidence because the actor will not
accept ethnically demeaning parts.   As recently as 1963,
Marshall declined an anti-black role which was subsequently
converted to white in Term of Trial, co-starring Laurence
Olivier and Simone Signoret.   The Hell with Heroes, an adventure film, was the vehicle in which the actor appears as
Al Poland, the owner of a cabaret in Algeria.   Suave, sophisticated, seen mostly in formal attire, Al is involved in
rather shady dealings.   The small role is reminiscent of
Humphrey Bogart's portrayal of Rick in Casablanca, without
the stellar emphasis and focus, of course.

With very few exceptions (W. C. Handy, Haile Selassie, Joe Louis), famous black men have not been portrayed
in American motion pictures.   Such a portrayal did occur in
The Boston Strangler.   William Marshall acted the role of
Edward W. Brooke, attorney general of Massachusetts at the
time in which the film's story transpires.   Brooke (Marshall)
has one important scene in which he summons John S. Bottomly (Henry Fonda), a criminal investigator, to his stately
office in Boston.   Making a personal appeal to the reluctant
Bottomly, Brooke persuades him to set up a "strangler bu-
reau" and head up the search for the elusive killer.

Sugar Ray Robinson joined an all-star cast in Candy,
a motion picture made from the best-selling novel by Terry

Southern. The former boxing champion had little to do in the role of Zero, chauffeur and friend to McPhisto (Richard Burton), a poet and seducer. Zero's lines included "Tell it like it is, baby" and "Gotcha man."[7] Apparently, the script writer and the director wanted Zero to communicate in what passes for a black vernacular. Zero was the only "devoted servant" among the Negro portrayals in 1968. During the year, Robinson also appeared briefly as himself in Paper Lion, a movie about George Plimpton.

A sub-plot of the motion picture, Madigan, dealt with the issue of police brutality to blacks. Dr. Taylor (Raymond St. Jacques) is a Negro clergyman whose son has been picked up by the police for interrogation about a crime of which he is innocent. When his son, whom we do not see, is released, Dr. Taylor seeks the police commissioner's guarantee that the officers involved in the false arrest will be punished. Commissioner Russell (Henry Fonda) reminds Dr. Taylor of his son's two previous convictions. Insisting that his son has changed, Dr. Taylor counters that his son is in a state of "mental collapse and anguish" due to "outrageous pressures" the officers have used in seeking a confession. Dr. Taylor is adamant in his quest for redress:

> TAYLOR: I came here for justice and I'm going to get it. I don't want a policeman's idea of justice. I want a little of the victim's idea of justice, from the bottom looking up, not from the top looking down.
>
> RUSSELL: I think you're talking about revenge, not justice.
>
> TAYLOR: Commissioner, during the Harlem riots, I, well I was called an Uncle Tom, for using whatever influence I had to bring about peace and understanding. Was I wrong?

RUSSELL: You were right, doctor.

TAYLOR: Prove it, commissioner. You prove it
    to me. [8]

Commissioner Russell takes Dr. Taylor's tacit threat under
advisement. At the end of the film, which is set over one
weekend, Russell speaks grudgingly of a Monday morning appointment with Dr. Taylor. By implication, the Negro will
not receive the satisfaction he demands from the police commissioner.

In three motion pictures, law provided the occupations
for Negro supporting characterizations. Bernie Hamilton
plays Lt. Harvey Atkins, a police detective in The Sweet
Ride. When he takes Collie Ransom (Tony Franciosa), a
middle-aged beach bum, into custody for questioning, he encounters insolence and condescension. Ransom insists upon
calling him Harvey. James Edwards plays Sgt. Wallace, a
police detective, in Coogan's Bluff. The surveillance of
Coogan (Clint Eastwood), a deputy sheriff from Arizona, is
performed by Wallace in the shabby guise of a derelict.
Coogan is extremely uncooperative, bringing on an outburst
of temper from Wallace in a scene at police headquarters.
Al Freeman, Jr. plays Robbie Loughren, a rookie plain-
clothesman, in The Detective. At the beginning of the film,
an inexperienced Loughren becomes physically ill at the sight
of a mutilated corpus delicti. Within a very brief time,
Loughren displays a distinct transformation of character. In
an accusatory conversation with a superior, Loughren reveals a newly acquired cynicism and opportunism. Thus, the
black male stars of One Potato, Two Potato, (Hamilton),
Home of the Brave (Edwards), and Dutchman (Freeman) are
relegated to playing detective "bits" incommensurate with

their proven ability to perform leading roles. Related to
but not quite the same, was the police officer role played by
Brock Peters in the motion picture, PJ. When PJ (George
Peppard), a hired bodyguard and reputed trouble-maker,
comes to a small island in the Caribbean, he is greeted and
cautioned by Waterpack (Peters), resplendently dressed in
white uniform. It is not long before Waterpack, as the island's chief of police, must deport PJ. Unlike the three
aforementioned policemen, all of whom were Americans,
Waterpack has a West Indian accent, which Peters simulated
for the role.

Medical careers served as occupational base for three
Negro supporting characterizations:

Juanita Moore had the small part of a nurse in a rest
home in a film starring Rosalind Russell entitled Rosie.
Considering the large numbers of black women engaged in the
nursing profession, there should be more nurses depicted in
films.

George Stanford Brown appears as a young hospital
physician in the motion picture, Bullitt. When a seriously
wounded man fails to respond to treatment, Chalmers (Robert Vaughn), a prominent political figure who has a stake in
the patient's recovery, castigates the black resident physician and threatens to have him removed from the case.
Shortly after the patient dies, Bullitt (Steve McQueen), a detective, asks the doctor to conceal the fact of the patient's
death from Chalmers and from the authorities. Incredibly,
the doctor agrees to the deception, perhaps out of personal
pique at Chalmers. Since the story is not mainly concerned
with the black doctor, the script does not pursue the consequences, if any, of his irresponsible action.

Percy Rodriguez contributed his portrayal of a physi-

cian to The Heart is a Lonely Hunter. His Dr. B. M. Copeland is a general practitioner who lives comfortably in a
small Southern town with his adult daughter, Portia, played
by Cicely Tyson, seen previously in A Man Called Adam
(1966). The doctor does not challenge the segregationist code
under which he must function. "I only treat my own," says
Dr. Copeland. Again we have conflict between conservative
parent and militant offspring. Dr. Copeland is willing to
sacrifice his dignity and endure white oppression if he can
advance the education and future of his daughter. On the other hand, Portia refuses to accept white middle-class values
as her own and cannot abide the pretentious ways of her
father:

> PORTIA: Don't make me choose between you be-
> cause if you do I'm going to choose Willie.
>
> COPELAND: Seems to me, you already did that
> three years ago.
>
> PORTIA: No father, I didn't choose between you.
> I only chose to marry him over your ob-
> jection.
>
> COPELAND: When I think of all the plans...
>
> PORTIA: Those were your plans, not mine.
>
> COPELAND: You should have done something,
> something worthwhile with your life.
>
> PORTIA: I did. I married the man I love and the
> man who loves me.
>
> COPELAND: I raised you to be something better.
>
> PORTIA: Well I wasn't better. I was different.
> All those years after mama died, all that
> time I was growing up, what was I? I
> don't know. I only know I wasn't white and
> you wouldn't let me be black. [9]

To assure her father that she is black, Portia has wed an
unschooled black laborer and has taken employment as a
maid.   When her husband, Willie, becomes permanently
handicapped as a result of a racial assault by whites, Portia
is drawn even further apart from her parent.   Immediately
following the incident, Dr. Copeland, in a move unprecedented
for him, seeks justice for Willie from an uncaring white
power structure.   Finally, Portia and Dr. Copeland are re-
conciled when she learns of his imminent death from an in-
curable lung ailment, a secret he has kept.   For different
reasons, then, both Portia and Dr. Copeland are "the unhappy non-white."   Discriminated against when he was on location with the film in Selma, Alabama, Rodriguez should not
have found too difficult the portrayal of a victim of Southern
racial injustice. [10]

　　　Military careers establish a framework for three portrayals of the Negro.   Over the years, a black actor has become an indispensable token in any motion picture dealing with
the armed forces.   Providing this service for The Sergeant,
a movie starring Rod Steiger, Philip Raye as Aldous Brown
is merely required to decorate some barracks scenes.

　　　In a more substantial portrayal, Jim Brown is Leslie
Anders, a marine captain, in Ice Station Zebra, based on the
novel by Alistair MacLean.   The essence of the characterization is hostility and toughness, which Anders explains:

>　　　ANDERS:　Lieutenant!　You will notify the men that
>　　　　　　　　there will be a showdown inspection at 0700.
>
>　　　LIEUT.:　Yes, sir.
>
>　　　ANDERS:　And Lieutenant, it will be a bitch!!
>
>　　　LIEUT.:　Yes, sir.

> ANDERS: I made a point of it. You see, Captain,
> that saves a lot of lives, my teaching them
> to jump when I speak.
>
> CAPT.: All right.
>
> ANDERS: The young lieutenant is a familiar type,
> popular with the men. As for me, I meas-
> ure an officer's weakness by every man
> that likes him personally. [11]

While we suspect that his attitude is partially defensiveness
at being the only black man aboard the nuclear submarine in
which the story is set, no reference is ever made to race.
In an ironical climax, Anders confronts a Russian espionage
agent, who has tried to sabotage the submarine. A third
man happens along and, assuming Anders to be the villain,
kills him. All the white members of the mission survive.
It is only the black man who dies.

The third portrayal of the Negro in the military was
that of Raymond St. Jacques in The Green Berets, as Sergeant McGee. His lengthiest scene comes at the opening of
the film, when a contingent of "Green Berets" are being in-
terviewed by the press. It is McGee, the only black officer,
who makes a pro-American intervention in Vietnam speech:

> McGEE: As soldiers,...we understand the killing
> of the military but the extermination of
> the civilian leadership, the intentional mur-
> der and torture of innocent women and
> children. ...
>
> REPORTERS: Yes, I guess horrible things happen
> in war but that doesn't mean they need us
> or even want us.
>
> McGEE: I'll try to answer that question for you.
> Let me put it in terms we all can under-
> stand. If this same thing happened here
> in the United States, every mayor in every
> city would be murdered. Every teacher

that you've ever known would be tortured
and killed. Every professor you've ever
heard of, every governor, every senator,
every member of the House of Representatives and their combined families all would
be tortured and killed and a like number
kidnapped. But in spite of this, there's
always some little fellow out there willing
to stand up and take the place of those
who've been decimated. They need us...
and they want us. [12]

It is noteworthy that the lone black man in the film should be
selected to make a patently propagandistic speech. When
McGee returns to Vietnam he resumes his duties as a military medic, ministering to the health needs of Vietnamese
civilians as well. McGee is depicted as being kind and sympathetic to the very young and the very old. Finally wounded
in action, he does survive.

Twenty-seven years ago, Gunnar Myrdal, Swedish so-
ciologist, observed that the American motion picture screen
was practically closed to serious Negro actors, with very
few pictures portraying Negroes, even as minor characters,
in roles other than as buffoons. [13] Since then, the Negro has
been depicted in various other ways but the buffoon is still
very much present.

Richard Pryor, a young black comedian who appeared
in The Busy Body (1967), played Stanley X in Wild in the
Streets. An off-screen narrator introduces the twenty-one-
year-old Stanley as an anthropologist, trumpeter and author
of "The Aborigine's Cookbook." However, only his musicianship is substantiated in the film. Stanley X is the black
member of a group of white hippies who plan to gain control
of the United States. Always playing the buffoon, Stanley's
response to a comment that he doesn't read the papers is,
"Yeah, I read them on Wednesdays." Mercifully, the part

is brief.

The hippy scene is also the center of action in <u>Psych-Out</u>, a movie aimed at the teen-age market. Elwood (Max Julian), a cynical black hippy, saves the white heroine (Susan Strasberg) from a gang rape. Lest we associate blacks with the performance of good deeds, the script hastens to explain that a drug hallucinatory experience prompted Elwood's heroism.

Black comedian Godfrey Cambridge found work as a buffoon in two 1968 motion picture releases. In the first of these, <u>The Biggest Bundle of Them All,</u> Cambridge is seen as Benjamin Brownstead, an opportunist who finds himself without funds in Italy. He joins a group of ineffectual whites in a five-million dollar robbery scheme. Similar to the buffoons played by Stepin Fetchit, Mantan Moreland, Willie Best and others in the 1930's and 1940's, Benjy is hopelessly incapable as the would-be-thieves make plans:

> BENJY: Fellows, I'd like to do this for all of us but I've never handled a gun before. I mean, I could hurt somebody if I got excited or something, you know?
>
> CELLI: It will be all right Beniamino.
>
> BENJY: But suppose I shot somebody? Suppose I shot myself? [14]

One might prefer to attribute these remarks to a non-violent nature rather than to comic stupidity, but another scene removes reasonable doubt:

> BENJY: I'm a union man. I can't cross a picket line.
>
> HARRY: That's no picket line. Can't you read? That's a bunch of nuts protesting The Bomb. [15]

In a contradiction of characterization, Benjamin is clever
enough, though, to identify Ming jade, on sight. In addition
to being a refugee from alimony payments, Benjy is a classical musician. About this vocation, Cambridge said:

> When I went to Italy to do..., I was supposed to
> play a jazz musician. I said, 'No, no, darling;
> Negro jazz musicians are a glut on the market.
> Let me be a classical violinist' so I was, and we
> got much more out of the part that way.[16]

In another funny touch, the rotund (Cambridge was, then)
Benjy jogs breathlessly around a lake in Italy, wearing shorts
and a tee-shirt marked "N. Y. ACADEMY OF MUSIC."

Cambridge made his other comic film appearance of
the year in Bye Bye Braverman, adapted from the Wallace
Markfield novel, To An Early Grave. He portrays a Negro-
Jewish taxi cab driver from Brooklyn. His hack is involved
in a minor accident with another car which is taking four
white Jewish pals to the funeral of their mutual friend, Leslie Braverman. The entire portrayal takes place briefly on
Eastern Parkway in Brooklyn. The cab driver attempts to
ingratiate himself with the four men, volunteering his personal credo:

> CAB DRIVER: I don't know the kind of Jew you
> are. Maybe you pass all day Yom Kippur
> or maybe you look at it like me. You fig-
> ure it's all a crock. What's caused all
> the war, made all the hate? Religion,
> right? And what's religion? Temples,
> praying? Holidays? Nah! It's making
> the other fellow feel nice inside. It's
> treating him like he's also a person,
> right?[17]

Just as though he were doing a sequel to The Troublemaker
(1964), Cambridge strives for "minority" laughs. As a black
Jew, he says he needs a St. Francis medal like he needs a

sun lamp. Compulsive references to a wife's test for cancer
at Mt. Sinai, a son with summer employment as a bellhop in
the mountains, and his own copy of a B'nai B'rith newsletter,
coupled with a rising voice inflection and a liberal use of
such words as "oi" and "mazel," make the taxi driver more
a caricature than a characterization.

Although Sammy Davis, Jr.'s concern over the image
of the Negro in motion pictures is a matter of public record,
once again he turns to buffoonery for his role of Charles
Salt in Salt and Pepper. He and Christopher Pepper (Peter
Lawford) own the Salt and Pepper Club, a nightspot in the
Soho district of London. The pair are suspected of murder
in the "not to be taken seriously" plot. Salt wears at various times a bright red Nehru suit, leather pants, a colorful
turtle neck shirt adorned with necklace, and Victorian styled
suits. Although Salt sings one musical production number as
an entertainer in his own club, the portrayal is essentially
comic, as for instance:

> SALT: You mean it's all of those guys against the
> two of us?
>
> PEPPER: Yes.
>
> SALT: You're looking at one scared African. [18]

When a police inspector tells the white Pepper, "All London
knows your father was a black sheep," Salt says, I beg your
pardon." In a reversal of the well-known discriminatory remark, Salt quips, "They all look alike," referring to an Ori-
ental. In addition to his comic antics, Salt has to shoot to
death a white girl who is about to murder Pepper. Never
have so few blacks protected and saved so many whites as
in the medium of motion pictures. Typical of Salt's cinematic love life is a scene in which he approaches three show

girls, one at a time. After the first and second girls (both
colored) rebuff him, he contemplates the third girl (white)
for a split second and without even trying, Salt says "Nah!"

The buffoonery of Howard, performed by Al Freeman,
Jr. in the musical film, Finian's Rainbow, becomes a positive rather than a negative factor. Howard is a college senior at Tuskegee in the stage show but in the film he is a research botanist trying to grow mentholated tobacco. His one
major scene remains unchanged. Howard seeks temporary
employment at the colonial home of Senator Rawkins (Keenan
Wynn), a mint julep-drinking Southern reactionary. Howard
is informed that as a black member of the domestic staff he
is required to shuffle. Mentioning that he is working toward
a Master's degree, Howard is reluctant to accept the job under such terms. Soon Rawkins becomes overwrought and
asks for a Bromo-Seltzer. Performing his first act of service, the newly-hired Howard shuffles very slowly toward Rawkins carrying a foaming glass of Bromo-Seltzer. The more
Rawkins gasps for breath, the more "Comin' massa"'s are
uttered by Howard, whose shuffling has been perfected. The
scene concludes with a near apoplectic Rawkins awaiting Howard's interminably delayed delivery. Praising the portrayal,
Arthur Knight says, "His slow-motion portage, à la Stepin
Fetchit, of a glass of Bromo-Seltzer must be the comedic
highlight of the entire film."[19] Howard demolishes "the devoted servant" stereotype with his buffoonery.

His portrayal of Joseph Winfield Lee, a fugitive slave,
in The Scalphunters, brought Ossie Davis full cycle as an
actor. Only five years earlier, Davis had assailed the peculiar institution of slavery with his characterization of Purlie Victorious in the satirical film, Gone Are the Days
(1963). There is nothing satirical about the life and times

of the fictional Lee. When Indians rob Joe Bass (Burt Lancaster) of the furs he has trapped, they give him the fugitive
slave by way of amends. Lee immediately attempts to gain
his freedom from Bass, who refuses. Lee is depicted as
spirited, crafty, literate and well-accustomed to eating regu-
larly. The film credits these last two characteristics to the
fringe benefits of servitude. Lee is not above trying to pass
as a Comanche, if it will bring him freedom. He bandies
such phrases as "caveat emptor," makes historical reference
to Julius Caesar, and chides Bass, his temporary owner, on
his illiteracy. Initially, Lee is non-violent but his dealings
with a succession of captors throughout the film lead to his
ultimate militancy. In the final reel of the film, after Lee
has killed a man in order to save the life of the overbearing
Bass, Lee addresses him as man to man, not as slave to
master:

> LEE: You are the most stubborn mule-headed
>   love yourself man that ever walked God's
>   creation. And some day, if I get a chance
>   to, I'll knock some sense into your hard
>   boiled head. [20]

Lee gets his chance sooner than he expects. In a rarely
seen on-screen contest between a black man and a white man,
Lee and Bass match fisticuffs with neither one winning victory. At the fadeout, in overdue recognition of Lee's humanity, Bass offers him a drink of whiskey. This symbolic gesture is comparable to one made at the finale of In the Heat
of the Night in which Gillespie carries Tibbs' valise. The
unreality of the portrayal of Joseph Winfield Lee was ex-
pressed by critic Vincent Canby, who termed him "a slave
with a 1968 black awareness."[21] But when Film and Television Daily announced its selections for 1968, Ossie Davis

was named best supporting actor for this role.[22]

One of the three 1968 American films to portray the Negro on the wrong side of the law was If He Hollers, Let Him Go. Indicting Hollywood for its preoccupation with the profit system, James Baldwin stated:

> In such a system, it makes perfect sense that Hollywood would turn out so 'liberal' an abomination as 'If He Hollers, Let Him Go,' ... for that matter it makes perfect sense that Hollywood lifted the title 'If He Hollers, Let Him Go' from a fine novel by [black] Chester Himes ...?[23]

Raymond St. Jacques became a full-fledged star in this movie as James Lake, a fugitive from a Georgia prison. Lake has been unjustly convicted of the rape-murder of a Southern white girl. Before he can change from his prison uniform he is picked-up by Leslie Whitlock (Kevin McCarthy), a scheming white man. Whitlock first offers Lake the hospitality of his home, then tries unsuccessfully to coerce him into murdering the wealthy Mrs. Whitlock (Dana Wynter). Fleeing once more, Lake reflects on the events leading up to his predicament. Through flashbacks, Lily, his girl friend, is introduced. This role is played by Barbara McNair, a Negro songstress, which is also Lily's status in the film. Lake and Lily, both semi-nude, enact a love-making scene, something new in the motion picture portrayal of blacks. Their relationship terminates with Lake's confinement. When Lily visits Lake in prison, he finds it necessary to call her "a two-bit whore" in order to get her to leave him irrevocably and, of course, for her own good. Before some incredible plot maneuvers bring the film to its conclusion, Lake demonstrates an appreciation of Bach sonatas, a natural talent as an artist, an immunity to the romantic overtures of white females and an ability to establish his innocence of the crime of murder, almost single-handedly. In a final cliché, Lake risks his own life and freedom to save the life of a white woman who had previously been his accuser. When Ellen Whitlock asks for his explanation, Lake says:

> I really surprise myself. I became involved with you. I'm fed up with all this brutality. In a way, you're my sister. Do you believe that?[24]

Mrs. Whitlock replies in the affirmative but it is doubtful whether the audience believes any of it. So ends the characterization of James Lake, another example of the super-hero, a new stereotype. The characterization of Lily was concluded even earlier. Taking Lake's advice to forget him, Lily does just that by marrying his brother. Dispelling any doubt about the film's message, Lily's voice, actually Mc-Nair's, is heard during the final credits, singing:

> ...a man has to fight to be free
> Though his task may be great,
> He must fight greed and hate
> We're all part of the same
>   family tree....[25]

Drayton's Devils was a rather amateurish film about a plot to relieve a California Air Force base of $1,000,000. Black actor George Stanford Brown portrays Theon Gibson, a participant in the attempted heist.

Dealing in a more professional fashion with a black man's involvement in robbery is The Split, a film co-starring Jim Brown as McClain and Diahann Carroll as Ellie. This time the black man is leader of a group of white criminals who plan to steal the receipts of a football game at a Los Angeles stadium. Since not all of his associates welcome his leadership, McClain is required occasionally to demonstrate his physical and mental superiority. All but one

of the participants in the illicit scheme meet a violent end.
In a marked change from the customary pattern, it is the
black, McClain, who survives.   Ellie is McClain's partly estranged wife.   Early in the story, McClain returns to Ellie,
whom he had deserted.   "You had the whole world to mess-
up, why me?"   Although McClain probably loves her in his
fashion, he is self-centered:

> McCLAIN: You opened the front door fast enough.
>
> ELLIE: Oh Mc! I'm weak with you. That's an
> entirely different problem. That's my
> problem. What did I do? I married you.
>
> McCLAIN: Marrying me was the only thing you
> ever did in your life that you really wanted
> to.
>
> ELLIE: Wrong! There were two things. The sec-
> ond was divorcing you and there's about
> to be a third, telling you to get the hell
> out of here and never come back. [26]

Ellie is depicted as an attractive, intelligent young woman
who loves McClain despite her better instincts. She knows
that she is being used. Of all the characters in the film,
black or white, Ellie is the most sympathetic. Her senseless and gory murder in an attempted rape by her white landlord is sad. The Split is noteworthy for presenting two black
stars, one male, one female, in a manner previously reserved for white stars. Their love scenes leave no more to
the imagination than the love scenes played by whites in comparable movies. They are in the foreground of the plot development. Brown has a distinctive swagger which could become an asset in an occupation where unique mannerisms are
almost prerequisite to lasting stardom. Reviewing The Split,
Renata Adler says, "We may be well on the way to a whole

cast of black matinee idols, with genuine starring parts to
evolve for them in the course of time."[27]

LeRoi Jones, black playwright, views the motion picture portrayals of Jim Brown in a different way. His poem,
"Jim Brown On The Scene," written after he had seen The
Split, denounces McClain and other recent Brown film characterizations as sterile, white-imitative, accommodating ren-
ditions of past stereotypes presented in new packages. The
poem does conclude on a surprising note of optimism:

> jim you can be more than that anyway, more than
>   a new amos in space
> more than uncle thomas from inner plantation psychotic
> cotton salvation you could be a man, jim, our man
>   on the land
> our new creator and leader, if you would just do
>   it and be it
> in the real world
> in the new world of yo own black people
> I hope you do
> it, Jim
> I hope you unmaniquin yo
> self, you can
> do it, if you
> want it, you can
> you
> sho
> can[28]

In a much lighter vein were the Negro characterizations in For Love of Ivy. Ivy Moore (Abbey Lincoln), a maid
for the Austins, a wealthy suburban family, decides to re-
sign, attend secretarial school and by so doing, achieve a
better life. Jack Parks (Sidney Poitier), a partner in a
trucking business, becomes a romantic distraction for Ivy,
prearranged by the son of her employers. His trucking enterprise conceals floating gambling casinos in the rear of the
vehicles. If he does not date Ivy, Tim Austin will expose
Parks to the authorities. In the tradition of countless film

comedies of the past, Ivy and Jack fall in love, separate
temporarily over a misunderstanding and reunite for a happy
finale. The screenplay was written by Robert Alan Arthur,
a white man, from an original story outline by Sidney Poitier.
The first black actor to win an "Oscar" created in Jack
Parks and Ivy Moore two characters that easily fulfill his
own stated professional goal:

> I've wanted to work with a Negro actress in a man-
> woman situation that was warm and positive. I'm
> not interested in having a romantic interlude on the
> screen with a white girl. I'd much rather have ro-
> mantic interludes with Negro girls.
>
> This is not a put-down of white girls, ... But, in
> the lives of most black men are Negro women, and
> vice-versa. [29]

Jack Parks is thirty-six years old, a veteran, sophisticated
and cultured. When he takes Ivy to a fashionable Japanese
restaurant he orders in Japanese. "Maybe because I'm pretentious," he says. Jack seemed, at least before Ivy, committed to bachelorhood. "I was married. It's a bad scene."
he explains. Parks is overtly sensitive to racial issues as
can be observed from his almost involuntary quiver when
Tim Austin uses the phrase "spade cats" to refer to black
men. When he is asked for his opinion of the 'black power"
movement, he replies, "I think about it a lot, but I don't
talk about it." For no obvious reason, the dialogue on two
occasions establishes Jack Parks as a West Indian. Display-
ing a keen sense of humor, Jack takes pleasure in mocking
the biases of whites. The Austin youths, Tim and Gena, are
only too willing to believe, with a little encouragement from
Jack, that he is swallowing "goof-balls" rather than aspirins.
Jack is kind to black children, permitting several to feed
the tropical fish in his apartment. Certain aspects of the

characterization are inadequately developed. Avarice cannot
fully explain why Jack risks a flourishing legitimate business
with involvement in illicit activities. Even his obvious aver-
sion to a second marriage does not explain remarks like:
"...that piranha strikes at anything in its way. That's me,
and with little chicks like you, I'm murder," spoken to Ivy.[30]

Ivy Moore has not nearly the complexity of characterization of Jack Parks. She is shy, congenial and lonely, at-
tending civil rights meetings because it's a "place sometimes
to meet people." Reared by a grandmother and virtually independent since she was twelve, Ivy boasts, "I'm not giving
that up for no two-bit hustler." Not exactly certain what it
is she wants in life, Ivy explains, "I just know I haven't got
it now." An education and her own man are two distinct
possibilities, as Ivy asks, "Ain't it better if you don't go ignorant and alone?" Although she is a pretty girl with an ap-
pealing naïveté, at twenty-seven she lacks self-assurance in
personal relations.

> JACK: You're something!
>
> IVY: Well you don't want me, so I can't be
> very much.
>
> JACK: Suppose I did want you?
>
> IVY: I wouldn't mind.
>
> JACK: You just throw yourself at anybody?
>
> IVY: Well, you're not just anybody.
>
> JACK: That's right.
>
> IVY: I like you![31]

Yet, despite the reticence, there is a refreshing honesty
from Ivy about her emotional attraction to Jack. The bed-

room love-making scenes between the black couple, although
a "first" for a Poitier film, were actually the third such occurrence in 1968, the other two being If He Hollers, Let Him
Go and The Split. Reactions to the film and its characterizations seemed to involve two major points of difference. Troy
DeBose did his criticism in the form of a fictitious letter
written by a black girl, Beulah, who is a summer visitor to
New York City, to her sister, Hattie Mae, back home. [32]
Set-down in what is intended as "Negro vernacular," the main
idea of the piece was that Poitier played the part as if he
were a white man. DeBose found the portrayal of Ivy to be
more realistic, failing on only two counts, her possession of
expensive straight hair wigs and, as a presumably mature
adult, her reliance upon a young white girl for birth control
information. Archer Winsten took issue with the false characterization of the film:

> It might be said that for many long years Negroes
> suffered the phony characterizations of themselves
> created by white writers who knew what the white
> public would buy and didn't give a damn for the
> truth. [33]

Winsten found that the pendulum has swung the other way in
For Love of Ivy, with Ivy's white employers becoming objects
of comic ridicule. Hollis Alpert attributes the films weak-
nesses to the lack of a black director:

> One would think that Sidney Poitier would have the
> power by now to request one of several talented
> Negro directors (of stage and television) for a film
> in which he is the prime attraction.... [34]

Jay Weston, co-producer of the movie, offers an insight on
that score. It seems Poitier took his story to established
film-makers who had profited from previous associations with
him, but they rejected it as being uncommercial. [35] Vincent

Canby found that the film "marks the final step in the metamorphosis of Sidney Poitier from a fine character actor into
a Hollywood super-star, with all the mythic cool and sexual
prerogatives of a Clark Gable."[36] Roy Wilkins, Executive
Director of the National Association for the Advancement of
Colored People, found such a metamorphosis acceptable, asking, "Has Clark Gable, one of the great greats of the films,
suddenly become a tarnished target now that Poitier approaches?"[37] With this query, Wilkins takes the position
that blacks are as entitled as whites to a motion picture superhero, in this case, Sidney Poitier as Jack Parks. Since
Abbey Lincoln as Ivy Moore has been clearly stereotyped as
Reddick's "the natural-born cook" in her white employers'
household, one cannot quite equate her as the black counterpart of white motion picture star, Doris Day. A final noteworthy achievement of For Love of Ivy is the advent of a
side-kick for the black hero. Leon Bibb fulfills this role as
Billy Talbot, silent-partner and confidant to Parks. Negro
actors have been cast as side-kicks for years but not in this
relationship to other blacks.

Up Tight is a fitting film with which to conclude this
glimpse at Negro portrayals for 1968. It is the first motion
picture about the black revolution in the United States. The
film is a transposition of The Informer, a novel by Liam O'-
Flaherty about the Irish during "the time of the troubles."
The new setting is Cleveland, Ohio's Hough ghetto in the period immediately following the assassination of Martin Luther
King. The opening scenes of the film include footage of Dr.
King's funeral and the sound of his voice. This beginning almost gives the film the tone of an important social documentary. Jules Dassin, the producer and director, wrote the
screenplay with the assistance of two black artists, Julian

Mayfield, novelist-author, and Ruby Dee, actress. Both
Mayfield and Dee also star in the film. The story in outline
concerns the attempted robbery by black militants of a muni-
tions warehouse, the betrayal of their leader by a frustrated
member of their own ranks and the traitor's ultimate penance.
The telling brings into play a broad range of Negro characterizations. Tank (Julian Mayfield), an unemployed steel-
worker, drinks to forget his inability to provide for his woman. He is disgruntled over his ostracism by the group of
black militants. "If I don't have you guys, I don't have nobody," he says. Full of self pity, Tank is morally bankrupt.
This makes him vulnerable to the notion of becoming an in-
formant. As to his physical appearance,

> Mayfield sets an entirely new image of a black
> leading man.... His hair is bushy, his eyes are
> large and fierce, his face is grizzly and his clothes
> are unkempt. The image is big, black and burly.
> He is--in a word--Every-nigger.[38]

Tank is not without a lively sense of humor and he aims it
at a group of whites who happen to be slumming in an amuse-
ment arcade he visits. Deriding them with an imaginative
fabrication of what will happen when blacks take over in this
country, Tank laughingly remarks, "I gave 'em a little black
lash."

Laurie Hudson (Ruby Dee), Tank's mistress and by
need a part-time prostitute, receives public welfare assistance as an unwed mother. She is desperate for money to
care for her children. She confesses to Tank, "You don't
like me to be on welfare? That lousy check don't buy nothing. I have to do a whole lot of other things I don't like."
Laurie genuinely loves Tank but she also despises his weakness. She is plainly-dressed but still attractive.

B. G. (Raymond St. Jacques), a junior high school
teacher, is leader of the group of militants. A large map of
Africa decorates his apartment. He wears rimless spectacles,
a mustache and beard, and a Nehru jacket. B. G. mistrusts
all whites. He is a type described by William Grier and
Price Cobbs:

> Black men have stood so long in such peculiar
> jeopardy in America that a black norm has devel-
> oped--a suspiciousness of one's environment which
> is necessary for survival. Black people, to a de-
> gree that approaches paranoia, must be ever alert
> to danger from their white fellow citizens. It is
> a cultural phenomenon peculiar to black Ameri-
> cans.[39]

B. G. manifests the syndrome that the two black psychiatrists
described:

> B. G.:   We got to make them know that every time
> they even think of picking up a gun against
> a black man, there's a black gun waiting
> for them.[40]

His bitterness extends even to a white "liberal" whom he has
known for a long while. When the man asks how he can help
the movement, B. G. replies, "You want to help us? Send
us some guns. You folks can buy them easier than we can."

Kyle (Frank Silvera), a politician, is a conservative
civil rights leader who still has faith in the system. Kyle
has a fundamental belief in integration and conciliation. He
suggests a program rather than guns as a method of achieving first-class citizenship for blacks. Kyle says, "The poor
people of this country are going to be organized. There's
your power, and not just a black caucus, everybody." He
fits the paradigmatic man sketched by Grier and Cobbs:

> This man is always described as 'nice' by white
> people. In whatever integrated setting he works,

> he is the standard against whom other blacks are
> measured. 'If they were all only like him, every-
> thing would be so much better.' He is passive,
> nonassertive, and nonaggressive. He has made a
> virtue of identification with the aggressor, and he
> has adopted an ingratiating and compliant manner.[41]

Kyle is frightened of the possible consequences of the black
militant movement: "You'll bring a whole military machine
down on our heads. You will be the excuse for fascism in
this country. You'll bring on the camps." Interestingly, the
film-makers have cast a light-complexioned actor in the part
of accommodator.

Clarence (Roscoe Lee Browne), a homosexual and col-
laborator with the police, persuades Tank to become a traitor to his friend. Cultured and articulate though he may be,
his lines have a theatricality and artificiality about them, as
for example, "That's the trouble with every black man I know.
He has no sense of the ridiculous." He refers to Tank as
"James Bond in colored town."

Jeannie (Janet MacLachlan), B. G.'s girl and sister of
the betrayed, is the personification of the recently emanci-
pated black woman in American society. Her "Afro" hair
style is visual proof of her liberation. Grier and Cobbs comment on the prototype which Jeannie exemplifies:

> It is against this endless circle of shame, humilia-
> tion, and the implied unacceptability of one's own
> person that a small but significant number of black
> women have turned to the 'natural hairdo',.... The
> effect is...so psychologically redemptive, that we
> can only wonder why it has taken them so long,
> and why even yet there are so few.[42]

Explaining why old acquaintances no longer recognize her,
Jeannie says, "I'm off my knees now. I like my man with
a gun."

Other minor portrayals include Johnny (Max Julian), the betrayed leader; Mama Wells (Juanita Moore), Johnny's critically ill mother; and Corbin (Dick Williams), a militant leader.

It should be obvious from this lengthy catalog of characters that Dassin has added to O'Flaherty's one-man character study, characterizations prerequisite to telling the story of the black militant movement. The remote resemblance between Up Tight and The Informer, which Dassin admits, [43] ought easily to be understood. George Bluestone explains:

> What happens, therefore, when the filmist undertakes the adaptation of a novel, given the inevitable mutation, is that he does not convert the novel at all. What he adapts is a kind of paraphrase of the novel--the novel viewed as raw material. He looks not to the organic novel, whose language is inseparable from its theme, but to characters and incidents which have somehow detached themselves from language and, like the heroes of folk legends, have achieved a mystic life of their own. [44]

In addition to the new black images it presents, Up Tight depicts aspects of the black experience as they have not been revealed previously in a major American motion picture. The sidewalk evangelist is seen warning, "Jesus is the answer"; the prostitutes promenade back and forth on the street; "Blood Donor" signs are conspicuous; the strained gaiety of the taverns is shown. The numbers racket man is greeted with, "Here's my man, my main man." A black power group is soliciting on the street:

> SPEAKER: You don't think. That's the truth. He tells you, you are unskilled. He tells you, you are unskilled and semi-skilled and you believe him. But didn't you clear the land?
>
> CROWD: Yeah!!

SPEAKER: Didn't you lay the tracks?

CROWD: Yeah!

SPEAKER: Didn't you build the cities?

CROWD: Yeah!

SPEAKER: Now what you got? You got equip-
          ment?

CROWD: No!

SPEAKER: You got factories?

CROWD: No!

SPEAKER: You got a membership card in the
          white man's union?

CROWD: No!

SPEAKER: Do you have any money?

CROWD: No!

SPEAKER: You ain't got nothing.

CROWD: LAUGHTER[45]

The speaker continues to stir the emotions of those in the
crowd until in a final frenzy they are all yelling, "Power!
Black Power!"

The film has the mark of timeliness with its attention
to the prevalent schism between black militants and white lib-
erals of the civil rights movement. This message is clearly
delineated in the film's enactment of a private strategy meeting held by black community activists:

B. G.:   We're wasting time. Selma, lunch coun-
         ters, Birmingham, --yesterday! A place we
         went through together. Now we don't walk
         together any more. Now no whites. It's
         policy.

TEDDY: It's great. Stomped on, spilled blood, but
you can't work here any more. Disquali-
fied, wrong complexion.

CORBIN: Don't shout, friend. We got to do it
alone.

TEDDY: You can't do it alone. Without me, you
can't win. Without me, you're gonna get
killed!

CORBIN: Teddy, we got to do it, alone. We don't
want your know how. We got to develop
our own or die. Think about it. Go help
the white brother. He's in deep trouble.
Change him. That's your job.[46]

Renata Adler, film critic, questions the reality of the
film's depiction of the black movement. She supports her
argument with an unqualified statement of what black militant
meetings are and are not. According to Adler, the casting
of a black hero as a member of a violent revolution in progress in America makes no emotional sense.[47] Julian Mayfield, star and co-author of Up Tight, bases his rebuttal of
Adler's position on her personal qualifications--or lack of
them in this instance. Mayfield maintains that Adler, as a
white woman, is not competent to comment on the inner machinations of a black militant group. Pointing out that the black
frame of reference is often different from the white, Mayfield
challenges the right of whites to insist that a story about
blacks written by blacks is false. Mayfield justifies his
views:

Writing and playing the currently fashionable Super
White Negroes is a welcome relief from the old
Amos 'n' Andy days, and profitable to several individuals, but some black artists want to use their
crafts to warn their people...during the dangerous
period we are entering.[48]

As 1968 came to a close, it was evident that the American motion picture medium still trailed far behind the legitimate theatre in providing black writers with opportunities to communicate their unique message.

Notes

1. The World Almanac and Book of Facts, 1969, (New York: Newspaper Enterprise Association, Inc., 1969), pp. 48, 70-77, and 917.

2. The New York Times, December 12, 1968, p. 32.

3. The World Almanac and Book of Facts, 1969, (New York: Newspaper Enterprise Association, Inc., 1969), p. 238.

4. Kay Gardella, "TV Casts Diahann As a Pioneer," Sunday News, September 1, 1968, p. 39C.

5. Charles Champlin, "Sidney Poitier: The Burden of a Pioneer," New York Post, February 3, 1969, p. 48.

6. Motion Picture Association of America, The Motion Picture Code and Rating Program. A System of Self-Regulation (New York: n. d.).

7. Candy (Cinerama Releasing Corporation, 1968).

8. Madigan (Universal Pictures, 1968).

9. The Heart Is a Lonely Hunter (Warner Brothers-Seven Arts, 1968).

10. Ellen Holly, "How Black Do You Have To Be?," The New York Times, September 15, 1968, p. D5.

11. Ice Station Zebra (Metro Goldwyn Mayer, 1968).

12. The Green Berets (Warner Brothers-Seven Arts, 1968).

13. Gunnar Myrdal, An American Dilemma, The Negro

Problem and Modern Democracy, (New York: Harper, 1944), p. 988.

14. The Biggest Bundle of Them All (Metro Goldwyn Mayer, 1968).

15. Ibid.

16. Joan Barthel, "The Black Power of Godfrey Mac-Arthur Cambridge," The New York Times, November 20, 1966, p. D13.

17. Bye Bye Braverman (Warner Brothers-Seven Arts, 1968).

18. Salt and Pepper (United Artists, 1968).

19. Hollis Alpert, "SR Goes to the Movies," Saturday Review, November 23, 1968, p. 49.

20. The Scalphunters (United Artists, 1968).

21. Vincent Canby, "Screen," The New York Times, April 3, 1968, p. 40.

22. New York Amsterdam News, April 5, 1969, p. 10.

23. James Baldwin, "The Price May Be Too High," The New York Times, February 2, 1969, p. D9.

24. If He Hollers, Let Him Go (Cinerama Releasing Corp. , 1968).

25. Ibid.

26. The Split (Metro Goldwyn Mayer, 1968).

27. Renata Adler, "Screen," The New York Times, November 5, 1968, p. 55.

28. LeRoi Jones, "Jim Brown On The Scene," (Unpublished poem.)

29. Carolyn H. Ewers, Sidney Poitier: The Long Journey (New York: The New American Library, 1968), p. 122 (by permission of the Author and Henry Morrison, Inc. her Agents).

30. *For Love of Ivy* (Palomar Pictures International, 1968).

31. Ibid.

32. Troy DeBose, "The Maid Wore Costly Wigs and Dressed Like No Maid We'll Ever See," The New York Times, September 1, 1968, p. D9.

33. Archer Winsten, "Reviewing Stand," New York Post, July 18, 1968, p. 26.

34. Hollis Alpert, "SR Goes to the Movies," Saturday Review, August 3, 1968, p. 35.

35. Jay Weston, "Movie Mailbag," The New York Times, October 1, 1967, p. D15.

36. Vincent Canby, "The Screen," The New York Times, July 18, 1968, p. 26.

37. Roy Wilkins, "Poitier's Ivy," New York Post, July 27, 1968, p. 27.

38. "Up Tight," Ebony, November 1968, p. 52.

39. William H. Grier and Price M. Cobbs, Black Rage (New York: Basic Books, Inc., 1968), p. 206.

40. Up Tight (Paramount Pictures, 1968).

41. Grier and Cobbs, op. cit., p. 66.

42. Grier and Cobbs, op. cit., p. 45.

43. "Up Tight," Ebony, November 1968, p. 54.

44. George Bluestone, Novels into Film (Baltimore: The Johns Hopkins Press, 1957), p. 62.

45. Up Tight (Paramount Pictures, 1968).

46. Ibid.

47. Renata Adler, "Critic Keeps Her Cool on 'Up Tight,'" The New York Times, December 29, 1968, pp. D1, 29.

48.   Julian Mayfield, "Explore Black Experience," The
      New York Times, February 2, 1969, p. D9.

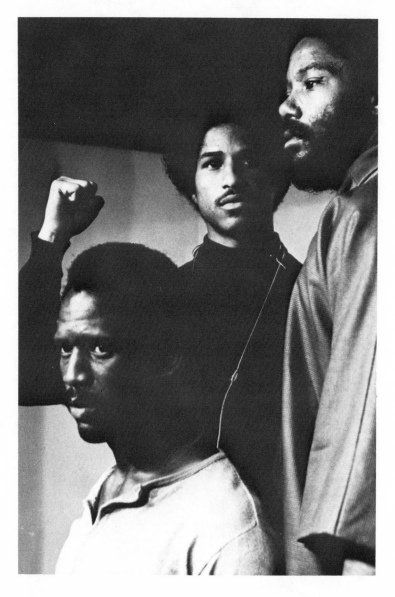

Starring in Herbert Danska's <u>Right On</u>, "The Last Poets":
Kane, Felipe Luciano and David Nelson (Photo courtesy
Herbert Danska)

Chapter 13

1969

Following protest by civil rights groups, President
Nixon's nomination of Clement F. Haynsworth, an anti-liberal
jurist from South Carolina, for a vacant seat on the Supreme
Court was not confirmed. Police shootouts with leaders of
the Black Panther Party transpired in two major cities, Chicago and Los Angeles. James Foreman, director of the National Black Economic Development Council, launched a campaign and presented a manifesto calling for reparations from
U.S. churches and synagogues for past injustices to black
people. Charles Evers, brother of the assassinated Medgar
Evers, became the mayor of Fayette, Mississippi. Replac-
ing its fifteen-year "with all deliberate speed" decision, the
Supreme Court ordered an immediate end to the operation of
separate school systems for blacks and whites. In the performing arts, The Great White Hope, a play about a black
prizefighter, won the Pulitzer Prize for drama. Black folk
singer Josh White and black actor Rex Ingram died. [1]

As in previous years, old stereotypes recurred and
new stereotypes emerged with reference to the depiction of
blacks in American motion pictures.

Several "bit" appearances which William Burke has
labeled appropriately "background" presentations were seen
in 1969. [2]

Easily the most moving of these is Anthony McGowan's
portrayal in Goodbye, Columbus. As a little black boy, he

201

is avidly seeking information and culture in the public library. His poignant bid for attention is repulsed by one character in the film but Neil Klugman (Richard Benjamin), the
hero of the story, encourages the winsome boy in his pursuit of knowledge. Stanley Kauffmann wrote, "The incident
of the Negro boy who comes into the library to look at Gau-
guin seems phony today. Not that it couldn't happen; anything can happen; but its use here seems coyly humane."[3]

In The Mad Room, a grade "B" film, Carol Cole has
the small role of Chris in a tale of insanity, suspense and
horror. This appearance certainly did little to enhance the
image of blacks in films or the screen career of Nat "King"
Cole's actress-daughter.

Alfred Hitchcock's film production of Leon Uris' best
selling novel Topaz included a sequence in Harlem. A Cuban
delegation has taken up residence in the Theresa Hotel.
Phillippe Du Bois (Roscoe Lee Browne), a local florist who
doubles as an espionage agent, is asked to photograph some
secret documents in the possession of a Cuban leader. Pos-
ing as a reporter, Du Bois visits the hotel ostensibly seeking
an interview. When he returns to his shop after the mission,
the florist places a "rest in peace" ribbon on a floral piece.
This gesture is a supreme bit of irony, considering that he
has just been an instrument of murder.

Reddick's "the unhappy non-white" was on display in
several motion pictures during the year, most prominently in
Vixen and Change of Mind.

In the latter film, a white terminal cancer victim has
his brain transplanted into the body of a black man played by
Raymond St. Jacques. His sexual and other readjustments
comprise the remainder of the plot. To what professional
heights can a newly transformed black District Attorney as-

pire amid a community of white bigots? Will the white man's
wife caress the black body? Will the black man's widow
"dig" the white mind? It is easy to understand why David
Rowe (St. Jacques) is the "unhappy non-white." The white
wife recoils from his touch and the black wife finds his love
making inadequate. As the black wife, Janet MacLachlan
must simultaneously evoke sympathy and suggest a "soul"
sexuality.

Another "unhappy non-white" is evident in Vixen, one
of Russ Meyer's sexploitation films. Throughout the story
which is set in British Columbia, Vixen racially baits her
brother's young black friend, a U.S. draft dodger named
Miles (Harrison Page). Eventually Miles can no longer ignore
Vixen's cruel insults. At the perverse behest of Vixen's
brother, no less, Miles attempts to assault her sexually but
demurs at the last minute. He fares no better with an invi-
tation to flee to Cuba. No sooner is Miles airborne than he
is degraded racially, this time by a Cuban-bound communist.
Harrison Page acts with dignity the absurd role of Miles.

The year's films did not neglect "the natural born musician," but what talented black musicians they are! Louis
"Satchmo" Armstrong, not seen on screen since A Man Called
Adam (1966), performs his unique rendition of the title song
in Hello Dolly! The parade sequence of this film depicts the
10th Cavalry, one of five black regiments prominent about a
century ago. This kind of recognition of Afro-American participation in the military history of the country is rare. The
film version of the popular musical Sweet Charity allowed
Sammy Davis, Jr. to register another "natural born musician" performance. The role written into the screenplay especially for him allowed him to entertain as only he can.
Davis is seen as Big Daddy, spiritual leader of a flower

group called "Rhythm of Life."

When Lawrence Reddick identified "the devoted servant" as one of several Negro stereotypes in the medium of
motion pictures, his reference to servant was in the traditional context of employee. Twenty-five years later, a different sort of servant appears in films, equally enslaved by
another kind of bondage. Two examples of this new stereotype involve attractive black women.

Although Death of a Gunfighter marks the return to
motion pictures of Lena Horne, as co-star, after a twelve-
year hiatus from films, her characterization of Claire Quintana is not the major focus of attention, as one might guess
from the film's title. As the mistress of Sheriff Frank
Patch (Richard Widmark), Claire is the operator of a racially-integrated brothel. Miss Horne admittedly relished a dramatic role that did not require her to sing. However, her
singing is heard off screen during the final credits. Casting
a black woman (Horne) as Claire adds a dimension of ambi-
guity to the characterization, intentional or otherwise. The
attractive Claire seems unduly thankful for Patch's affection:

> CLAIRE: I want you to go away with me, Frank.
> You don't have to marry me. You don't
> even have to love me.[4]

This "devoted servant" clearly asks for very little. Later,
when Patch does offer marriage, Claire responds:

> CLAIRE: You did mean it, didn't you?
>
> PATCH: Mean what?
>
> CLAIRE: About marrying me?
>
> PATCH: Yes.
>
> CLAIRE: When, Frank?

> PATCH: Right now.
>
> CLAIRE: Can a bride have an hour to get ready?
>
> PATCH: All right but hurry up.[5]

Can Claire's subservience be attributed solely to the insecurity of her occupation as whore-house madam or is her grati-
tude motivated by a black woman's hope of marriage to a
white man? Since the script does not mention race, audiences will make their own inferences. A film critic for The
New York Times raises still another question: Would such a
despicable community as the one in this story "have permitted a Negro woman to operate a bawdy house in the center of
the town."[6] Despite the fact that the aforementioned self-ef-
facing dialogue makes Claire Quintana "a devoted servant,"
Miss Horne did succeed finally in abandoning roles that merely required her to stand against a pillar singing. "I did that
20 times too often," she says.[7]

In a similar role, Barbara McNair, as Ahn Desaje in
Stiletto, is more interested in the welfare of her white boy
friend Cesare (Alex Cord), a Mafia hoodlum, than in her own
safety. In one scene, wearing a helmet and riding a motor-
cycle, Ahn (McNair) actually comes to Cesare's rescue. In
another episode, the interracial couple visit an all-black night
spot. Ahn trots out her Afro wig for this occasion. As the
club they see Hannibal Smith (Lincoln Kilpatrick), a menac-
ing black leader of the New York branch of the Mafia. Ahn's
willingness to be an updated version of "the devoted servant"
brings about her destruction at the hands of Hannibal whose
allegiance is not to the Black Panther Party (as one might
expect) but to the Italian Mafia. Ahn's sacrificial gesture
is for a white man whom she knows to be in love with a
white woman. Thus, the script succeeds in pitting black

against black in the interest of whites.

Nineteen sixty-nine could be considered the year of
Jim Brown.   The black actor starred in three American motion picture productions.   In each of these films, Brown
brought to full fruition the newly emerged stereotype of superhero.

A prison rebellion is the backdrop for Jim Brown's
appearance in Riot.   Cully Brixton (Brown), a white character in the novel, finds himself the reluctant leader of the riot, an outbreak more than a break out.   Riot is a departure
for films of its genre: no Negroes singing "Swing Low Sweet
Chariot" as James Cagney moves stoically through death row;
no blacks taking orders from V. I.P. white convicts.   In this
flick, Brown as Cully makes decisions, confronts prison of-
ficials, disciplines renegade convicts, resists homosexual
overtures and protects prison hostages during the unrest.   He
is morally and physically heroic.   In fact, audiences might
properly wonder how such a clean-cut, fair-minded fellow
ever became a convict in the first place.   Cully is even allowed the luxury of feminine companions.   A dream sequence
shows an assortment of beautiful girls of varying brown com-
plexions, clad in swim suits and waiting eagerly for Cully's
attentions.   The movie permits Cully to imbibe strong drink,
a prison-brewed mash with raisins.

As Cully, Brown is wary, militant, aloof and possessed of an inner vision of man's basic aloneness. Whether
Brown is actually any of these things is irrelevant; what really counts is the proud black image he projects as superhero.[8]

Playing the title role in Kenner, Jim Brown is a sea-
man-adventurer seeking revenge in Bombay.   He wants to
find and kill a rogue who has previously double-crossed him.
Instead, he falls in love with a lovely Indian woman and ends

up adopting her little boy when she dies. The boy persuades
Kenner to place himself above revenge. As is the practice
in most Jim Brown films, the dialogue is anything but complex. "I hear you play a mean sitar," Roy Kenner tells his
lady fair. [9]

Westerns have been traditionally "no man's territory"
as far as black performers are concerned, despite the existence of real black heroes like Nat (Deadwood Dick) Love.
This breach has been filled by Jim Brown in 100 Rifles. As
Sheriff Lydecker, he goes to Mexico to capture a bank rob-
ber and becomes entangled in a Yaqui Indian revolt against
the Mexican government. Although race is not a paramount
factor in 100 Rifles, it is always somewhere within close
range. Yaqui Joe (Burt Reynolds) asks Lydecker, "How come
they gave you a badge in the first place?" Lydecker admits
he took a job nobody wanted. The Mexicans refer to Lydecker as the "black gringo," perhaps a Spanish equivalent
of Norman Mailer's term, the "white Negro." Lydecker asks
Sarita (Raquel Welch) why several Mexican children are star-
ing at him. "They have never seen a black man before,"
she replies.

In what can only be an attempt to pit minority against
minority, the script endows the black Lydecker with a pro-
clivity toward racial bigotry. Making a point of calling Yaqui
Joe a half-breed, Lydecker admits, "I don't much like Indians anyway." Lydecker's sense of personal security does appear to extend beyond racial lines: "I know what I am. I
don't have to go looking for it." Brown's torrid love-making
scene with the voluptuous Raquel Welch represents something
of a milestone in the portrayal of blacks in American cinema.
"Brown acknowledged he 'got a kick out of getting the chick'
in the film, a privilege not often granted blacks cinemati-

Sidney Poitier gained prominence in the Stanley Kramer production, <u>The Defiant Ones</u>, which co-starred Tony Curtis. (Photo courtesy Stanley Kramer)

cally..."[10] Yet he wins the girl only to lose her. The same unofficial code that mandated the death of Brown's Hindu love
in Kenner, exacted the death of his Mexican amour in 100
Rifles.

Apparent in all three Jim Brown movies described is
the pattern of the bare torso observed by Burke:

> 'Shirtlessness' proves to be a recurring condition
> among Negro males in American films. It is one
> of the more curious repetitive scenic 'events' to
> be traced in the films.... [21]

The female counterpart of Reddick's stereotype, "the
sexual superman," came to the fore in two American films
in 1969. She is the "hot mama" or "Negro sexpot."

Judy Pace appears as Eulice in Three in the Attic.
The black co-ed and student teacher in a New England college community is one of a trio of girls, all recipients of
the sexual attention of one white man. Where he, at least
initially, is the aggressor with the two white girls, it is the
reverse with Eulice--she chases him. Aiming to teach the
campus Romeo a lesson, the three girls imprison him in a
dormitory attic, taking turns at exacting hourly sexual satisfaction from him. Eulice is characterized as being more
exotic and sensuous than the two white girls.

In an equally sleazy film, Russ Meyer's Finders
Keepers, Lovers Weepers, Lavelle Roby plays Claire, entre-
preneur of a house of prostitution. Even the most casual ob-
server of films would recognize this as an increasingly frequent occupation for black women in movies. Apparently a
completely dedicated madam, Claire personally replaces one
of her lovely white call girls in bed, presumably offering the
girl rest and the client sexual and ethnic variety.

Superficial liberality has brought "the token Negro"

to American motion pictures. He is seen in westerns and
war films, although his occurrence is not confined to these
two categories. It is not unusual for "the token Negro" to
be imbued with a forced militancy, making the characterization anachronistic to its own setting.

Castle Keep presents Al Freeman, Jr. as Pfc. Alistair
P. Benjamin, one of several soldiers billeted in a medieval
castle in Belgium during World War II. Benjamin's sharp
and witty dialogue is compatible with his occupational goal of
becoming a writer. Explaining his relationship to the white
soldiers, Benjamin says, "These kind gentlemen rescued me
from a slaver. They thought they could learn Swahili from
me." Once bivouaced in the castle, he asks, "You think my
living here will lower the real estate value? " "Your lecture
on art turned me on." he tells another soldier who happens
to be an art historian. These lines are more in the tempor-
al context of Da Nang, 1970 than Bastogne, 1944. All members of the military detachment are killed in a grand finale
battle at the castle, all except the black Pfc. Benjamin. His
commanding officer has given instructions, 'When it's all
over, I want you to get her [the white leading lady] out."
Accordingly, Benjamin, the only black soldier, is denied the
option of an heroic death, granted to all the whites. The Negro and the female, second-class citizens both, are to be
spared, it seems. [12]

Ossie Davis as Jedidiah Hooker, a blacksmith, is "the
token Negro" in Sam Whiskey, a western spoof. It is difficult to believe that an independent black man with a skilled
trade would risk all to join up with a cocky white rascal in
some crazy scheme, especially in the racially sensitive post-
Civil War era. For his labors, the blacksmith gets what
blacks usually get in these stories, nothing. Jedidiah also

engages the white male lead in fisticuffs, just as Davis did in
The Scalphunters (1968). The motivational force behind these
interracial bouts in recent films might be a concerted effort
to sublimate racial hostility. Certainly in this single respect,
American movies have progressed considerably in the thirty-
six years since Emperor Jones (1933). That film was ex-
pressly edited to eliminate a scene depicting a black man
(Paul Robeson) striking a white man. Sam Whiskey was not
the only film to include a match between black and white in
1969.

Ned McCaslin (Rupert Crosse) "has at" Boon Hoggan-
beck (Steve McQueen) in one scene of The Reivers, based upon the William Faulkner novel. Unlike the novel, the film
depicts Ned not as an ordinary stablehand, but as clever,
outspoken, and swift in defense of his rights. Ned even man-
ipulates an unwilling Boon into taking him along on an automobile trip to Memphis. In a turn-of-the-century Mississippi
setting, the brassy characterization of Ned is anachronistic.
For his work in The Reivers, Rupert Crosse received an
Academy of Motion Picture Arts and Sciences nomination for
the best performance by a male actor in a supporting role.
The Reivers also included two "good darky" portrayals:
Juano Hernandez as Uncle Possum and Vinnette Carroll as
Aunt Callie struggle valiantly to lend stature to Negro roles
one customarily associates with the historic South.

Another film during the year with a Southern setting
was Slaves. Filmed in Shreveport, Louisiana and written in
collaboration with black novelist, John O. Killens, Slaves
shows blacks being wrested from their families, sold at auc-
tion, mistreated and abused. Resisting this inhuman oppression is Luke, a noble and courageous slave, played by Ossie
Davis. In the course of the movie, Luke makes a prototypal

transition from "Uncle Tom" to "Nat Turner." Slaves
abounds in incongruities including a plantation mansion decorated with African art, a house slave adorned with jewelry
by Richelieu and a slaveowner who spouts black history. [13]
One can be critical of Slaves and yet applaud it for utilizing
brilliant black acting talents (Davis, Barbara Ann Teer, Robert Kya-Hill, Julius Harris, Eva Jessye, Dionne Warwick).
Miss Warwick, a popular musical recording star, made her
motion picture acting debut as the spirited slave mistress of
a white plantation owner. The advertisement for the film was
frankly exploitative of the sexual relationship between white
slave master and black slave: "He bought me for $650 but
I own him." The movie can also be hailed for its attempt
to portray the true plight of blacks in bondage prior to the
Civil War. The squalor of the huts, the brutality of the whip,
the indifference to human life is clearly depicted. Herbert
Biberman, co-author and director of Slaves, wrote:

> our slow deliverance from the effects of slavery is
> still being written all over this country.[14]

> ...a charming elderly lady, talked with me about
> the use of her plantation if we should decide to
> film in Louisiana.... 'There is one condition. You
> can see that I am an upholder of the old traditions.'
> ... 'I mean, I can't allow any niggers in my house.
> And I am not prejudiced....'[15]

The scenarists do not explain why the privileged house
slaves were the ones to chance an escape rather than the
brutalized field slaves. Nor do they make clear the reason
Luke is willing to die in order that the slave mistress of the
white master can go free. It would have seemed more plausible for him to have chosen to live in the hope of being reunited someday with his wife and family.

The Learning Tree is really the first film since A

Harry Belafonte, seen here with Gloria Foster, is "angelicized" in <u>The Angel Levine.</u> (Photo courtesy United Artists)

Raisin in the Sun (1961) to treat the black family with some
sensitivity.   In signing a contract with Warner Brothers-
Seven Arts to direct the screen version of his autobiographi-
cal-novel, Gordon Parks became the first black man in the
history of American cinema to direct a major Hollywood production.[16] The movie is about a black youth and the problems he encounters while growing up in a small Kansas town
during the 1920's.   The range of roles for blacks in any
given film is usually limited to one or two familiar stereotypes.   The Learning Tree presents a diverse assortment of
characterizations, young and old, hero and villain, passive
and militant.   The three most interesting characters are
Sara, Newt and Marcus.   Sara (Estelle Evans) is the understanding mother who teaches Newt to use incidents as his
"learning tree."   Newt (Kyle Johnson), her son, has the sensitivity and character which comes from a happy home and
devoted parents.   The contrast between Newt and Marcus
(Alex Clarke) is sharply drawn.   Although he is about the
same age as Newt, Marcus is the victim of a broken home
and the abuse of an embittered father.   One scene not particularly relevant to the plot is nonetheless memorable.   As
Newt leaves an outdoor carnival free-for-all fistfight, an innocent little white boy congratulates him by saying, "I'm
glad you won, Sambo."   When Newt yells, "Get outta here,
you little. . . ," the bewildered child is frightened.[17]   This
is a sardonic commentary on the nature of racism.   The
process which Burke termed "the gentling of the Negro" has
evolved into a new stereotype, "the Negro who cannot harm
whites."[18]   No matter what the provocation this fellow will
not lift his hand against whites.   Booker Savage, the father
of Marcus, seizes a gun but does not turn it against a crowd

of whites who are yelling, "Get the Nigger!" Although Booker
has an explosive temper and despises whites, he decides to
shoot himself instead of the mob. Essentially, The Learning
Tree is a Huckleberry Finn tale, related for the first time in
terms of the black experience. The film nearly missed this
distinction. A producer offered to purchase the property from
Mr. Parks if he would change the black characters to white.[19]

Fully at the other end of the convention spectrum is
Robert Downey's Putney Swope, a comedy about an advertising agency taken over by a group of blacks committed to the
overthrow of the Establishment. Putney (Arnold Johnson), by
a strange fluke, is elected Chairman of the agency because
each "liberal" board member voted for him, thinking no one
else would. Putney promptly renames the agency Truth and
Soul (TS for short). He replaces most of the white staff with
black militants. Those whites allowed to remain are sub-
jected to indignities. This film reverses the standard black,
white images and actions. A wealthy black couple have a
lazy white maid. A black employer turns down white job ap-
plications. A black orders a white delivery man to go back
down 30 stories in order to come up on the service elevator.
The Truth and Soul Agency commercials (photographed in col-
or) are highlights of buffoonery. There is the black youth
(Ronnie Dyson) and his white girl friend strolling through the
woods for "Face-Off Pimple Remover." A black chick in a
gold lamé dress whirls around a slum, ballyhooing a new experience in 'lectric fans. "You can't eat an air-conditioner."
she sings.[20] Arnold Johnson is adequately abrasive and arrogant as Putney. Laura Greene lends the proper blend of
bitchiness and sexiness to the part of his lover, mistress
and wife in that order. Both characterizations border on
anti-black but if this criticism holds, then the film must be

deemed equally anti-semitic, anti-Oriental and anti-white.
Critics used such adjectives as sophomoric, disjointed, obscene, amateurish, disgusting, zany and unintelligible to describe Putney Swope. Its producer, Robert Downey, who also contributed "the voice" of Putney states:

> I wanted to show that if you hook yourself into a
> system that's a toilet, it doesn't matter if it's a
> black toilet or a white toilet.[21]

No one should be surprised by Downey's thesis that blacks
can be as corrupted as whites by power and cash.

The militancy of Putney Swope seems mild when compared to that of The Lost Man starring Sidney Poitier. This
film moves one step beyond the revolutionary and separatist
doctrine introduced in Up Tight (1968). Commenting about
Poitier's new role, Alexander Walker says:

> The same ability to humanise and personalise the
> negro, [sic] which saved many of his goody-goody
> roles from being stereotypes, serves him well in
> the opposite extreme. The thoughtful and well-ad-
> justed negro [sic] who competed with whites by his
> skilled labour, or showed them up by his moral
> superiority, has been replaced by a wised-up ene-
> my of white society who looks on violence as a
> self-justifying act of rebellion.[22]

The role of Jason Higgs is a departure from the usual antiseptic characterizations associated with Poitier. Jason is
indeed the "lost man," a veteran who plans and perpetrates
a robbery in order to obtain funds for the families of imprisoned black brothers. The payroll heist goes wrong because Jason won't fire on a hostage ("the Negro who cannot
harm whites"). Consequently he is wounded and becomes the
object of a police dragnet. Seeing Poitier wearing dark
glasses with a scarf to mask his identity and a revolver
drawn against the law is a nearly incomprehensible image.

Several unanswered questions surround the portrayal. Why does Jason, who once advocated non-violence, suddenly become a black "Robin Hood"? What sort of organization does he work for without question? If "black is beautiful" to this dedicated revolutionary, why is he so quickly attracted to a white social worker? Although Poitier is not allowed the sexual aggressiveness of Jim Brown, he does get to kiss his white leading lady full on the lips, for what little that means in terms of cinematic progress. It is her ineffectual assistance in facilitating Jason's escape that leads to their ultimate destruction. Inevitable doom for an interracial romance is now a familiar film pattern. Poitier feels:

> . . . there is significance in the fact that both the hero and the heroine are killed at the end of the movie. 'We do have a tendency to kill off a lot of good people in our society, don't we?'[23]

Members of Jason's gang (Bernie Hamilton, Leon Bibb, Lincoln Kilpatrick) have little to do, with the possible exception of Al Freeman, Jr. Dennis (Freeman, Jr.), a civil rights demonstrator, is reluctant to participate in the robbery. Subsequently convinced, he uses pickets to distract police from the crime in progress. While on the run, Jason encounters Sally (Beverly Todd), an endearing black beautician. In the process of helping Jason elude the police, the pathetic Sally admits calling herself Dorothy Starr in honor of the late black actress Dorothy Dandridge. This reference originally was made to Marilyn Monroe, prior to a revision of the script. The Lost Man fails to come to grips with the black revolution in much the same way as Up Tight. Both films were hybrids of a sort, based upon previous dramas of the Irish rebellion, the former on Odd Man Out and the latter on The Informer. Larry Neal likens the problems involved

in the portrayal of blacks in motion pictures to the Tar Baby
episode of the Brer Rabbit tales:

> . . . We are locked into such a prison of distorted
> symbols and images that the very attempt to extri-
> cate ourselves only leads to more confusion.
>
> Black people were much easier to portray, from
> the point of view of Hollywood and the Establish-
> ment theater, when white racism simplified human
> relationships. Now because of the revolutionary
> tempo of these times, Hollywood and its satellites
> have been forced to confront the black experience
> in all of its human complexity. But they are sel-
> dom successful. . . . [24]

Renata Adler notes the apparent inability or unwilling-
ness to "draw upon some of the experience, the personal and
social history, the drama and the look of Negro American
life." She remarks:

> You wouldn't know from current movies that there
> have been black men of great courage, intelligence,
> and gentleness working in the south. You wouldn't
> know there has been a Watts, or ghetto life, or a
> Negro family. . . . It is all a blank where the richest
> fiction and documentary material should be. [25]

Notes

1. The World Almanac and Book of Facts, 1970, (New
       York: Doubleday, 1969), pp. 47-49, 459, 906-
       928.

2. William L. Burke, "The Presentation of the Ameri-
       can Negro in Hollywood Films, 1946-1961: An
       Analysis of a Selected Sample of Feature Films,"
       (Unpublished Ph. D. dissertation, Northwestern
       University, 1965), p. 146.

3. Stanley Kauffmann, Figures of Light, Film Criticism
       and Comment, (New York: Harper & Row,
       1971), p. 155.

4. Death of a Gunfighter (Universal, 1969).

5. Ibid.

6. Howard Thompson, "Screen," The New York Times,
    May 10, 1969, p. 34.

7. New York Amsterdam News, May 3, 1969, p. 25.

8. Vincent Canby, "The Movies That Still Haunt Holly-
    wood," The New York Times, January 26, 1969,
    p. D15.

9. Kenner (Metro Goldwyn Mayer, 1969).

10. Jerry Tallmer, "Jim Brown: A New Ball Game,"
    New York Post, March 29, 1969, p. 33.

11. Burke, op. cit., p. 128.

12. Castle Keep (Columbia Pictures, 1969).

13. Vincent Canby, "Screen," The New York Times,
    July 3, 1969, p. 21.

14. Herbert Biberman, "We Never Say Nigger In Front
    of Them," The New York Times, January 19,
    1969, pp. D1, D11.

15. Ibid.

16. Patricia Bosworth, "How Could I Forget What I
    Am? The New York Times, August 17, 1969,
    p. D11.

17. The Learning Tree (Warner Brothers-Seven Arts,
    1969).

18. Burke, op. cit., p. 321.

19. Bosworth, op. cit.

20. Joseph Morgenstern and Stefan Kanfer, eds. Film
    69/70: An Anthology By The National Society of
    Film Critics (New York: Simon and Schuster,
    1970) pp. 157-164.

21. Lindsy Van Gelder, "A Talk with: Robert Downey, New York Post, August 15, 1970, p. 11.

22. Alexander Walker, Stardom The Hollywood Phenomenon (New York: Stein and Day, 1970), p. 354.

23. Guy Flatley, "Sidney Poitier as Black Militant," The New York Times, November 10, 1968, p. D15.

24. Larry Neal, "Beware of the Tar Baby," The New York Times, August 3, 1969, p. D13.

25. Renata Adler, "The Negro That Movies Overlook," The New York Times, March 3, 1968, p. 1.

Chapter 14

1970

Riots by blacks occurred in cities throughout the nation including Asbury Park, New Jersey; New Bedford, Massachusetts; New Brunswick, New Jersey and Miami, Florida. Kenneth A. Gibson became Newark's 34th mayor and the first black man to win this office in a major Eastern city. Following criticism by civil rights groups, Judge G. Harrold Carswell of Florida became the second Nixon nominee to be rejected for a vacant Supreme Court seat. Angela Davis, a black university instructor and avowed communist, was apprehended and booked for her alleged role in the killing of a California judge. A nation-wide "Free Angela Davis" movement emerged. The conviction of Black Panther Party cofounder Huey P. Newton, on charges of voluntary manslaughter, was overturned by a California Court of Appeals. Jackson State College in Mississippi, a predominantly black institution, closed temporarily after two black students were killed and nine wounded by police gunfire. James Edwards, Juano Hernandez, Frank Silvera, Earl Grant and Jimi Hendrix were among black performing artists who died during the year.[1] A black soldier killed in Vietnam was finally buried in an all-white cemetery in Fort Pierce, Florida by court order.[2]

American motion pictures released during 1970, with one or two exceptions, failed to depict the black revolution in progress, the social and political upheaval in our cities,

Bernie Hamilton, in The Losers (Photo courtesy the Fanfare Corporation)

the problems of the black Vietnam War veteran or the struggle for racial equality being waged in the courts. All but
one or two of the Negro stereotypes identified previously
were present, blatant in some films, thinly disguised in
others.

Black buffoonery was in sufficient demand to effect
the motion picture "comeback" of Mantan Moreland. The
comedian, who had not shuffled in films for years, played a
counterman in Watermelon Man starring Godfrey Cambridge.
Cambridge portrays Jeff Gerber, a white (courtesy of heavy
make-up) insurance agent, who awakens in the middle of the
night to discover he has mysteriously turned black. Not so
mysterious is the change in attitude of the counterman (Moreland). His long-time breakfast customer, Mr. Gerber, is
routinely addressed as Jeff now that he is black. When Gerber becomes hysterical over his unwanted pigmentation, Moreland, a true 1970 Uncle Tom, says, "Cool it, that's why they
don't want us in these places now."[3] Cambridge, who is no
stranger to buffoonery either, says, "Look at my skin!"
Moreland replies, "I don't have to look at your skin. I can
look at my own."[4] If Cambridge has an understandable contempt for the title Watermelon Man (originally titled "The
Night the Sun Came Out on Happy Hollow Lane"), one is
drawn to speculation about his feelings on the portrayal itself. Surely this fine performer, recognized for his stage
work in Genet's The Blacks, cannot enjoy being a perpetual
buffoon in films. How sad to watch as he anoints his black
skin with a variety of skin bleaches and to hear him remark,
"These creams don't work. No wonder Negroes riot."[5] Of
course, as soon as Gerber turns black, he starts wearing
flashy clothing, beds down with a blonde Norwegian secretary who is attracted to black men, and drills with potential

black revolutionaries (who use brooms and mops). Primarily
"the buffoon," Gerber incorporates as many other Negro
stereotypes as possible. Watermelon Man marked the Hollywood directorial debut of Melvin Van Peebles, a black film
maker.

One More Time (hopefully the last) brings back Sammy
Davis, Jr. as Charles Salt, teamed again with Peter Lawford as Christopher Pepper in a sequel to Salt and Pepper
(1968). The comedy is mostly slapstick, with Salt (Davis)
invoking the memory of Stepin Fetchit, Willie Best et al. In
the course of the plot, Salt is fearful in the extreme, even
to the point of tears. A few of the "double entendre" gags are
on the dirty side. When a beautiful girl offers to reveal her
intimate knowledge of a singular difference between identical
twins Sidney and Christopher Pepper, Salt quips, "It must be
something big!"[6] Like the earlier film, One More Time is
self-conscious in its racial awareness. "All these books and
not one Ebony," Salt is forced to remark. When Jerry Lewis (who directed this film) acts the zany comic, he is merely
that. When Sammy Davis, Jr. rolls his eyes and makes
faces as he does in One More Time, he exemplifies "the buffoon" and the "happy darky," two images that many people
want to keep alive.

Perhaps buffoonery is a legacy bequeathed to black
comedians. For there is Redd Foxx being unduly ridiculous
as Uncle Bud in Cotton Comes to Harlem, a film discussed
previously in connection with other stereotypes. Who would
believe that a black junk dealer sharp enough to outsmart cops
and robbers out of $87,000 would do so just to hide away in
some jungle spot in a grass skirt and floral head wreath and
be fanned by black servants. What a lack of imagination attributed to blacks!

Wherever interracial comedy teams are on view, it is the black member of the duo who becomes the "number one" buffoon. The Busy Body (1967) and Salt and Pepper (1968) were precursors of The Man From O.R. G.Y. which teamed Slappy White, a black comedian, with white singer, Steve Rossi as Mafia agents. For reasons that should be apparent, one can accept Rossi as Luigi but White as Vito is quite another matter. With a black performer appearing as a member of the Mafia in Stiletto (1969) as well as in Man from O. R. G. Y. and Cotton Comes to Harlem this year, Hollywood must have concluded that seeing one minority is seeing them all.

Four movies found destructive work for "the social delinquent" in an equal number of fictional institutions. Max Julian as Ellis, a militant university student, in Getting Straight, singlehandedly goes about the business of smashing windows and doors with no immediate purpose other than destruction. In an almost identical role, Paul Winfield portrays Steve Dempsey, black student leader of "Hudson Afro," a campus group in R. P. M. High on the list of demands of those students who have liberated the computer center is the appointment of a black trustee. In discussing the demands, Dempsey asks, "How can you negotiate ghettos?" Dempsey's militancy is rewarded when he is offered a job as the first black recruitment officer.

James A. Watson, Jr. is J. T., the rebellious student in Halls of Anger. His hostility is aimed at the few white students bused into the all-black high school he attends. Inevitably the chip on J. T. 's shoulder is knocked off. Although J.T. is the ring leader, other black students in the school qualify as "social delinquents." A group of black girls strip a white girl nude in a school dressing room.

Calvin Lockhart, star of the movie states:

> ... The black girls didn't want to do it. Maybe that's
> something that whites would do to a black in the
> South, but it's just not a part of black people's
> culture. I don't think they're that interested, real-
> ly. ... I really think it is in bad taste.[7]

In End of the Road, the violence of Doctor D (James
Earl Jones), a deranged psychiatrist, is committed within an
insane asylum. When Doctor D is not permitting, nay en-
couraging, coition between his patients, he is running about
the place ranting and raving.

The "sexual superman" appears in several of the
year's film characterizations in varying degree. Jim Brown
as Luke in El Condor carries forward the image of virility
established without contradiction in the earlier 100 Rifles.
This time instead of to Raquel Welch, Jim is making love
to another white beauty, Mariana Hill, who plays the mistress of a Mexican general. The mere sight of Jim's bulg-
ing biceps prompts this woman to betray her lover and an
entire fortress. Completely under Jim's spell, she says,
"I want whatever you want."[8]

Capitalization on the Negro sexuality myth reached absurd proportions in Last of the Mobile Hot Shots, a film
based upon Tennessee Williams' The Seven Descents of
Myrtle. Robert Hooks portrays Chicken, the Negro half-
brother of a terminally-ill white man. Chicken sets out to
seduce Myrtle, his brother's white bride. Myrtle, seated
directly in front of a standing Chicken, begs him to be seated
also so that she can see his face. "You don't have to look
at my face," Chicken replies suggestively, just before a fade
out. In a subsequent scene, Myrtle protests that she has
never done anything like that [engage in oral sex] before,

clearly not meaning the more conventional sexual relations.
Flashbacks show Chicken making love to attractive girls,
white and black, while his brother looks on as voyeur.

Not even the motion picture version of Howard Sack-
ler's award-winning The Great White Hope could resist making reference to the sexual equipment of the Negro. For
most of the film Jefferson (James Earl Jones) is "the black
buck," putty in the hands of an insipid white mistress. Finally, in frustration, he tells her, "Ah don wanna give you
nothin, Ah cut it off first."[9]

Occasionally "the sexual superman" emerged spoofing
himself. When Harry (Elliott Gould) tells Ellis (Max Julian)
in Getting Straight that blacks will have to be better than
whites in our society, Ellis responds, "I already am in one
area [sex]."[10] Harry retorts that this seems to be the one
stereotype blacks are not eager to deny.

In similar "tongue in cheek" vein is the remark of
Emerson Thorne (Harrison Page) in Beyond the Valley of the
Dolls. He tells his girl she loves him "because I am the
ballsiest cat you ever did meet."[11]

In The McMasters, Benjie (Brock Peters), a black
rancher, is presented with a beautiful and willing squaw by
some Indians he has befriended. For no apparent reason he
brutally rapes the girl. Other scenes showing Benjie as capable
of tender love and sensitivity were edited out of the final version of the movie. Peters protested the cuts and asked that
the scenes be restored on moral and artistic grounds. He
claimed that without scenes depicting Benjie's remorse over
the rape, the character is distorted and dehumanized, and a
brutish stereotype is perpetuated. Finally, both versions of
the film were released in New York.[12]

The "hot mama-Negro sex pot," female counterpart

of "the sexual superman," is not overlooked in films of the
year.   Judy Pace fulfills this function in both Cotton Comes
to Harlem and Up in the Cellar.

In Cotton, Judy is the "stone Fox" who reduces a
white police officer to ridicule.   The lure and sexual promise
of her nude body prompts him to strip naked and cover his
face (repugnant to her) with a paper bag.

For Up in the Cellar, Judy, as Harlene, becomes the
sexual object of two white men, this time around, compared
to only one white man in Three in the Attic (1969).   As the
black mistress of a college president, she becomes not unwilling prey for a radical student who seeks to embarrass
the executive by seducing her.   Perhaps one redeeming aspect is that the student is compelled to "pass for black" in
order to succeed with his seduction.   Harlene feels she cannot live up to any white man's sexual fantasy of a black woman.   If we are to believe American movies, young black
women are a prescribed extra-curricular activity for white
males on campuses everywhere.   In the aforementioned Getting Straight, we find Harry (Elliott Gould), a graduate student, in bed with a pretty black co-ed as a consequence of
having been rejected by his white steady.   Copulation completed, the black girl asks Harry for a list of his favorite
books.   She hops out of bed "au naturel" for a notebook, revealing her entire anatomy.   Harry's white girl friend, despite scenes of sexual intimacy, is never as completely ex-
posed.   An obvious authority, the black girl pronounces
Harry's love-making satisfactory but somewhat repressed.

The entire plot of The Liberation of L. B. Jones centers on the marital infidelity of a black mortician's attractive young wife.   Rejecting her husband's plea to drop her
white lover, an ignorant and corrupt policeman, Emma Jones

(Lola Falana) tells him "No daddy, why he's twice the man ...." [13] Every time her callous white lover enters her bedroom, Emma cannot seem to undress fast enough.

Moving to Tell Me That You Love Me, Junie Moon, we discover much the same situation. In the small role of Solana, Emily Yancy is a lovely black intellectual, capable of reciting classical poetry. We are given no explanation of her instant attraction to a white paralyzed homosexual. Shortly after meeting this fellow, Solana virtually rapes him in an all-night beach session. The sexuality of the black woman is so strong that she is capable of making a man of this human wreck, we are to believe. Apparently bringing white males to manhood is a new mission for "the hot mamas."

Not one, but two black women are assigned this responsibility in The Landlord, starring Beau Bridges in the title role. While her black militant husband is imprisoned, Fanny (Diana Sands), "Miss Sepia of 1957," seduces the young blond owner of the tenement in which she dwells. A reduction of rent, renovation and repair of her apartment, plain old loneliness, or an insatiable sexual appetite are possible motivations for Fanny's act of adultery. According to Clayton Riley, the film makers possibly want to reinforce a notion held by white American males that black women are "aching to seduce all the white flesh their bedsprings will support." [14] The other black woman who yields eagerly to the landlord is a Negro stereotype not seen in recent films, "the tragic mulatto," and small wonder too, considering that black women with whom she works brand her "a high yeller heifer."

They Call Me Mister Tibbs! offers us a mini-skirted Beverly Todd as Puff, prostitute and mistress to her white bi-sexual pimp. A notch over the previously described "hot mamas" who were exclusively white in sexual orientation, Puff is not averse to accommodating the black detective played by Poitier.

Two other "Negro sexpots" offer their sexual favors to black men. Marlene Warfield recreates her stage performance as Clara, the hot-passioned and jealous common-law wife of the black boxing champion in The Great White Hope. Since the pugilist has jilted her for a white woman by the time the film begins, Warfield's sexuality can only be inferred from her earthy language. It would seem most unlikely that "the Negro sexpot" stereotype could ever resist the sexual overtures of a Jewish angel, particularly the one played by handsome Harry Belafonte in Angel Levine. Disregarding her better judgment and heeding her sexual impulses, Sally (Gloria Foster) jumps into bed with Alexander Levine (whom she no longer even likes) in the spare bedroom of an elderly Jewish couple, who are not merely strangers to her but likely to interrupt at any moment.

There Was a Crooked Man features Claudia McNeil as the madam of a racially-integrated brothel, similar to the one in Death of a Gunfighter (1969) presided over by Lena Horne. Negro actresses as "hot mamas" do have a monopoly on the marketing of sex.

Before leaving the subject of black sexuality in American films one further observation is necessary. Now that the black man is finally overcoming years of psychological and economic emasculation in our society, the American motion picture seems bent on the promulgation of a new stereotype: "the sexually impotent black" [Sweet Love, Bitter (1967), Up Tight (1968)], out of proportion with the miniscule frequency of total black appearances in films. Lester Clotho,

(Moses Gunn), a black in W.U.S.A., cradling a baby in his arms, says, "Things being the way they are I may bring him up as a girl. I really may."[15] A minor black character in the same film is a transvestite who poses as his sister (with minimum effort) in order to cash her welfare checks. Reuben Greene plays Bernard, the black member of the "gay set" depicted in The Boys in the Band. In Myra Breckinridge, Calvin Lockhart plays Irving Amadeus, an effeminate actor who dusts his hair with sequins. Apparently, where perversions, social ills and negative images are concerned, there seems to be little difficulty integrating blacks. If "the sexual superman" is to coexist with "the sexually impotent black," American film makers will have succeeded in having it both ways, as it were.

The emergence of new stereotypes in no way implies the demise of older ones. "The devoted servant" is alive and well in Patton. As performed by the late black actor James Edwards, Sgt. William George Meeks, military orderly to General George S. Patton, seems content to pack and unpack for the general, draw a hot bath, fetch a glass of milk or minister a sleeping pill. "I thought you might be feeling kind of low,"[16] says Meeks, comforting Patton over some bad news. In an early scene, Meeks holds a helmet aloft before positioning it with precision on Patton's head. Later, discussing the coronation of an historical conqueror, Patton remarks, "a slave stood behind with a golden crown."[17] The parallel of master-slave relationship seems unmistakable.

As motion picture casts become increasingly integrated, we can expect to see more of "the superior athlete." His presence within the context of most screen stories can be explained conveniently. Fred Williamson undertakes the

role of "Beachboy," a vacation resort employee and part-
time hustler in Tell Me That You Love Me, Junie Moon.
The muscular black actor displays his physique by lifting a
white paralytic about from place to place during the course
of the movie. Again enacting "the superior athlete," this
time in M. A. S. H., a satire on the U.S. Army Medical Corps,
Williamson is on view as Dr. Oliver Harmon Jones, a neuro-
surgeon. The M. A. S. H. group requests Jones for his athletic prowess, not for his medical expertise. It appears that
Jones, better known as "Spearchucker," a javelin thrower
and football player with the 49'ers, can help the M.A.S.H.
team win a football game against another military unit. A
white Southerner, hearing about the imminent arrival of
"Spearchucker," asks, "What about the social problem?"
Actually, there is no social problem other than some race
baiting during the big game.

Although we do not see the football field in The
Grasshopper, Jim Brown conveys "the superior athlete" image in the role of a former football star who is currently
host in a cocktail lounge. His fame fleeting, his business
ventures failing, Tommy Marcott (Brown) is preoccupied with
his lovely white wife. Not letting us forget for a moment
that this black man is an athlete, the script calls for him to
defend his wife's honor on a golf course and to be slain
vengefully on a basketball court.

Boxing provides an arena for two occurrences (one
minor, one major) of "the superior athlete." Neither the image of the Negro nor the image of the athlete is enhanced by
the characterization of Randy Black (Jim Iglehart), the boxing champion in Beyond the Valley of the Dolls. Randy seduces another man's girl friend and subsequently attempts to
run the fellow down with an automobile. An off-screen nar-

rator summarizes Randy as an animal and beast.

In a slightly different vein, but eligible nevertheless for categorization as "the superior athlete," was the portrayal of Jack Jefferson (derived from facts about heavyweight champion Jack Johnson) in The Great White Hope. Despite a fine performance by James Earl Jones which garnered him an Academy of Motion Picture Arts and Sciences nomination for the best performance by an actor in a leading role, Jack Jefferson emerges as a brawny and brainless black. When it is suggested that he will win and become champion of the century, Jack says, "or lose and be the nigger of the minute."[18] A clean-shaven head, shirtlessness again, excessive sweating (white pugilists seldom perspire in films), a wide grin revealing pearly white dentures, and endless strutting and posturing make for an amalgamation of Negro stereotypes with strong emphasis on "the superior athlete." Even stereotype characterizations are not without their touching moments, such as the one in which a black youngster who had been cheering for Jefferson spits at him when he withdraws from the ring a defeated man.

It would appear that all progress made by blacks in motion pictures is coupled with certain constraints. In the past, a movie with a school setting would cast Negroes, if at all, only as menials. Now we find Calvin Lockhart, a black actor, playing the part of Quincy Davis, a high school principal in Halls of Anger. What is the catch? It is simply that Quincy Davis is more "the superior athlete" than the academician. As a former basketball champion who "made good," Davis is reassigned from a white middle-class school to an explosive school in the black ghetto. There, the script maneuvers him into a basketball game, lest we forget after all that he is "the superior athlete."

"The vicious criminal" and "the knife toter," almost

archaic stereotypes, were revived in isolated incidents during the year. Where's Poppa?, one of those slick sick
films, makes a stark statement about blacks in American society. Four black men are depicted as Central Park
muggers and one has the reprehensible name of "Mutha
Fucka." Explaining their crude language and criminal actions, one of them says, "It's our heritage."[19] When the
gang discovers that their white victim has no money, they
steal all his clothing and leave him nude on Central Park
West. Although these antics are ostensibly aimed at the destruction of stereotypes, they reinforce them in fact. Oper-
ating with considerably more finesse is Deke O'Malley (Calvin Lockhart), the phony preacher manipulating a "back to
Africa" swindle in Cotton Comes to Harlem. Even this
smooth con man qualifies for "the vicious criminal" label
when he socks a woman and pushes some children around.

Not frequently, since Louise Beavers portrayed Delilah in Imitation of Life (1934), have we seen "the natural
born cook," one of the oldest stereotypes assigned to Negroes
in films. Yet she appears again, acted in modern mammy
fashion by Pearl Bailey, in The Landlord. Marge, one of
several colorful tenement dwellers, is characterized as an
ex-vaudevillian, a fortune-teller and especially a fine cook.
Faster than you can say chitterlings and grits, she will pre-
pare anyone a "soul food" dinner in her apartment. When a
snobbish white society matriarch is unable to swallow another
morsel, Marge offers impromptu "take home" service.
Watching the internationally acclaimed Bailey struggle to
make something of this part, one can only wonder how this
happened to Dolly Levi.

Juano Hernandez, that grand old character actor, did
his final film role in They Call Me Mister Tibbs! Regret-

fully, his "swan song" amounted to one more rendition of
"the mental inferior" which Hernandez perfected in The Pawnbroker (1965). Mealie Williamson, the character he enacts
in Tibbs, is nervous, confused and inarticulate, with nary a
trace of the charisma exhibited as Lucas in Intruder in the
Dust (1950). "I never killed nobody," is Mealie's feeble response to confrontation by the police over a crime he did not
commit. Mealie nearly becomes "the sacrificial lamb" who
protects guilty whites in the film. While the script eventually relieves him of this burden, black characters in other
films during the year were not so successful.

In My Sweet Charlie, Al Freeman, Jr. is a black activist attorney from the North who is a fugitive from a killing in connection with a civil rights demonstration. He becomes involved with an unmarried pregnant white Southern
girl, possibly the worst kind of trouble a black man can have
in a Gulf Coast town. The relationship between the two cir-
cumstantial allies evolves from a position of hostility to one
of mutual respect. Instead of proceeding with his planned
escape, Charlie risks capture in order to bring medical help
for the girl and is slain. That this ultimate black sacrifice
could be genuinely appreciated by the ignorant and frightened
white heroine is problematical. The distortion of priority
which demands black sacrifice for white need is a monu-
ment to the American cinema's racism.

A different sort of sacrifice is made by Louis Gos-
sett as Copee, black husband and father in The Landlord.
Ax in hand, he angrily pursues the white landlord who has
cuckolded him. When Copee catches up with the young lover,
he is mysteriously unable to wield the ax and exact his revenge. Why? The script gives no explanation beyond calling for the immediate mental collapse and hospitalization of

Copee, "the sacrificial lamb," "the Negro who cannot harm whites."

The achievement of motion picture stardom by black actors has signaled the occurrence of the superhero. This invincible brother, paragon of perfection, has been played to the hilt since 1963 by Sidney Poitier, Jim Brown, Raymond St. Jacques and Robert Hooks.

Brock Peters joined their illustrious ranks in 1970 with his portrayal of Benjie in The McMasters, an anything-but-traditional western. Benjie, an ex-slave and Union Army veteran, returns after the Civil War to his home town. His two major undertakings, marriage and ranching, are threatened by hostile whites. Benjie is insulted, intimidated, mocked, beaten, tortured, shot at and burned, but Benjie, "the superhero," is determined to see it through. At the conclusion of The McMasters, Benjie's tenacity is evident but his survival is questionable.

Jim Brown does a "superhero" act in Tick Tick Tick as a newly elected black sheriff who succeeds a popular white sheriff in a Southern County. Local bigots throw darts at his campaign poster, smash his car, insult him and assault his black deputy. Still the sheriff does not lose his "cool." His sense of justice transcends racial animosity, so naturally he does not employ a Negro who is overtly anti-white. The most abhorrent whites in the community are eventually converted to his cause. Five minutes with this "black Messiah" and George C. Wallace of Alabama would purchase lifetime membership in the N.A.A.C.P. Brown saw this role as a transitional point in his film career, a change-over from action stuff to more sensitive material.[20]

Sidney Poitier, the original "superhero," follows his own footsteps in recreating the role of Virgil Tibbs for They

Call Me Mister Tibbs! Poitier introduced this omniscient
character to motion picture audiences in In the Heat of the
Night (1967). In the sequel, Detective Tibbs has a wife
(Barbara McNair) and two children. This time the action
takes place in San Francisco instead of the South.[21] Little
else has changed, though, as Tibbs proceeds to investigate
the murder of a white prostitute. In his best unruffled manner, Tibbs questions suspects, shoots it out with hoodlums,
places a well-regarded preacher friend under arrest for murder, outsmarts fellow sleuths and finds time to romance his
wife, discipline his son and instruct his daughter in calisthenics. Vincent Canby considers the film a milestone in
that it casts a black actor (Poitier) in a role that ordinarily
might have gone to a white star like Frank Sinatra.[22] As in
The Slender Thread (1965), Poitier's blackness is not mentioned in They Call Me Mister Tibbs! Abandonment of ethnic identity is high price indeed to pay for the status of "superhero. "

From progressive observation of the saintly attributes
of "the superhero" one would have expected him inevitably to
be angelicized. This happens in fact to Harry Belafonte as
Alexander Levine in the Belafonte Enterprises production of
Angel Levine, a liberalization of Bernard Malamud's story.
What is "the superhero's" mission? An angry young black
thief must perform the miracle that will save the life
of a dying white woman. How is this feat to be accomplished? Within twenty-four hours, he must convince the
"old girl's" husband, an elderly destitute Jewish tailor, to
accept him as a Jewish angel from God, leather jacket and
all. Believing as he does in black fulfillment, Belafonte's
high expectations for this film, which is neither black nor
Jewish reality, is incredulous.[23]

The women's liberation movement must be vying for
its share of Negro stereotypes in films. The female counterpart of "the superhero" is manifest in Change of Habit. Barbara McNair appears as Sister Irene, a Catholic nun who,
with two white nuns, discards her habit for contemporary
dress and assignment to an urban slum area. A ghetto product herself, Sister Irene recalls, "When little white girls
were playing with dolls in their party dresses, I was dodg-
ing drunks and praying that I wouldn't be just another nigger."[24] Black militants question her Negritude, feeling she's
"a white who is dipped in maple syrup." They challenge her,
"Get it together or get out."[25] She surprises them by doing
both. But first she does nursing work and launches a one-
girl crusade against exploitative shop owners and a local loan
shark. Accomplishing more than she set out to do for the
poor Latinos and blacks, Sister Irene, "superheroine," dons
her habit anew and slips back into the convent.

It should not be inferred from the above analyses of
a wide variety of Negro stereotypes that no truthful images
of blacks were projected in American motion pictures during
1970. Several portrayals, major and minor, depicted blacks
as thinking, feeling, human beings, free from the bondage of
restrictive categorizations.

Janet MacLachlan portrays Noreen, a maid, in Darker
Than Amber. For once, we learn something about the personal concerns of a black servant other than preoccupation
with white employers. None of the fantasy associated with
the maid in For Love of Ivy (1968) is seen here. Noreen's
statement, "I don't mess with no white guys," is compatible
with her proud carriage and Afro hair style. Some of the
best acting in the world is done by black domestics in white
homes across America. This point is made by Noreen when

A picture designed to "blow the mind" is Sweet Sweetback's Baadasssss Song, starring Melvin Van Peebles.

she is questioned about her Aunt Jemima accent. "That goes with the job," she confides.[26]

Miss MacLachlan manages to capture illuminating roles or at least to ameliorate the damnation and insidious nature of other roles. In Halls of Anger, she is Lorraine Nash, a teacher in a black inner-city school. The enormity of the school's educational and ethnic problems frustrates her, but not to the point of desertion. Her romance with the new black principal begins as both soak their tired feet in a pail of water, surely realism with a capital "R."

A different sort of teacher is depicted by Melvin Stewart in The Landlord. Prof. Duboise operates a black nationalist school for ghetto children. He drills black pride into the youngsters, preparing them for future lives as revolutionaries. Duboise is the one black in the film who demonstrates a realistic grasp of the schism, between blacks and whites in American society.

Black actress Barbara McNair counterbalanced her previously described appearance as "superheroine" with another role in 1970 which was reasonably liberated from stereotype. Valerie Tibbs, whom she portrays in They Call Me Mister Tibbs!, is a composite of every middle-class American housewife. She wears fashionable middle-class clothing, oversees an attractively decorated middle-class suburban home, does her own gardening and is tyrannized by her children. Blacks and whites alike will recognize and identify with this ultra bourgeois characterization.

In the same film, there is a refreshing blood and flesh performance by George Spell as Andrew, the strong-willed 11 year old Tibbs son. In addition to disobeying his mother, bullying his little sister, keeping a sloppy room and playing television too loudly, Andy likes to sneak a smoke

when mom and dad are not around. Concerning his life
goals, the precocious boy tells his father, "If you're poor
I'll be a bum, if you're rich I'll be a playboy."[27] Andrew's
scenes are highlights of the movie.

Bit parts sometimes provide avenues of expression
for black dignity. Playing an airline stewardess in the popular movie Airport, Ena Hartman makes it possible for audiences to perceive an attractive and well-groomed colored
woman in an occupation not customarily associated with
blacks in films.

Bernie Hamilton brings some much needed realism to
the part of a black army captain in The Losers. The film
was branded by some "the dirty dozen of the motorcyclist
crowd," due to its contrived involvement of a group of cyc-
lists with the Vietnam War. It is here that Captain Jackson
(Hamilton) encounters again an earlier love, a native girl
who has given birth to his baby. The necessity of linking
the lone black character among a cast of white males to il-
legitimacy cannot be ignored easily despite Hamilton's strong
performance.

William Marshall, another once prominent black actor,
gives an authoritative performance as an attorney in the
courtroom scenes of a "potboiler" entitled Skullduggery.
Marshall infuses a bit of "black experience" into the small
part. In his cross examination of a white witness from
South Africa, he remarks, "What you're really trying to tell
the world is that the black man is not human."[28]

In W. U.S.A., an embittered black mother (Susan Batson),
whose tubercular baby has been taken from her by the "procedures" of whites in authority, reminds us that these same "procedures" seem incapable of preventing white mothers from killing unwanted babies and leaving them in shoe-boxes.

One split-second scene in Where's Poppa? shows a
respectable looking black woman hailing a taxi on Central
Park West. It passes her by, only to stop for a bizarre
looking gorilla a few yards away. This episode must have
been applauded by Godfrey Cambridge and other black Americans who have experienced this particular brand of "My
Country 'Tis of Thee, Sweet Land of Bigotry."

The outstanding heroism of Dorie Miller at Pearl
Harbor in 1941 is documented in Darryl F. Zanuck's production of Tora! Tora! Tora! In the midst of heavy strafing by
Japanese aircraft, with white crew members dropping everywhere, Miller (Elven Havard) rushes to an unmanned gun.
The black navy man promptly downs an enemy plane. This
visually heroic scene (no dialogue) must be deemed progress
in light of past exclusion from American motion pictures of
any reference to black participation in America's wars
(cited in Chapters 4 and 6).

Another salutary portrayal of the black man within
the framework of the military occurred in Suppose They Gave
a War and Nobody Came. Sgt. Raymond Jones (Ivan Dixon)
is a member of the peace-time army stationed near a small
town in the South West. His main ambition and goal when
he is discharged is to own and operate a highway gas station. Jones has the security and strength that comes from
knowing who he is and where he is going. After sipping
some strongly laced punch, Jones says, "If I die, send my
body to Diahann Carroll."[29] When a fellow-black soldier
gets huffy, he quips, "We should never have given them their
freedom."[30] The sergeant encounters an act of racial bias
with intelligence and sophistication.

"Undertaking" is an extremely common occupation
among black Americans and the source of many black for-

tunes. Yet it was not until 1970 that a major black characterization in motion pictures was seen as a mortician. Lord
Byron Jones, skillfully played by Roscoe Lee Browne, is the
most prominent member of the black community in Somer-
ton, Tennessee. His slight build and reserved demeanor conceal a powerhouse of dignity and determination. Though it
means overturning the unwritten racial code of a Southern
town, Jones insists upon a divorce from his sexy black wife.
Her blatant affair with a local white sheriff has shamed him
to the point of no return. He meets insults, threats and
physical abuse not in the manner of "the superhero" but like
a sensitive human being caught in circumstances beyond his
control. The portrayal of L. B. Jones is multi-faceted.
Humorous are his encounters with potential customers. His
unrequited love for an adulterous wife reveals elements of
tenderness, compassion and grief. Jones' final courageous
reaffirmation of his manhood, "I'm not running anymore."
brings on his violent death and mutiliation. So successful is
the characterization that one almost feels a real sense of
loss as a black choir sings at the grave site, "I Hear Music
in the Air. There Must Be a God Somewhere."

There is validity in the characterization of Sonny Boy
Mosby (Yaphet Kotto) in the same motion picture. Sonny
Boy represents "the sleeping tiger" in each one of us. He
bears a long-term and justifiable grudge against a cruel white
farmer who abused him as a child. Sonny Boy's all-consum-
ing mission in life is personal revenge. Finally, the opportunity arises and Sonny Boy cannot pull the trigger of his
gun. This is not "the Negro who cannot harm whites" but
a truly non-violent soul. Sonny Boy weeps for joy at welcome liberation from his personal prison of hate. This
early establishment of his basic gentility gives added strength

and meaning to a subsequent unspeakably violent act he must
commit to avenge the murder of L. B. Jones when Southern
justice will not.

Grave Digger Jones and Coffin Ed Johnson are the
black heroes of Cotton Comes To Harlem. The film is an
updated version of Chester Himes' 1964 novel about the two
detectives and their search for stolen money. Grave Digger
(Godfrey Cambridge) and Coffin Ed (Raymond St. Jacques)
connote equalization for blacks in American motion pictures.
Simon "The Saint" Templar, Sam Spade, Ellery Queen, Inspector Clouseau and James Bond have never been fictional
heroes with whom blacks could readily identify. Grave Digger and Coffin Ed fill this function admirably. The two detectives are tough, sharp, honest (no graft) and facile at re-
partee: "Black folk need hope like anybody else."[31] White
colleagues begrudgingly concede their professionalism but re-
sent their arrogance. Like true detectives, they know every
inch of Harlem and are knowledgeable about its underworld.
Yet their basic fallibility prevents them from attempting "superheroics." In preparation for his role, Cambridge actually spent time with the 28th Detective Squad in Harlem.[32]
Most importantly, Grave Digger Jones and Coffin Ed Johnson
are proud and black, a combination too rarely observed in
American motion pictures. They set the standard against
which future portrayals along similar lines will be measured.
More films like Cotton Comes to Harlem, written, directed
and acted by blacks, will be forthcoming. There is true
prophesy in the film's theme song, "Ain't Now But It's Gonna
Be."

Notes

1. The World Almanac and Book of Facts, 1971, (New York: Doubleday, 1970), pp. 914-939, 944-946.

2. Information Please Almanac Atlas and Yearbook, 1971, (New York: Simon and Schuster, 1970), p. 83.

3. Watermelon Man (Columbia Pictures, 1970).

4. Ibid.

5. Ibid.

6. One More Time (United Artists, 1970).

7. Judy Klemesrud, "Calvin: Champagne, Yes, Coca-Cola No," The New York Times, April 19, 1970, p. D11.

8. El Condor (National General Pictures, 1970).

9. The Great White Hope (Twentieth Century Fox, 1970).

10. Getting Straight (Columbia Pictures, 1970).

11. Beyond the Valley of the Dolls (Twentieth Century Fox, 1970).

12. Jesse H. Walker, "Ex-Slave Brock Peters Asking For His Freedom," New York Amsterdam News, August 1, 1970, p. 1.

13. The Liberation of L. B. Jones (Columbia Pictures, 1970).

14. Clayton Riley, "When the All-American Boy Meets Miss Sepia of 1957," The New York Times, August 2, 1970, p. D27.

15. W.U.S.A. (Twentieth Century Fox, 1970).

16. Patton (Twentieth Century Fox, 1970).

17. Ibid.

18. The Great White Hope (Twentieth Century Fox, 1970).

19. Where's Poppa? (United Artists, 1970).

20. Judy Stone, "Jim Brown, Fighting Southern Sheriff," The New York Times, July 27, 1969, p. D9.

21. William Hoffman, Sidney (New York: Lyle Stuart, Inc., 1970).

22. Vincent Canby, "Milestones Can be Millstones," The New York Times, July 19, 1970, p. D1.

23. Nick Browne, "Would You Believe Belafonte as a Jewish Angel," The New York Times, April 27, 1969, p. D17.

24. Change of Habit (Universal Pictures, 1970).

25. Ibid.

26. Darker Than Amber (Cinema Center Films, 1970).

27. They Call Me Mister Tibbs! (United Artists, 1970).

28. Skullduggery (United Pictures, 1970).

29. Suppose They Gave a War and Nobody Came (A Cinerama Releasing Corp., 1970).

30. Ibid.

31. Cotton Comes to Harlem (United Artists, 1970).

32. Lindsay Patterson, "In Harlem, a James Bond with Soul?", The New York Times, June 15, 1969, p. D15.

Chapter 15

EPILOGUE

In the preceding chapters, the author has attempted
to trace the evolution of black people in American motion pictures over the years. Precious little research had been done
on this highly specialized topic. The scant and scattered literature pertinent to the Negro in American motion pictures
seemed lacking in objective assessment. Critical reviews
tend to be either too laudatory or too condemnatory, depending frequently upon whether the critic is black or white.
There is a schism between black film critics and white film
critics on the subject of Negro characterization in American
motion pictures. In question is the ability of white film critics to evaluate film portrayals of a black experience, alien
to their own existence.

A steady increase in the number of appearances of
blacks in American films is evident in major and minor characterizations. The increased frequency of major Negro portrayals led to the emergence of full-fledged black motion picture stars such as Sidney Poitier, Jim Brown, James Earl
Jones and Harry Belafonte. An interesting corollary to the
phenomenon of the black male star is the conspicuous absence of his counterpart, the black female star. We have
noted the screen performances of many talented black actresses including Judy Pace, Gloria Foster, Lola Falana,
Beverly Todd and Janet MacLachlan to name just a few. So
far not one has managed to garner the stellar eminence at-

tached to the late Dorothy Dandridge with the possible exception of Diahann Carroll, Diana Sands and Barbara McNair,
each of whom established reputations in other media.
During the last decade, especially, blacks were portrayed in various vocations with which they had not been associated previously on screen. It has become not uncommon
to see a black psychiatrist, nun, police officer, teacher,
lawyer, physician, detective, secretary or salesman. This
represents progress even since Daisy Balsley's 1959 study
of occupational roles assigned to Negroes in the mass media,
including motion pictures.[1]

Greater participation by black artists in the writing,
direction and production of American motion pictures is another salutary development which we have seen can liberate
a film from stereotype. One need only recall the positive
black images established in Dutchman (LeRoi Jones), The
Learning Tree (Gordon Parks), and Cotton Comes to Harlem
(Chester Himes, Ossie Davis). There is some indication
that this trend will continue in the future. A new "western,"
co-starring Harry Belafonte and Sidney Poitier, also marks
the directorial debut of Poitier in a Belafonte Enterprises
production. The Third World Cinema Corporation was formed
recently to produce films and utilize the talents of blacks,
Puerto Ricans and other minority groups. The organization
founded by Ossie Davis, Diana Sands, Rita Moreno, Brock
Peters, James Earl Jones, Piri Thomas and others has announced a film biography of the late black jazz singer Billie
Holiday as its first project (to star Miss Sands).[2] These
seeming advances may be illusory when measured against the
difficulties encountered by Raymond St. Jacques, Ivan Dixon
and Robert Hooks in their abortive attempts to bring such
properties as The Numbers, The Spook Who Sat by the Door

and Ceremonies in Dark Old Men to the screen. The American motion picture industry still remains under almost total
white dominance.   If it is true as Kracauer[3] states that "images of 'in-group' peoples surpass those of 'out-group'
peoples in reliability" then increased participation by blacks
in all areas of motion picture production could give them the
power base to which Kracauer alludes.   Lindsay Patterson
sees benefit performances by successful black artists and
stock ownership by black audiences as practical methods of
financing black entrepreneurs in the motion picture industry.[4]

It should be possible to bring the abundance of "black
experience" materials to the screen.   James Baldwin's Go
Tell It On the Mountain or his Another Country, John O.
Killens' And Then We Heard the Thunder or his Cotillion,
Charles Wright's The Messenger or his The Wig, John A.
Williams' Sissie or Louise Meriwether's Daddy Was a Num-
ber Runner are merely several of many literary works by
blacks which would be suitable for screen adaptation.

More than two decades ago, Hortense Powdermaker,
a noted anthropologist, wrote: "Attitudes stem from the past
and change slowly.   In a rapidly changing society such as
ours, some attitudes born out of a past situation continue under new conditions even when inappropriate."[5]   Dr. Powdermaker's view of the Hollywood film has been reaffirmed in
these pages.   The more objectionable Negro stereotypes, for
example "the shufflin' dolt" and "the mammy," have virtually disappeared.   Others such as "the sexual superman" and
"the superior athlete" continue.   "The superhero" has
emerged as a highly conspicuous new Negro stereotype re-
placing "the happy slave."   In this work, he was identified
in Guess Who's Coming to Dinner?; A Patch of Blue; Tick,
Tick, Tick; If He Hollers, Let Him Go; In the Heat of the

Night and 100 Rifles among other films. "The superhero" is
a saintly character without imperfection who is capable of
confronting overwhelming obstacles. Somehow it seems appropriate then for Sidney Poitier to bring "the superhero"
stereotype to full fruition with his portrayal of the title role
in Brother John (1971). Literally playing God's messenger
in the drama could have been Poitier's bid for equal-time
with Belafonte's Angel Levine but more probably Brother
John represents the logical ultimate step in a career of progressive role-deification.

Black culture and history were almost completely neg-
lected by the motion pictures discussed in this work. The
changing social climate for black Americans, documented in
the opening passages of Chapters 6 to 14 is not reflected in
the majority of films discussed. Among notable exceptions
were The Learning Tree and Nothing But a Man (problems of
black family life), The Cardinal (parochial school desegregation) One Potato, Two Potato (interracial marriage), Madigan (police brutality), Hotel (discrimination in public accommodations), Up Tight (black militancy), Lost Man (racial
demonstrations), They Call Me Mister Tibbs! (community control), Sweet Love, Bitter (jazz musicianship), R. P. M. (Afro-
American student demands) and The Landlord (liberation
schools).

Future motion pictures may well deal with issues relevant to the lives of black Americans in new ways. Herbert
Danska and Woodie King's Right On! (1971) is such a film,
innovative in content and form. Revolutionary poetry is
spoken by three young black men (The Last Poets) on a Harlem rooftop. The camera probes the ghetto streets comple-
menting the poets' fiery words. Right On! is proof that
films of its kind can be entertainment as well as documentary

in orientation.

Another motion picture designed to "blow the mind" and titillate the visual senses is Sweet Sweetback's Baadasssss Song, the product of one black man's virtuosity. Melvin Van Peebles, director of Watermelon Man (1970), wrote, produced, directed, scored, edited and played the leading role in Sweet Sweetback's Baadasssss Song. The by now familiar plot of a black brother's flight from the consequences of his own violent acts committed in reaction to the injustice of "whitey's" laws is secondary. The power and significance of SSBS comes from its experimental and liberated camera techniques (montage, superimposition of multiple images) and its uncompromising black chauvinism. For much the same reason as Putney Swope (1969), SSBS has been called vulgar, tasteless, disgusting, "a shocking soul on vice" and exploitative of blacks. Peebles does not deny that SSBS is about the exploitation of blacks (by others), believing that a true black consciousness must be preceded by full awareness of the degradation brought on by the white power structure. Dedicating SSBS to all the brothers and sisters who have had enough of "The Man," Peebles hopes that his film will decolonize the Negro mentality, offsetting to a degree the genocide perpetrated upon black minds. Clayton Riley comments, "The survival of the Sweetbacks of the world, their ability to maintain their lives, is possibly America's most significant current event."[6]

It should be unmistakably clear that an increasing number of American motion pictures are granting blacks equality of opportunity with whites in the achievement of a fantasy portrayal and the avoidance of realism. For Love of Ivy earned Abbey Lincoln parity with Doris Day. Jim Brown traveled the John Wayne route in 100 Rifles and El Condor.

It only remained for blacks to attain their own "private eye."
For did not whites possess Sam Spade, James Bond, Philip
Marlowe, Mike Hammer and a host of other unreal sleuths.
Enter John Shaft. The M.G.M. production of Shaft (1971) introduces Richard Roundtree in the title role and represents
the second feature film to be directed by Gordon Parks.
Following in the tradition of his white counterparts with a
"soul style" all his own, Shaft proceeds to handle a kidnap-
ping, the Mafia, the police and black militants, all with great
aplomb. He is arrogant, tough, fearless, a satisfying lover,
a sharp dresser and above all invincible; the last, a prerequisite for fictional detectives.

However slow, the force of change in the American
motion picture portrayal of blacks cannot be denied. In his
book, The Black Panthers, Gene Marine recalls a scene
from a 1930's Tarzan movie. [7] Several whites are moving
along a dangerous mountain trail when one of their "native"
bearers slips and falls, screaming to his death. One of the
white characters peers down and asks with indifference,
"What was in that pack?" In 1971, a different black character tumbles to his death, this time out of a window in John
Shaft's office. Shaft couldn't care less. Tempus fugit!

Notes

1. Daisy F. Balsley, "A Descriptive Study of References
    Made to Negroes and Occupational Roles Repre-
    sented by Negroes in Selected Mass Media, "
    (Unpublished Ph. D. dissertation, University of
    Denver, 1959).

2. New York Amsterdam News, February 27, 1971,
    pp. 1, 43.

3. Siegfried Kracauer, "National Types as Hollywood
    Presents Them, " in Mass Culture; the Popular

Arts in America, ed. by Bernard Rosenberg
and David Manning White (New York: The Free
Press, 1957), p. 274.

4. Lindsay Patterson, "In Movies, Whitey Is Still
   King," The New York Times, December 13,
   1970, p. D17.

5. Hortense Powdermaker, Hollywood: The Dream
   Factory. An Anthropologist Looks at the Movie-
   Makers (Boston: Little, Brown, 1950), p. 309.

6. Clayton Riley, "What Makes Sweetback Run?"
   The New York Times, May 9, 1971, p. D11.

7. Gene Marine, The Black Panthers (New York:
   New American Library, 1969), p. 216.

Bibliography

Abramson, Doris E. Negro Playwrights in the American Theatre, 1925-1959. New York: Columbia University Press, 1969.

Adams, William B. "A Definition of Motion Picture Research," Quarterly of Film, Radio, TV, 7 (Summer, 1953), pp. 408-421.

Adler, Renata. "Critic Keeps Her Cool on 'Up Tight'," The New York Times, December 29, 1968, pp. D1, 29.

_____. "The Negro That Movies Overlook," The New York Times, March 3, 1968, pp. 1, 10.

_____. "Screen," The New York Times, November 5, 1968, p. 55.

Alpert, Hollis. "The Problem," Saturday Review, January 21, 1967, p. 35.

_____. "SR Goes to the Movies," Saturday Review, August 3, 1968, p. 35; November 23, 1968, p. 49.

Amberg, George. "The Ambivalence of Realism: Fragment of an Essay." The Visual Arts Today. Edited by Gyorgy Kepes. Middletown, Conn.: Wesleyan University Press, 1960, pp. 150-153.

Bailey, Pearl. The Raw Pearl. New York: Harcourt, 1968.

Baldwin, James. "The Price May Be Too High." The New York Times, February 2, 1969, p. D9.

_____. "Sidney Poitier," Look, July 23, 1968, pp. 50-58.

Balsley, Daisy F. "A Descriptive Study of References Made
    to Negroes and Occupational Roles Represented by
    Negroes in Selected Mass Media." Unpublished
    Ph.D. dissertation, University of Denver, 1959.

Bart, Peter. "The Still Invisible Man," The New York
    Times, July 17, 1966, Section II, p. 13.

Barthel, Joan. "Black Power of Godrey MacArthur Cam-
    bridge," The New York Times, November 20, 1968,
    pp. D13, 18.

Berelson, Bernard. Content Analysis in Communication Re-
    search. Glencoe, Illinois: The Free Press, 1952.

Biberman, Herbert. "We Never Say Nigger in Front of
    Them," The New York Times, January 19, 1969,
    pp. D1, D11.

Bloom, Samuel W. "A Social Psychological Study of Motion
    Picture Audience Behavior; A Case Study of the Ne-
    gro Image in Mass Communication." Unpublished
    Ph.D. dissertation, University of Wisconsin, 1956.

Bluestone, George. Novels into Film. Baltimore: The
    Johns Hopkins Press, 1957.

Bosworth, Patricia. "How Could I Forget What I Am?"
    The New York Times, August 17, 1969, p. D11.

Braithwaite, Edward R. To Sir, With Love. Englewood
    Cliffs, New Jersey: Prentice-Hall, 1959.

Britannica Book of the Year, 1965, 1968. Chicago: Encyc-
    lopaedia Britannica, Inc., 1965, 1968.

Browne, Nick. "Would You Believe Belafonte As a Jewish
    Angel?" The New York Times, April 27, 1969,
    p. D17.

Buchanan, Singer A. "A Study of the Attitudes of the Writers
    of the Negro Press toward the Depiction of the Negro
    in Plays and Films: 1930-1965." Unpublished Ph.D.
    dissertation, The University of Michigan, 1968.

Budd, Richard W. Content Analysis of Communications.
    New York: The Macmillan Co., 1967.

Burke, William L. "The Presentation of the American Ne-
    gro in Hollywood Films, 1946-1961: Analysis of a
    Selected Sample of Feature Films." Unpublished
    Ph.D. dissertation, Northwestern University, 1965.

Canby, Vincent. "Milestones Can be Millstones," The New
    York Times, July 19, 1970, p. D1.

_____. "The Movies that Still Haunt Hollywood," The
    New York Times, January 26, 1969, p. D15.

_____. "Screen," The New York Times, April 3,
    1968, p. 40; July 18, 1968, p. 26; July 3, 1969,
    p. 21.

Carmen, Ira H. Movies, Censorship and the Law. Ann
    Arbor: The University of Michigan Press, 1966.

Champlin, Charles. "Sidney Poitier: The Burden of Power,"
    New York Post, February 3, 1969, p. 48.

Chaudhuri, Arun. "A Study of the Negro Problem in Motion
    Pictures." Unpublished Master's thesis, University
    of Southern California, 1951.

Colle, Royal D. "The Negro Image and the Mass Media."
    Unpublished Ph.D. dissertation, Cornell University,
    1967.

Cripps, Thomas R. "Death of Rastus: Negroes in Ameri-
    can Films Since 1945," Phylon, 28 (Fall, 1967), pp.
    267-275.

_____. "The Reaction of the Negro to the Motion Pic-
    ture Birth of a Nation," The Historian, XXV (May,
    1963), pp. 344-362.

Crist, Judith. "The New Movie," World Journal Tribune,
    January 31, 1967, p. 15.

_____. The Private Eye, The Cowboy & The Very
    Naked Girl, Movies from Cleo to Clyde. New York:
    Holt, Rinehart & Winston, Inc., 1968.

Critics' Guide to Movies and Plays, v. 1 no. 5, 1967, 36 p.

Crowther, Bosley. "Screen," The New York Times, July

26, 1962, p. 17; February 16, 1965, p. 40; February 2, 1966, p. 24; January 20, 1967, p. 27; November 1, 1967, p. 37.

Dale, Edgar. The Content of Motion Pictures. New York:
The Macmillan Co. , 1935.

Danska, Herbert. Telephone communication, New York City,
March 3, 1969.

Davis, John P., ed. The American Negro Reference Book.
Englewood Cliffs, N. J. : Prentice-Hall, Inc., 1966.

Davis, Sammy, Jr. ; Boyar, Jane; and Boyar, Burt. Yes I
Can: The Story of Sammy Davis, Jr. New York:
Farrar, Straus & Giroux, 1965.

De Bose, Troy. "The Maid Wore Costly Wigs and Dressed
Like No Maid We'll Ever See. " The New York Times,
September 1, 1968, p. D9.

Drotning, Phillip T. Black Heroes in Our Nation's History:
A Tribute to the Negroes Who Helped Shape America.
New York: Cowles, 1969.

Ebony. The Negro Handbook. Chicago: Johnson Publishing
Co. , 1966.

Ewers, Carolyn H. Sidney Poitier: The Long Journey. New
York: The New American Library, 1969. (By permission of the Author and Henry Morrison, Inc. her Agents)

Fernow, Donald. L. "The Treatment of Social Problems in the
Entertainment Film. " Unpublished Master's thesis,
University of Southern California, 1952.

The Film Daily Year Book of Motion Pictures, 1968. 50th
ed. New York: The Film Daily, 1968.

Film Facts, 1962, 1963, 1964, 1965, 1966, 1967 and 1968.
New York: Motion Picture Producers and Distribu-
tors of America, Inc. 7 v.

Fishel, Leslie and Quarles, Benjamin. The Negro American:
A Documentary. New York: Morrow, 1967.

Flatley, Guy. "Sidney Poitier as Black-Militant. " The New
York Times, November 10, 1968, p. D15.

Frazier, Edward F. Black Bourgeousie. Glencoe, Illinois:
   The Free Press, 1957.

French, Philip. "Violence in the Cinema." Sight, Sound
   and Society, Motion Pictures and Television in America. Edited by David Manning White and Richard
   Averson. Boston: Beacon Press, 1968. pp. 320-
   334.

"From Pigskin to Redskins," Life, September 18, 1964, pp.
   67-68.

Fyock, James A. "Content Analysis of Films: New Slant
   on an Old Technique," Journalism Quarterly, 45
   (Winter, 1968), pp. 687-691.

Gardella, Kay. "TV Casts Diahann as a Pioneer," Sunday
   News, September 1, 1968, p. 39C.

Gelber, Jack. The Connection. New York: Grove Press,
   1960.

Gent, George. "Exit Darkies, Enter Blacks," The New
   York Times, July 3, 1968, p. 71.

Gerbner, George. "On Content Analysis and Critical Research in Mass Communication," Audio-Visual Communications Review, 6 (Spring, 1958), pp. 85-108.

Gessner, George. The Moving Image, A Guide to Cinematic
   Literacy. New York: E. P. Dutton & Co., Inc.,
   1968.

Greeley, Andrew M. "Black and White Minstrels," The Reporter, March 21, 1968, p. 40.

Grier, William H. and Cobbs, Price M. Black Rage. New
   York: Basic Books Inc., 1968.

Griffith, Richard. The Movies; The Sixty-Year Story of the
   World of Hollywood and Its Effect on America from
   Pre-Nickelodeon Days to the Present. New York:
   Simon & Schuster, 1957.

Gross, Seymour L., and Hardy, John, eds. Images of the
   Negro in American Literature. Chicago: The University of Chicago Press, 1966.

Halliwell, Leslie, ed. The Filmgoer's Companion: From
    Nickelodeon to New Wave. New York: Hill and
    Wang, 1965.

Handel, Leo A. Hollywood Looks at Its Audience; A Report
    of Film Audience Research. Urbana: University of
    Illinois Press, 1950.

Hansberry, Lorraine. "Me Tink Me Hear Sounds in De
    Night," Theatre Arts, 44 (October, 1960), pp. 9-11.

Harnick, Barbara Barrie, Letter, New York City, January
    4, 1969.

Herridge, Frances. "Movie Scene," New York Post, July
    21, 1964, p. 17; November 6, 1967, p. 82.

Hirsch, Foster. "Uncle Tom's Becoming a Superhero,"
    Readers & Writers, November/January 1968, pp.
    12-14.

Hoffman, William. Sidney. New York: Lyle Stuart, 1971.

Holly, Ellen. "How Black Do You Have to Be?," The New
    York Times, September 15, 1968, p. D5.

_____. "Living a White Life--For a While," The New
    York Times, August 10, 1969, p. D13.

Horne, Lena, and Schickel, Richard. Lena. New York:
    Doubleday, 1965.

Hughes, Langston, and Meltzer, Milton, eds. Black Magic:
    A Pictorial History of the Negro in American Enter-
    tainment. Englewood Cliffs, N.J.: Prentice-Hall,
    1967.

Information Please Almanac Atlas and Yearbook, 1971.
    New York: Simon and Schuster, 1970.

Isaacs, Edith J. The Negro in the American Theatre. New
    York: Theatre Arts, 1947.

Jacobs, Lewis. The Rise of the American Film, A Critical
    History with an Essay, "Experimental Cinema in
    America, 1921-1947." New York: Teachers College
    Press, 1968.

Jerome, V. J. The Negro in Hollywood Films. New York:
    Masses & Mainstream, 1950.

Johnson, Albert. "Beige, Brown or Black," Film Quarterly,
    13:1 (Fall, 1959), pp. 39-42.

Johnson, Beulah V. "The Treatment of the Negro Woman
    as a Major Character in American Novels, 1900-
    1950." Unpublished Ph. D. dissertation, New York
    University, 1955.

Jones, Dorothy B. "Quantitative Analysis of Motion Picture
    Content," Public Opinion Quarterly, 14 (Fall, 1950),
    pp. 554-558.

Jones, LeRoi. "Jim Brown on the Scene." Unpublished
    poem, n.d. 3 p.

Kael, Pauline. I Lost it at the Movies. Boston: Little,
    Brown, 1965.

_____. Kiss Kiss Bang Bang. New York: Atlantic-
    Little, 1968.

Kaplan, Abraham. "Realism in the Film: A Philosopher's
    Viewpoint," Quarterly of Film, Radio, TV, 7 (Sum-
    mer, 1953), pp. 370-384.

Katz, William L. Eyewitness: The Negro in American His-
    tory. New York: Pitman, 1967.

Kauffmann, Stanley. Figures of Light, Film Criticism and
    Comment. New York: Harper & Row, 1971.

_____. A World on Film. New York: Harper & Row,
    1966.

Killens, John O. "Hollywood in Black and White." The
    State of the Nation. Edited by David Boroff. Engle-
    wood Cliffs, N. J.: Prentice-Hall, 1966. pp. 100-
    107.

Klemesrud, Judy. "Calvin: Champagne, Yes, Coca-Cola
    No," The New York Times, April 19, 1970, p. D11.

_____. "St. Jacques: Our Next Black Matinee Idol?,"
    The New York Times, December 8, 1968, p. D19.

Kracauer, Siegfried. "National Types as Hollywood Presents
    Them." Mass Culture; The Popular Arts in Amer-
    ica. Edited by Bernard Rosenberg and David M.
    White. New York: The Free Press, 1957. pp.
    257-277.

Kramer, Stanley. "The David Frost Show." W.N. E.W. tele-
    cast, August 29, 1969.

Landry, Robert J. "The Movies; Better Than Ever?"
    Prejudice and the Lively Arts. Edited by Nathan C.
    Belth and Morton Puner. New York: Anti-Defama-
    tion League, n. d. pp. 10-11.

Lichtenberg, Philip. "A Content Analysis of American Mo-
    tion Pictures with Special Respect to 4 Classes of
    Characters." Unpublished Ph.D. dissertation, West-
    ern Reserve University, 1952.

Mailer, Norman. An American Dream. New York: Dial,
    1965.

Marine, Gene. The Black Panthers. New York: New Amer-
    ican Library, 1969.

Mason, Clifford. "Why Does White America Love Sidney
    Poitier So? " The New York Times, September 10,
    1967, pp. 1, 21.

Mayfield, Julian. "Explore Black Experience." The New
    York Times, February 2, 1969, p. D9.

Mitchell, Loften. Black Drama: The Story of the American
    Negro in the Theatre. New York: Hawthorn Books,
    1967.

Morganstern, Joseph and Kanfer, Stefan, eds. Film 69/70:
    An Anthology By The National Society of Film
    Critics. New York: Simon and Schuster, 1970.

Motion Picture Association of America, Inc. The Motion
    Picture Code and Rating Program: A System of
    Self-Regulation. New York: The Association, 1968.

Myrdal, Gunnar. An American Dilemma: The Negro Prob-
    lem and Modern Democracy. New York: Harper,
    1944.

Nafziger, Ralph O., and White, David M., eds. Introduction
to Mass Communications Research. Baton Rouge:
Louisiana State University Press, 1963.

Nasir, Sari. "The Image of the Arab in American Popular
Culture." Unpublished Ph. D. dissertation, University of Illinois, 1962.

Neal, Larry. "Beware of the Tar Baby." The New York
Times, August 3, 1969, p. D13.

Newquist, Roy. A Special Kind of Magic. Chicago: Rand
McNally & Co., 1967.

New York Amsterdam News, April 5, 1969, p. 10; May 3,
1969, p 25; August 30, 1969, p. 19; February 27,
1971, pp. 1, 43.

The New York Times, December 12, 1968, p. 32.

The New York Times Index, 1962-1970.

Noble, Peter. The Negro in Films. London: Skelton Robinson, 1948.

Patterson, Lindsay, ed. Anthology of the American Negro in
the Theatre: A Critical Approach. New York:
Publishers Co., Inc., 1967.

_____. "In Harlem a James Bond with Soul? " The
New York Times, June 15, 1969, p. D15.

_____. "In Movies, Whitey Is Still King." The New
York Times, December 13, 1970, p. D17.

_____. "To Make the Negro a Living Human Being,"
The New York Times, February 18, 1968, p. D8.

Peper, William. "The Peper Mill." New York World Tele-
gram & Sun, April 3, 1965, p. 20.

Ploski, Harry A., and Brown, Roscoe C., comps. The Negro Almanac. New York: Bellwether Publishing
Co., 1967.

Pool, Ithiel De Sola, ed. Trends in Content Analysis. Ur-
bana: University of Illinois Press, 1959.

Poussaint, Alvin F.   "Education and Black-Self-Image."
     Freedomways: A Quarterly Review of the Freedom
     Movement, 8:4 (Fall, 1968), pp. 334-339.

Powdermaker, Hortense.   Hollywood, the Dream Factory;
     An Anthropologist Looks at the Movie-Makers.
     Boston: Little, Brown, 1950.

Randall, Richard S.   Censorship of the Movies, The Social
     and Political Control of a Mass Medium.   Madison:
     The University of Wisconsin Press, 1968.

Reddick, Lawrence D.   "Educational Programs for the Im-
     provement of Race Relations: Motion Pictures,
     Radio, the Press, and Libraries." Journal of Negro
     Education, 13 (Summer, 1944), pp. 369-389.

Reed, Rex.   "Our Man Flint, Meet Georgy Girl." The New
     York Times, June 8, 1969, p. D15.

Riley, Clayton.   "What Makes Sweetback Run?"   The New
     York Times, May 9, 1971, p. D11.

_____. "When the All-American Boy Meets Miss Sepia
     of 1957." The New York Times, August 2, 1970,
     p. D27.

Robinson, Henry M.   The Cardinal.   New York: Simon and
     Schuster, 1950.

Rotha, Paul.   Rotha on the Film: A Selection of Writings
     about the Cinema.   Fairlawn, N.J.:   Essential Books,
     Inc., 1958.

Sanders, Charles L.   "Sidney Poitier: Man behind the Super-
     star." Ebony, April 1968, pp. 172-182.

Schickel, Richard and Simon, John, eds.   Film 67/68: An
     Anthology by the National Society of Film Critics.
     New York: Simon and Schuster, 1968.

Schumach, Murray.   The Face on the Cutting Room Floor:
     The Story of Movie and Television Censorship.
     New York: Morrow, 1964.

Schwartz, Jack.   "The Portrayal of Education in American
     Motion Pictures, 1931-1961." Unpublished Ph.D.

dissertation, University of Illinois, 1963.

Screen World, 1962, 1963, 1964, 1965, 1966, 1967, 1968.
New York: Crown.

Shuey, Audrey M. "Stereotyping of Negroes and Whites."
Public Opinion Quarterly, 17:2 (Summer, 1953), pp.
281-287.

Simon, John. Movies into Film; Film Criticism 1967-1970.
New York: Dial Press, 1971.

Slavitt, David. "Movies." Newsweek, August 3, 1964, p. 72.

Stone, Judy. "Jim Brown, Fighting Southern Sheriff." The
New York Times, July 27, 1969, p. D9.

Thomas, Bob. "Power Is Difference to Richer Belafonte."
The Plain Dealer, August 11, 1957, p. 10 quoted in
Simpson, George E., and Yinger, J. Milton. Racial
and Cultural Minorities: An Analysis of Prejudice
and Discrimination. 3rd ed. New York: Harper &
Row, 1965, p. 481.

Thompson, Howard. "Golden Boy Turns to the Trumpet for
Film." The New York Times, November 26, 1965,
p. 44.

_____. "Screen." The New York Times, February 27,
1964, p. 28; May 10, 1969, p. 34.

Time, October 5, 1962, p. M18; April 23, 1965, p. 103.

Time-Life Bks., eds. I Have a Dream: The Story of Martin Luther King in Text and Pictures. New York:
Silver Burdett, 1968.

"Up Tight." Ebony, November 1968, pp. 46-47, 52-54.

Van Gelder, Lindsy. "A Talk with: Robert Downey." New
York Post, August 15, 1970, p. 11.

Wagenknecht, Edward. The Movies in the Age of Innocence.
Norman: University of Oklahoma Press, 1962.

Wahls, Robert. "Footlights." Daily News, September 8,
1968, p. S2.

Walker, Alexander. Stardom, The Hollywood Phenomenon.
    New York: Stein and Day, 1970.

Walker, Jesse H. "Ex-Slave Brock Peters Asking For His
    Freedom." New York Amsterdam News, August 1,
    1970, p. 1.

_____. "Theatricals." New York Amsterdam News,
    June 7, 1969, p. 43.

Walker, Wyatt T. "Nothing but a Man." Malcolm X: The
    Man and His Time. Edited by John Henrik Clarke.
    New York: Macmillan, 1969. pp. 64-68.

Westen, Jay. "Movie Mailbag." The New York Times, Oc-
    tober 1, 1967, pp. D15, 26.

Wilkins, Roy. "Poitier's Ivy." New York Post, July 27,
    1968, p. 27.

Wilner, Daniel M. "Attitude as a Determinant of Perception
    in Mass Media of Communication: Reactions to the
    Motion Picture, 'Home of the Brave'." Unpublished
    Ph.D. dissertation, University of California, Los
    Angeles, 1951.

Winsten, Archer. "Reviewing Stand." New York Post, April
    21, 1964, p. 22; June 16, 1966, p. 58; July 18,
    1968, p. 26.

Wolfe, Bernard. "Ecstatic in Blackface." The Scene before
    You: A New Approach to American Culture. Edited
    by Chandler Brossard. New York: Rinehart, 1955.
    pp. 51-70.

Wolfenstein, Martha, and Leites, Nathan. "Two Social Sci-
    entists View 'No Way Out,' The Unconscious vs. The
    Message in an Anti-bias Film," Commentary, 10
    (November 1950), pp. 388-391.

Worden, James. "The Portrayal of the Protestant Minister
    in American Motion Pictures, 1951-1960." Unpub-
    lished Ph.D. dissertation, Boston University, 1962.

The World Almanac and Book of Facts, 1966, 1967, 1969,
    1970, 1971. New York: New York World Telegram
    & Sun, 1966; Newspaper Enterprise Association,

Inc., 1967, 1969, 1970.

The Writers' War Board. How Writers Perpetuate Stereotypes. New York: The Board, 1945.

Index